# INTERNATIONAL LAW AND CHILD SOLDIERS

This book commences with an analysis of the current state of child soldiering internationally. Thereafter the proscriptive content of contemporary norms on the prohibition of the use and recruitment of child soldiers is evaluated, so as to determine whether these norms are capable of better enforcement. An 'issues-based' approach is adopted, in terms of which no specific regime of law, such as international humanitarian law (IHL), is deemed dominant. Instead, universal and regional human rights law, international criminal law and IHL are assessed cumulatively, so as to create a mutually reinforcing web of protection. Ultimately, it is argued that the effective implementation of child soldier prohibitive norms does not require major changes to any entity or functionary engaged in such prevention; rather, it requires the constant reassessment and refinement of all such entities and functionaries, and here, some changes are suggested. International judicial, quasi-judicial and non-judicial entities and functionaries most relevant to child soldier prevention are critically assessed. Ultimately the conclusions reached are assessed in light of a case study on the use and recruitment of child soldiers in the Democratic Republic of the Congo.

**Volume 53 in the series Studies in International Law**

Studies in International Law

Recent titles in this series

For the complete list of titles in this series, see 'Studies in
International Law' link at www.hartpub.co.uk/books/series.asp

# International Law and Child Soldiers

Gus Waschefort

·HART·
PUBLISHING

OXFORD AND PORTLAND, OREGON
2017

**Hart Publishing**

An imprint of Bloomsbury Publishing Plc

Hart Publishing Ltd
Kemp House
Chawley Park
Cumnor Hill
Oxford OX2 9PH
UK

Bloomsbury Publishing Plc
50 Bedford Square
London
WC1B 3DP
UK

www.hartpub.co.uk
www.bloomsbury.com

Published in North America (US and Canada) by
Hart Publishing
c/o International Specialized Book Services
920 NE 58th Avenue, Suite 300
Portland, OR 97213-3786
USA

www.isbs.com

**HART PUBLISHING, the Hart/Stag logo, BLOOMSBURY and the
Diana logo are trademarks of Bloomsbury Publishing Plc**

First published in hardback, 2015
Paperback edition, 2017

© Gus Waschefort, 2017

**British Library Cataloguing-in-Publication Data**
A catalogue record for this book is available from the British Library.

ISBN: HB: 978-1-84946-520-5
PB: 978-1-50991-383-1

Typeset by Compuscript Ltd, Shannon
Printed and bound in Great Britain by
Lightning Source UK Ltd

To find out more about our authors and books visit www.hartpublishing.co.uk. Here you will find extracts, author information, details of forthcoming events and the option to sign up for our newsletters.

# *Acknowledgements*

It is rather unjust that the dedicated efforts of a host of people culminate in one person's name appearing on a book's cover. Indeed, there are more people who have contributed to my writing this book—both in the form of substantive assistance and emotional support—than I can thank individually. Nevertheless, a core group of people absolutely deserve individual acknowledgement.

My career path has been rather unorthodox. I left school when I was 15 to pursue a career in photojournalism. My first exposure to child soldiers came when I myself was a 17-year-old child, during a photography assignment to Angola. None of this would have been possible without the unwavering support and trust that my parents, Hein and Christine Waschefort, showed towards me.

My partner, Lee Stone, was the one person whose support of me and the project covered the full spectrum, from tremendously helpful substantive input to emotional support when I needed it most. She often set aside her own research to read every word I wrote, making invaluable comments and in the process refining my language and thinking. The greatest satisfaction I have yet received through this project came in the form of her encouragement and enthusiasm.

Without the generous financial support I received as the first recipient of the FirstRand Laurie Dippenaar Scholarship for Postgraduate International Study, this project would not have been possible. However, my indebtedness to Laurie and Estelle Dippenaar, and Adrian Arnott, goes beyond the financial aspect. The level of genuine interest they continuously showed in my work came as a great surprise, and served as real encouragement. I also remain indebted to one of my oldest friends, Jaco Oosthuizen, who contributed a significant sum of money for me to be able to finish this project.

Thanks should also go to my PhD supervisor, Dr Catherine Jenkins at the School of Oriental and African Studies at the University of London, my examiners Professor Robert Cryer and Dr Chaloka Beyani, and the anonymous peer reviewers, all of whom played a most valuable role in informing my understanding of international law and child soldiering. So too must I thank the academics and scholars who have mentored me over the years, in particular Professors Christof Heyns, Frans Viljoen and Andre Thomashausen.

# Contents

# 1

# *Situating the Debate*

## I. A BRIEF CHRONOLOGY OF THE PREVENTION OF CHILD SOLDIERING

F OR MOST OF human history, children's participation in armed conflict was not a matter of concern. Indeed, there are many accounts in history, theology and mythology of children's heroism in battle, notably the boy David defeating Goliath, the giant Philistine warrior. The origin of the word 'infantry' is said to be derived from the Latin word *infans*, meaning 'a very young child or baby'.[1] The infantry were those soldiers in the Roman legions who were too young, or of too low rank, to form part of the cavalry.[2] Many small towns in the United States have monuments and statues in honour of children who fought in the American Civil War: for example, the grave of Avery Brown is a landmark in Elkhard, Indiana.[3] Brown enlisted in Abraham Lincoln's Union Army during the Civil War, aged 8 years, 11 months and 13 days.[4] More recently, significant numbers of children participated in hostilities during the Second World War; yet the Geneva Conventions of 1949 did not prohibit the recruitment and participation of children in armed conflict.[5]

By 1977, a shift in the mores of the international community had occurred and the first instruments directly prohibiting child soldiering had been adopted in the form of the Two Additional Protocols to the Geneva Conventions.[6] For more than a decade after the adoption of

---

[1] C Soanes and A Stevenson (eds), *Concise Oxford English Dictionary*, 11th edn (Oxford, Oxford University Press, 2006).

[2] Ibid. The origin of the word 'infantry' is attributed to *infanterie* in French, and *infanteria* in Italian. The root of both these words is attributable to the Latin word *infant*, which means 'a very young child or baby'.

[3] MD Banks, 'Avery Brown (1852–1904), Musician: America's Youngest Civil War Soldier', *America's Shrine to Music Newsletter*, February 2001; also cited in DM Rosen, *Armies of the Young: Child Soldiers in War and Terrorism* (New Brunswick, NJ, Rutgers University Press, 2005) 5, note 12.

[4] Ibid.

[5] See generally Chapter 3.I below.

[6] Art 77(2) of Protocol I Additional to the Geneva Conventions of 12 August 1949, and relating to the Protection of Victims of International Armed Conflicts, adopted 8 June 1977 (entered into force 7 December 1978) 1125 UNTS 17512; and Art 4(3)(c) of Protocol II Additional to the Geneva Conventions of 12 August 1949, and relating to the Protection

1

the Additional Protocols there were no further developments. During 1989, the UN Convention on the Rights of the Child (CRC) was adopted which (inter alia) prohibited child soldiering and mandated the creation of the Committee on the Rights of the Child (CRC Committee).[7] Two vital decisions were taken at the Committee's third session, during 1993. It was decided to submit a request to the Secretary-General of the UN to appoint an expert to launch an in-depth investigation into the protection of children during armed conflict.[8] It was also decided to entrust a member of the Committee with drafting a first preliminary text of a Protocol to the CRC on the involvement of children in armed conflict (CIAC Protocol).[9]

Graça Machel was duly appointed in terms of a General Assembly resolution to investigate and report on the situation of children during armed conflict.[10] Although her mandate included the plight of all children during armed conflict, it was her ground-breaking report, released during 1996, that drew the international community's attention to the problem of child soldiering.[11] In her report, Machel states:

> The flagrant abuse and exploitation of children during armed conflict can and must be eliminated. For too long, we have given ground to spurious claims that the involvement of children in armed conflict is regrettable but inevitable. It is not. Children are regularly caught up in warfare as a result of conscious and deliberate decisions made by adults. We must challenge each of these decisions and we must refute the flawed political and military reasoning, the protests of impotence, and the cynical attempts to disguise child soldiers as merely the youngest 'volunteers'.[12]

This sentiment resonated across the divide between civil society and state actors. If ever the participation of children in armed conflict was wholly accepted, the turning point had been reached by the time this study was released. This is evident today in that not a single state, not even those most responsible for the use and recruitment of child soldiers, argues that such use or recruitment is lawful.

As recommended in the Machel report, the Office of the Special Representative to the Secretary-General on Children and Armed Conflict (SRSG) was created during 1998, and Olara Otunnu was appointed

---

of Victims of Non-International Armed Conflicts, adopted 8 June 1977 (entered into force 7 December 1978) 1125 UNTS 609.

[7] Convention on the Rights of the Child (entered into force 2 September 1990) 1577 UNTS 3 (CRC).

[8] Committee on the Rights of the Child, 'Report on the Third Session', CRC/C/16 (5 March 1993), para 176 and Annex VI.

[9] Ibid, para 176 and Annex VII.

[10] General Assembly Resolution 48/157 (20 December 1993).

[11] G Machel, 'Promotion and Protection of the Rights of Children: Impact of Armed Conflict on Children', UN Doc A/51/306 (26 August 1996) (Machel Report).

[12] Ibid, para 316.

as the first SRSG.[13] The SRSG has a multifaceted mandate that, in relation to children in armed conflict, includes: tracking progress, raising awareness, promoting information gathering, working closely with other role players, fostering international cooperation to ensure respect for children's rights and finally contributing to the coordination of efforts by governments and relevant UN bodies.[14]

Child Soldiers International is a non-government organisation (NGO) that was originally founded as The Coalition to Stop the Use of Child Soldiers (CSUCS), collaboratively formed by Amnesty International, Human Rights Watch, the International Save the Children Alliance, the Jesuit Refugee Service, the Quaker United Nations Office, and Terre des Hommes International Federation during 1998 as an NGO coalition. By this time, Rädda Barnen (Save the Children Sweden), Quaker United Nations Office, the International Committee of the Red Cross and others had already made significant contributions to the prohibition of child soldiering on both an advocacy and a research basis. Behind the driving force of the CSUCS, civil society spearheaded the campaign for the drafting and adoption of a protocol to the CRC on the involvement of children in armed conflict, originally the brainchild of the CRC Committee. The campaign called for a protocol that would lift the minimum use and recruitment age to a so-called 'straight-eighteen' threshold. Accordingly, the Optional Protocol to the Convention on the Rights of the Child on the Involvement of Children in Armed Conflict (CIAC Protocol) was adopted during 2000.[15] However, in my view, the final product is very disappointing. The adopted text presents a compromise on the straight-eighteen threshold that allows states parties to the CIAC Protocol to voluntarily recruit children between sixteen and eighteen, but not allowing them to use children younger than eighteen in direct participation in hostilities.

In another important development in 2000, the Security Council of the United Nations acknowledged that child soldiering 'may constitute a threat to international peace and security'.[16] It thus took a mere four years from when child soldiering was placed firmly on the agenda of the international community by the Machel report, for the organ of the UN with principal responsibility for the maintenance of international peace and security to recognise child soldiering as a problem potentially affecting such peace and security.

By 16 January 2002, the date upon which the Special Court for Sierra Leone was established, there had never been a prosecution for the use

---

[13] Ibid, paras 266–69.

[14] General Assembly Resolution 57/77 (12 December 1996).

[15] Optional Protocol to the Convention on the Rights of the Child on the Involvement of Children in Armed Conflict (entered into force 12 February 2002) 2173 UNTS 222.

[16] Security Council Resolution 1314 (11 August 2000), operative para 9.

and recruitment of child soldiers. To date, that Court has delivered four Trial Chamber judgments on the subject,[17] as well as appeal judgments in each of those cases.[18] All of these cases relate to the war crime of child soldier enlistment, conscription or use. Furthermore, in the International Criminal Court's (ICC) first conviction, the *Lubanga* case (appeal pending), the defendant was charged with the sole war crime of enlisting, conscripting or using children for active participation in hostilities.[19] In the Democratic Republic of the Congo (DRC), numerous prosecutions, in national courts have been finalised.[20] The first was during 2008.

During 2005, a comprehensive Monitoring and Reporting Mechanism (MRM) on child soldiering was established in terms of a Security Council resolution.[21] Otunnu, in his capacity as SRSG, first proposed the creation of such a mechanism to the General Assembly during his 2003 annual report.[22] The MRM serves to 'collect and provide timely, objective, accurate and reliable information' on those situations affecting children that have been identified by the SRSG as most urgently deserving attention,[23] which includes 'recruiting or using child soldiers'.[24]

The exact level of effectiveness of these measures is relatively unclear. What is clear, however, is that the recruitment and use of child soldiers internationally persists and no clearly visible inroads have been made as yet. This is not to say that current measures are wholly ineffective, but, as Drumbl suggests, 'although international interventions have helped reduce specific incidents, the practice of child soldiering still persists. It may shift locally, but it endures globally.'[25] Having said this, it is certainly also true that there are far fewer child soldiers today than during

[17] *Prosecutor v Sesay, Kallon and Gbao*, Trial Chamber I, SCSL-04-15-T (2 March 2009) (*RUF* case); *Prosecutor v Fofana and Kondewa*, Trial Chamber I, SCSL-04-14-T (2 August 2007) (*CDF* case); *Prosecutor v Brima, Kamara and Kanu*, Trial Chamber II, SCSL-04-16-T (20 June 2007) (*AFRC* case); *Prosecutor v Charles Taylor*, Trial Chamber II, SCSL-03-01-T (26 April 2012) (*Taylor* case).

[18] *Prosecutor v Fofana and Kondewa*, Appeals Chamber, SCSL-04-14-A (28 May 2008) (*CDF appeals* case); *Prosecutor v Brima, Kamara and Kanu*, Appeals Chamber, SCSL-04-16-A (22 February 2008) (*AFRC appeals* case); *Prosecutor v Sesay, Kallon and Gbao*, Appeals Chamber, SCSL-04-15-A (26 October 2009) (*RUF appeals* case); *Prosecutor v Charles Taylor*, Appeals Chamber, SCSL-03-01-A (26 September 2013) (*Taylor appeals* case).

[19] *Prosecutor v Thomas Lubanga Dyilo*, Trial Chamber I, ICC-01/04-01/06 (14 March 2012) (*Lubanga* case).

[20] See generally Chapter 7.B below.

[21] Security Council Resolution 1612 (26 July 2005).

[22] OA Otunnu, 'Protection of Children Affected by Armed Conflict', Report of the Special Representative of the Secretary-General for Children and Armed Conflict, A/58/328 (29 August 2003), paras 73–78.

[23] Security Council Resolution 1612, n 21 above, operative para 5(c).

[24] 'Report of the Secretary-General on Children in Armed Conflict', A/59/695, S/2005/72 (9 February 2005), para 68.

[25] MA Drumbl, *Reimagining Child Soldiers in International Law and Policy* (Oxford, Oxford University Press, 2012) 1.

the 1990s. What is less clear is whether this reduction has much to owe to the interventions of international law.

At the time of writing there are indeed a number of situations internationally where child soldiering is a real and a large-scale problem. The armed conflicts in Syria and the Central African Republic are key areas of concern, and reports that the Nigerian terrorist group Boko Haram are using child soldiers is equally worrisome. As such, the need for a strong international law response remains as acute as ever.

## II. CONCEPTUALISING AN 'ERA OF APPLICATION'

During 1999, the SRSG at that time, Olara Otunnu, reported to the General Assembly that:

> The Special Representative believes that the time has come for the international community to redirect its attention and energies from the juridical task of the development of norms to the political project of ensuring their application and respect on the ground. An 'era of application' must be launched. Words on paper cannot save children and women in peril. Such a project can be accomplished if the international community is prepared to employ its considerable collective influence to that end.[26]

The year prior to recommending this refocus of attention towards an 'era of application', Otunnu had already reported that 'the Special Representative believes that the most important and pressing challenge today is how to translate existing standards and commitments into action that can make a tangible difference to the fate of children exposed to danger on the ground'.[27] With reference to the establishment of the child soldier monitoring and reporting mechanism,[28] SRSG Otunnu contended that this mechanism 'marks a turning point in our collective campaign for the "era of application"—for transforming protective standards into compliance, and condemnation into accountability'.[29] Almost ten years after first introducing the era of application, on the occasion when Otunnu received the Harvard Law School Association Award and when he was no longer the SRSG on Children in Armed Conflict, he elaborated further on what an era of application entails.[30] On this occasion, he placed specific emphasis on the need that an era of application be 'embedded

---

[26] 'Promotion and Protection of the Rights of Children: Protection of Children Affected by Armed Conflict Note by the Secretary-General', A/54/430 (1 October 1999), para 165.

[27] 'Promotion and Protection of the Rights of Children: Protection of Children Affected by Armed Conflict Note by the Secretary-General', A/53/482 (12 October 1998), para 140.

[28] See generally Chapter 6.II.C.i below.

[29] OA Otunnu, '"Era of Application": Instituting a Compliance and Enforcement Regime for CAAC', statement before the Security Council, 23 February 2005.

[30] OA Otunnu, 'Era of Application', remarks on the occasion of receiving the Harvard Law School Association Award, 15 June 2007.

within formal, structured and binding compliance mechanisms'. This, however, has to be interpreted together with his earlier statement, quoted above, that a shift has to occur from norm creation to 'the political project of ensuring their [norms] application and respect on the ground'. As such, an era of application is dependent on a broad range of mechanisms that has the potential to contribute to child soldier prevention.

My conception of an era of application overlaps very much with that of Otunnu. In his work, Cassel speaks of 'rights protection',[31] whereas Dror, for example, focuses on 'social change'.[32] Rights protection is a narrower concept than social change in that the former occurs on individual bases, without necessarily affecting deeper systemic problems that account for the occurrence of the social problem in question. In this study, emphasis is placed on many mechanisms aimed at rights protection. This is done based on the argument that extensive rights protection is one of the primary components of broader social change. Such rights protection is central to an era of application. The notion that focus should shift to enforcement and compliance in human rights more broadly is not novel. It is, however, important to recognise that this shift of focus necessitates a move away from a preoccupation with doctrine, and an embracing of international institutional law. In 1950, Hersch Lauterpacht commented that

> no legal order, international or other, is true to its essential function if it fails to protect effectively the ultimate unit of all law—the individual human being. The two decades that followed the First World War lent weight, with ominous emphasis, to these now self-evident propositions. They resulted, in the Second World War, in the widespread conviction that the effective international protection of fundamental human rights, including some form of International Bill of Rights of Man, was a major purpose of the war inasmuch as it is an essential condition of international peace and progress.[33]

At present, there are in existence at least eight binding international instruments directly prohibiting the use and recruitment of child soldiers. Moreover, every state in the world bar Somalia has ratified at least one of these instruments.[34] In other words, regardless of the fact that the prohibition of the use and recruitment of child soldiers is undoubtedly a norm of customary international law,[35] all states except Somalia are also under a treaty obligation to refrain from such conduct. Few substantive norms of international law can make this claim. Lauterpacht would

---

[31] D Cassel, 'Does International Human Rights Law Make a Difference?' (2001) 2 *Chicago Journal of International Law* 121, 126–34.

[32] Y Dror, 'Law and Social Change' (1958–59) 33 *Tulane Law Review* 787, see generally.

[33] E Lauterpacht, *International Law and Human Rights* (London, Stevens & Sons, 1950) 79.

[34] Art 38 of the CRC prohibits the use and recruitment of child soldiers. All states except Somalia and the US have ratified this instrument. The US has, however, ratified the OPCRC, which also prohibits the use and recruitment of child soldiers.

[35] See generally Chapter 4.III below.

argue that this is pre-World War Two thinking. As discussed above, these treaty standards are by no means perfect. Nevertheless, the international community has been unable to ensure compliance or enforcement with even the weakest of these standards by some of its members.

I argue that international law has a role to play in the effective prevention of the use and recruitment of child soldiers.[36] Examples are discussed later in the book where the mobilisation of international law directly resulted in not only the demobilisation of active child soldiers, but also the cessation of their use and recruitment, even while hostilities were ongoing.[37] In order for international law to be an agent through which an era of application can be entered in the context of child soldier prevention, the focus must now be shifted from norm creation to norm enforcement. As President Kennedy said regarding law reform in the context of civil rights in the US, 'law alone cannot make men see right'.[38]

Buergenthal, in commenting on the 'evolving international human rights system', has divided this system into four sequential stages: 'the normative foundation'; 'institution building'; 'implementation in the post cold war era'; and 'individual criminal responsibility, minority rights and collective humanitarian intervention'.[39] In line with Otunnu's statement, this study is aimed at imagining an era of application, which would correspond with stages three and four of Buergenthal's evolution. It is important to note that, although it may be significant, the capacity and resources that the international community will expend on child soldier prevention is finite.[40] A rigid divide between these stages is unrealistic, as there will always be further development within each of these stages and a significant degree of overlap. What is more, this debate about evolution within international human rights law (IHRL) is framed within the context of the Human Rights Movement broadly. This is well evidenced from Buergenthal's stages, as the fourth stage includes 'minority

---

[36] International law is a broad concept; in this context, it means all the rules that emanate from the accepted sources of international law, including soft law that is relevant to the prevention of the use and recruitment of child soldiers. Of particular relevance in this regard are rules belonging to international humanitarian law, international human rights law and international criminal law.

[37] See, eg Chapter 7.B below.

[38] JF Kennedy, 'Civil Rights: Address to Nation' (11 June 1963), published in TJ McInnerny and FL Israel (eds), *Presidential Documents: Works that Shaped a Nation from Washington to Obama* (New York, Routledge, 2013) 271–74.

[39] T Buergenthal, 'The Normative and Institutional Evolution of International Human Rights' (1997) 19 *Human Rights Quarterly* 703, see generally. See also P Nikken, *La Proteccion Internacional de los Derechos Humanos: Su Desarrollo Progresivo* (Madrid, Institudo Interamericano de derechos humanos, 1987).

[40] The amount of resources and capacity that are allocated to preventing the use and recruitment of child soldiers is proportional to the level of commitment of states to combat this problem. Nevertheless, it will never be infinite. As such, any departure from a norm creation paradigm to a norm enforcement paradigm requires the reallocation of resources and capacity away from the former to the latter.

rights' and, as such, the developmental course of these rights lags behind most of the corpus of IHRL. For present purposes, this begs the question where child rights more broadly, and child soldier prohibitive rules in particular, factor in on this evolution of IHRL.

The CRC, which directly prohibits the use and recruitment of child soldiers, is the most rapidly and widely ratified human rights treaty.[41] Additionally, as previously stated, there are no less than eight binding international instruments prohibiting the use and recruitment of child soldiers, from within four regimes of international law (international humanitarian law (IHL), IHRL, international criminal law (ICL) and international labour law). Finally, such use and recruitment is a violation of customary international law.[42] Cumulatively, these factors strongly indicate that the time is ripe to progress from an era of standard setting to an era of application, or from Buergenthal's first two stages to his last two stages.

There is a very big gap between the existence of normative standards and the strength of these normative standards. The relative weakness of normative standards can for practical purposes be divided into two categories: first, those standards that are weak because the content of the norm fails to provide extensive protection, for example, instruments that prohibit the use and recruitment of children younger than fifteen, instead of eighteen; and secondly, those standards that are weak because of bad drafting, or the use of language that is imprecise and hard to apply to a concrete situation, for example, those standards that state that 'all feasible measures' must be employed to ensure that a child does not take a direct part in hostilities. As these examples indicate, instruments prohibiting child soldiering suffer from both these forms of relative weakness.

The first mentioned category poses less of a problem, as it does not directly affect the ability to enforce the norm. On the contrary, as the norm provides a lesser standard of protection than many would desire, it should be applicable to fewer situations, and only in those situations where there is very broad agreement that the conduct in question should be prohibited; as such, the enforcement of such norms should be easier. The argument can therefore be made that the international community should refrain from further norm creation until such time as the current norms enjoy a significant measure of enforcement. However, the second category directly impacts on the enforceability of the norms. If the norm itself inherently inhibits its own enforceability, the argument that emphasis should shift from norm creation to norm enforcement is likely to fail. However, there has never been an instance where the use of a child soldiers in hostilities was justified on the basis that 'all

---

[41] Art 38 of the CRC, n 7 above.
[42] See generally Chapter 4.III below.

feasible measures' were taken to ensure that the child would not be used in hostilities.

This may cast doubt on whether, in the context of child soldier prevention, the evolution of IHRL has really entered Buergenthal's third stage. Because of the nature of the law-making process on the international level, there is always compromise in agreeing to treaty norms. As such, no norms are perfect and there is a significant degree of overlap between the different stages.

There are numerous weaknesses in those instruments that prohibit the use and recruitment of child soldiers, and they are discussed in detail in Chapters 3 and 4. Some of these weaknesses may well impact on the level of enforceability of these norms. Accordingly, this issue forms one of the central research questions in determining whether it is feasible, and indeed possible, to progress to an era of application.

I am not arguing that all capacity and resources should be reallocated to enforcement instead of norm creation, just as all capacity and resources are not currently allocated to norm creation. Rather, a critical mass of these resources and capacity should be so reallocated. We should not simply accept the weaknesses of the positive law. Instead, we should now put greater emphasis on enforcing these imperfect, but necessary, standards.

## III. 'THE POLITICS OF AGE'[43]

As mentioned, the participation of children in armed conflict has been accepted throughout most of human history. Quénivet explains this, in part, on the basis that the concept of childhood did not exist during the Middle Ages.[44] That children under a predetermined age threshold should not be used or recruited as soldiers remains an assertion less obvious than most would imagine. The politics of age, as it manifests in the child soldier discourse, revolves around two central themes: the increased recognition of agency among children in the liberal rights discourse and cultural relativism.

Concrete age barriers are often challenged as young people develop at different rates, so that a particular eighteen-year-old may be less independent and less capable of making informed decisions than a particular sixteen-year-old. This argument has been further advanced on the basis that children have a greater capacity for making important decisions,

[43] This title is quoted from Rosen, n 3 above, 132–58.
[44] N Quénivet, 'The Liberal Discourse and the "New Wars" of/on Children' (2012–13) 38 *Brooklyn Journal of International Law* 1053, 1058, where Quénivet cites A James and AL James, 'Childhood: Toward a Theory of Continuity and Change' (2001) 575 *Annals of the American Academy of Political and Social Science* 25, 26.

such as enlisting in an armed force or group, than they are given credit for, although this in itself is not an argument against the creation of age barriers.

It is ironic that both the plight of child soldiers and the progression from viewing children as passive subjects to cogent agents were matters taken up at the same time, and largely among the same advocates. Van Bueren has argued that there is a tension between the protection of children and the participatory rights of children.[45] Similarly, in an interview I conducted with Jean Zermatten, Chairperson of the UN Committee on the Rights of the Child, Zermatten expressed the view that there is an ongoing paradigm shift from child protection to child rights.[46] However, Van Bueren has correctly warned: 'to regard the issue as only that of protection versus participation is too simplistic as some children will not survive unless taken into the armed forces'.[47]

The increased recognition of the agency of children notwithstanding, virtually all commentators assume the virtue in trying to prevent the use and recruitment of child soldiers. Rosen, however, takes a different approach. He challenges the assumptions that 'modern warfare is especially aberrant and cruel; that the world-wide glut of light-weight weapons makes it easier than in the past for children to bear arms; and that vulnerable children become soldiers because they are manipulated by unscrupulous adults'.[48] In this regard, he challenges a number of notions upon which the differentiation between age groups for protective purposes is based, arguing that the development of a child cannot be predicted in clear terms;[49] that 'the politics of age' is debated within a cultural and political context;[50] and that children have a far greater agency than they are given credit for by both those driving international law and civil society in general.[51] Rosen does not argue that the contemporary use of children in armed conflict is acceptable in all circumstances. However, where such use is unacceptable in his view, it is not inherently due to the fact that the child is a soldier, but rather due to the specific circumstances—for example, forced conscription.

There is much truth to Rosen's critiques. For example, Pinker has argued convincingly that 'we are living in the most peaceable era of our existence as a species'.[52] Thus Pinker, like Rosen, challenges the

---

[45] G Van Bueren, *The International Law on the Rights of the Child* (Amsterdam, Kluwer 1998), 335.

[46] Interview conducted with Mr Zermatten on 2 February 2011, Geneva, Switzerland.

[47] Van Bueren, n 45 above.

[48] Rosen, n 3 above, 1.

[49] Ibid, 1–4.

[50] Ibid, 4.

[51] Ibid, 131–38.

[52] S Pinker, *The Better Angels of Our Nature: Why Violence has Declined* (New York, Penguin, 2011) 1.

dominant humanitarian narrative, often fuelled by civil society, that 'modern warfare is especially abhorrent and cruel'. Nevertheless, there is a breakdown in reasoning in arguing that, because many of the premises upon which the abhorrent nature of child soldier use and recruitment is based are false, it is any less abhorrent, or, by extension, that children are any less deserving of protection. In this era of individual rights, sight is often lost of group dynamics. The fact that a given child develops at a different pace than his or her peers does not change the fact that juveniles, as a group, are less able to make life-changing decisions than adults.

Moreover, perspectives such as Rosen's gives scant attention to the fact that today the theory of cognitive ability (which associates age with cognitive ability), or some variations thereof, has become deeply entrenched in not only all municipal legal systems, but also international law in general.[53] It is inescapable that, although arguably at different ages, all children will, up to a certain phase in her/his development, not be in a position to make an informed decision as to whether or not to join an armed force or group, while many are subject to forced recruitment and adult manipulation. International law cannot be based on a system whereby the unique developmental characteristics of each young person are considered to inform a determination as to whether or not the specific child can make an informed decision whether or not to enlist. This argument is certainly not new: it is endorsed in every municipal criminal justice system, where differentiation based on age is used across the board for purposes of determining criminal capacity, sentencing and appropriate detention facilities.

In assessing municipal legal systems, Lowe argues that a state's freedom to create its own unique laws and legal systems plays a major role in creating a separate and unique identity and character for the relevant state.[54] The pursuits of international law, he argues, are quite the opposite.[55] International law exists to create a minimum threshold of norms to which all states are bound, and in so doing creates a degree of uniformity among states.[56] Thus, international law is, by definition, universalist. It goes without saying that a degree of dissent generally exists from a minority of states, or even a majority of weaker states, regarding a specific rule.[57] This dissent has often manifested itself in

---

[53] See generally Chapter 2.III.A.iii below.
[54] AV Lowe, *International Law* (Oxford, Oxford University Press, 2007) 7.
[55] Ibid.
[56] Ibid.
[57] In its most extreme form, this results in persistent objectors to the formation of customary international law. In general persistent objectors are not bound by the relevant rule. See, eg *Anglo-Norwegian Fisheries*, ICJ Reports 1951, 115, 131; *Asylum*, ICJ Reports 1950, 277; *Nicaragua*, ICJ Reports 1986, 107. Against: Judge Tanaka, Dissenting Opinion, *South West Africa Cases, Second Phase*, ICJ Reports 1966, 6, 291.

a divide, or at least in a perceived divide, between western and non-western states and ideas.[58]

Within the human rights paradigm, this has led to tension between a universalist approach to human rights and a culturally relative approach, and the cultural relativity of age goes to the heart of this debate. Sen speaks of 'world justice and the rule of law'.[59] Some argue that the notion of child soldiering and the international attention it has garnered of late is an example of western conceptions of childhood and ideals of child protection being forced upon non-western states.[60] In this regard, it is again useful to refer to Sen:

> I have also argued against considering the question of impartiality in the fragmented terms that apply only within nation states—never stepping beyond the borders. This is important not only for being as inclusive in our thinking about justice in the world as possible, but also to avoid the dangers of local parochialism against which Adam Smith warned nearly two and a half centuries ago. Indeed, the contemporary world offers much greater opportunity of learning from each other, and it seems a pity to try to confine the theorization of justice to the artificially imposed limits of nation states. This is not only because . . . 'injustice anywhere is a threat to justice everywhere' (though that is hugely important as well). But in addition we have to be aware how our interest in other people across the world has been growing, along with our growing contacts and increasing communication.[61]

Furthermore, in many instances non-western states have subscribed to legal provisions regarding the prohibition of the use and recruitment of child soldiers at a faster rate than western states.[62] Additionally, there are no persistent objectors to the customary international rule prohibiting the use and recruitment of child soldiers. The African Charter on the Rights and Welfare of the Child (the African Children's Charter) provides an apt example of the global response to child soldiering not only being accepted among some of the most traditional and culturally sensitive societies in the world, but even further developing such prohibitive norms.[63] This charter was the first convention to elevate the age threshold for the prohibition of the military use and recruitment of children to eighteen, as opposed to fifteen.[64] Furthermore, this convention provides:

---

[58] See, eg JJ Heckman, RL Nelson and L Cabatingan (eds), *Global Perspectives on the Rule of Law* (New York, Routledge, 2010).

[59] A Sen, 'Global Justice' in Heckman et al, ibid, 69.

[60] Rosen, n 3 above, 4.

[61] Sen, n 59 above, 69–70.

[62] See generally Chapter 4.III.A below.

[63] The African Charter on the Rights and Welfare of the Child (1990), OAU Doc CAB/LEG/24.9/49 (entered into force 29 November 1999).

[64] Ibid, Art 22.

States Parties to the present Charter shall take all appropriate measures to eliminate harmful social and cultural practices affecting the welfare, dignity, normal growth and development of the child and in particular:

(a) those customs and practices prejudicial to the health or life of the child; and

(b) those customs and practices discriminatory to the child on the grounds of sex or other status.[65]

It might seem contradictory to seek to enforce a global standard in a culturally sensitive way. However, I argue that this approach is justified, as today there is no dissent from the basic premise of the global standard—that young children should not be soldiers.

## IV. CONCEPTUALISING THE 'CHILD SOLDIER'

There are soft law instruments providing overarching definitions of child soldiering; for example, the Paris Principles provide that 'a child associated with an armed force or armed group' refers:

to any person below 18 years of age who is or who has been recruited or used by an armed force or armed group in any capacity, including but not limited to children, boys and girls, used as fighters, cooks, porters, messengers, spies or for sexual purposes. It does not only refer to a child who is taking or has taken a direct part in hostilities.[66]

However, it is clear that the customary norm that has crystallised prohibiting the use and recruitment of child soldiers has much less proscriptive content.[67] Furthermore, in order to assess the legal obligations incumbent upon a specific state, one has to have regard to the treaty norms the state has made itself subject to by acceding to or ratifying relevant treaties. At present, there are at least eight international treaties prohibiting the use and recruitment of child soldiers, as opposed to regional treaties.[68] The obligations created by each of these treaties are different from one another, some only slightly and others more materially. What is more, different states have ratified different combinations of

---

[65] Ibid, Art 21(1).

[66] Art 2(1) of the Paris Commitments and the Principles and Guidelines on Children Associated with the Armed Forces or Armed Groups (2007). See also the Cape Town Principles on Best Practices on the Prevention of Recruitment of Children into the Armed Forces and on Demobilisation and Social Reintegration of Child Soldiers in Africa (1997).

[67] See generally Chapter 4.III below.

[68] See generally Chapters 3 and 4 below for an analysis of such legal obligations. Additional Protocol I and Additional Protocol II, n 6 above; CRC, n 7 above; CIAC Protocol, n 15 above; the Rome Statute of the International Criminal Court (Rome Statute) (entered into force 1 July 2002) 2187 UNTS 90; ILO Forced Labour Convention No 29 (entered into force 1 May 1932) 39 UNTS 55; ILO Minimum Age Convention No 138 (entered into force 19 June 1976) 1015 UNTS 297; ILO Worst Forms of Child Labour Convention No 182 (entered into force 19 November 2000) 2133 UNTS 161.

these treaties, further complicating the assessment of the exact nature of the legal obligations to which a specific state may be subject vis-à-vis a specific child in a concrete case.

There are two ways in which to address this phenomenon. First, one can argue that if the law does not prohibit the enlistment of a child (a person younger than eighteen) into the military, that child will not be deemed a child soldier. Alternatively, one can argue that the child remains a child soldier, but that no legal norms were violated in recruiting or even using that child in military operations, where the relevant state has not subscribed to a legal obligation to the contrary. IHRL provides that 'a child means every human being below the age of eighteen years unless, under the law applicable to the child, majority is attained earlier'.[69] The United Kingdom, for example, has not subscribed to any legal norm that bars it from recruiting persons of sixteen years of age or older into its armed forces, and indeed, the UK does recruit such persons. In contrast, a number of states, such as Norway, have subscribed to such international norms. If one were to favour an interpretation in terms of which concept of the child soldier is the one which inherently denotes the unlawfulness of the child's enlistment, conscription or use, it would mean that a sixteen-year-old child would be deemed to be a child soldier if she/he were in the Norwegian Armed Forces but would not be deemed a child soldier if she/he were in the British Armed Forces. This results in a situation in which one would have to examine the treaty obligations to which a particular state has subscribed in every instance in which one wished to use the term 'child soldier'. Such a state of affairs will further be detrimental to the movement to progressively provide for more stringent prohibitive rules—such as achieving the straight-eighteen age barrier; which will also, over time, affect the content of customary international law.

The term 'child soldier' is thus broad and legally imprecise, but its use seems to me to be unavoidable. All instruments that predate the Rome Statute use the terms 'use' and 'recruit' in defining the proscribed conduct. The Rome Statute and those instruments that were drafted after the Rome Statute use the terms 'enlist', 'conscript' and 'use', which are broader than 'recruit'. This distinction is immaterial for the purposes of the present chapter, as well as Chapter 2. These chapters deal with child soldiering as a social phenomenon, which the international community wishes to regulate. The parameters of this regulation only become relevant in Chapter 3. The term 'child soldier' is therefore employed extensively in the first two chapters, whereas in the later chapters more precise and legally relevant terminology is employed, which is specific to the relevant legal norm under discussion in the given instance.

---

[69] Art 1 of the CRC, n 7 above.

The NGO community generally prefers concepts such as 'a child associated with an armed force or armed group' over that of a 'child soldier'.[70] In order to be a soldier, one has to engage or potentially engage in armed conflict,[71] whereas the NGO community and soft law instruments advocate for the non-use and recruitment of children in a broader context than direct military engagement only. However, the concept 'child soldier' can reasonably be interpreted as being broader than any of the relevant treaty norms or customary rules in existence. When considering international law, there is little use in employing concepts such as 'a child associated with an armed force or armed group' unless one wishes to advocate for the adoption of broader or higher legal standards, which I do not wish to do. I will therefore use the term 'child soldier' instead of broader concepts such as those discussed.

Like virtually any problem that is difficult to contain and address, child soldiering is multifaceted. Today it is clear that children participate, on a significant scale, in gang activity, whether it is on the streets of Los Angeles or in the context of narco-gangs in Mexico and other parts of Latin America.[72] Children are also extensively used in terrorist activities.[73] Nevertheless, for present purposes, child soldiering will for the most part be discussed in the context of military recruitment and participation in armed conflict. The response to child soldiering in armed conflict is very different to that of child gang and terrorist participation. Not only is the application of IHL limited to armed conflict, but the application of IHRL is different during armed conflict, in light of the fact that IHL is often the *lex specialis*.[74] The prevention of the use of children in gang and terrorist activity is much more reliant on municipal policing and law enforcement. International law does not create obligations for entities such as gangs and groups utilising terror tactics (outside of the context of armed conflict), whereas IHL does so in relation to state

---

[70] This phraseology is also used in the Paris Principles, n 66 above.

[71] See generally Chapter 3.II below.

[72] Edgar Jimenez Lugo, who is known as 'El Ponchis', is currently standing trial in Mexico for the murder, torture and decapitation of four people. His alleged crimes were all committed when he was fourteen years of age, and within the context of narco-gang warfare. Children participate in such gang activity on a significant scale. I Grillo, 'In Teenage Killers, Mexico Confronts a Bloody Future', *Time*, 8 December 2010.

[73] Terrorist activities in this context refers to the nature of the tactics used, eg bombings of civilian markets with the intention to inspire fear in the minds of a civilian population. The term is not used to connote a political determination regarding the nature of a specific group.

[74] There is some disagreement as to whether IHL is always the *lex specialis* and IHRL the *lex generalis*, or whether one has to consider the case at hand before determining which regime's norm is the *lex specialis*. Moreover, increasing commentators are considering other possibilities than the *lex specialis/lex generalis* construct to assess the relationship between IHL and IHRL. See generally Chapter 4.I below.

and non-state armed groups during armed conflict.[75] Outside the context of armed conflict, the international law duties to which states are subject in suppressing crime related to gangs and terror groups emanate from IHRL, not IHL. Therefore, although there is a margin of overlap, suppressing the use of children by gangs and terrorist entities requires a unique response.

The phenomenon of girl soldiers has rightly received increased attention from within the child soldier discourse. The use of girl soldiers adds several unique dimensions to the problem: most significantly, sexual exploitation.[76] Girl soldiers can broadly be divided into two categories: first, girls who are recruited to contribute to the war effort, in the same way as boys are recruited and used; and secondly, girls who are specifically recruited for the purpose of sexual exploitation, often called 'bush wives' in the African context.[77] Both groups are equally susceptible to sexual abuse by fellow soldiers, and especially commanders. Male child soldiers also sexually abuse young girls.[78] In many respects during the prevention of the use and recruitment of child soldiers the needs of girls require specific attention. This is particularly important during disarmament, demobilisation and reintegration processes. In this study, the particular experiences and needs of girls are acknowledged and addressed whenever this is relevant to the prevention of the military use and recruitment of children. However, this study has at its heart the concept 'child', not boy or girl. I therefore make no gender distinctions with regard to the reasons why children should not be used and recruited as soldiers.[79]

---

[75] See generally Chapter 3.II below. In the age of the war on terror, the concept of terrorism has become less precise. News media and the US administration routinely refer to belligerents in the ongoing conflicts in Iraq and Afghanistan as terrorists. These conflicts are conflicts properly falling within the IHL paradigm. As such, children who are used and recruited into structures engaged in these conflicts form part of the subject matter of this study.

[76] R Brett, 'Girl Soldiers Denial of Rights and Responsibilities' (2004) 23(2) *Refugee Survey Quarterly* 32, see generally.

[77] See, eg *AFRC appeals* case, n 18 above, 186.

[78] A Honwana, *Child Soldiers in Africa* (Philadelphia, PA, University of Pennsylvania Press, 2007) 91–92.

[79] I am of the view that the law cannot create a distinction based on sex for the purpose of prohibiting the enlistment, conscription or use of children. It is highly unlikely that such a differentiation will result in any greater enforcement. On the contrary, it is likely that such a differentiation will add a layer of complexity behind which armed groups can hide their use of boy soldiers. Furthermore, it was a hard fought battle in many states to gain the right for women to join the armed forces and positively contribute to the security and citizenship of their states. As it will be a step backwards to deny women the right to join the armed forces, it will equally be a retrogressive step to prohibit the enlistment, conscription or use of girl soldiers differently or for different reasons than boy soldiers.

## V. THE POTENTIAL ROLE OF INTERNATIONAL
## LAW IN PREVENTING CHILD SOLDIERING

In order to achieve social change with regard to a phenomenon as widespread and complex as the military use and recruitment of children, one has to recognise that there are many relevant disciplines and that any single contribution to the greater body of knowledge must identify the parameters and limitations not only of the relevant contribution, but also of the discipline from within which the contribution emanates. In this regard, Dror has stated:

> One of the more important devices used to initiate and control directed social change is law, a device the use of which is prima facie (and, in most cases, perhaps mistakenly) believed to be cheaper and quicker than education, economic development and other instruments and ways of directed social change.[80]

According to Tamanaha, the instrumentalist view of law 'is the notion that law is an instrument to achieve ends. At the systemic level, it has often been said that law is an instrument to serve the public good, or an instrument to direct social change.'.[81] He further acknowledges that the instrumentalist view of law has led some to argue that the 'law is an instrument of domination by one group over another within society . . . that lawyers instrumentally manipulate or utilise legal rules and processes to achieve the ends of their clients'.[82] His critique of an instrumentalist approach to law is premised on the importance of balancing interests among parties. If a lawyer manipulates the law to further the interest of her/his client, then the legitimacy of law, it may be argued, is at stake, as the legitimate interests of the opposing party to the dispute will not be safeguarded. However, when the law is used instrumentally to achieve social change by preventing the use and recruitment of child soldiers, there is no tension between such social change and the legitimate interests of the offending party. Both Dror and Tamanaha's approaches are outcomes based. As such, neither of these approaches will be of much value should law not be able to direct social change significantly. International law's ability to do so has, for the most part, been presumed by international lawyers,[83] whereas international relations scholars have been far more sceptical.[84]

---

[80] Dror, n 32 above, see generally.

[81] BZ Tamanaha, 'The Tension between Legal Instrumentalism and the Rule of Law' (2005–06) 33 *Syracuse Journal of International Law and Commerce* 131, 231.

[82] Ibid.

[83] B Kingsbury, 'The Concept of Compliance as a Function of Competing Conceptions of International Law' (1998) 19 *Michigan Journal of International Law* 345, 346. HH Koh, 'Why Do Nations Obey International Law?' (1997) 106 *Yale Law Journal* 2599, 2599–600.

[84] OA Hathaway, 'Do Human Rights Treaties Make a Difference?' (2001–02) 111 *Yale Law Journal* 1935, 1937–38.

As Schwebel has stated, 'compliance is a problem which lawyers tend to avoid rather than confront'.[85] This is even more apparent in the context of IHRL.[86]

After famously stating that 'almost all nations observe almost all principles of international law and almost all of their obligations almost all of the time', Henkin also stated that 'the forces that induce compliance with other law . . . do not pertain equally to the law of human rights'.[87] Unlike most other fields of international law, IHRL is primarily concerned with the manner in which a state treats people within its borders. The interests of other states are thus not directly at stake, as would be the case in the law of international finance, for example. Henkin thus argues that, without opposing state interest, the incentive to comply with rules of international law falls away to some extent. Yet the extraordinary amount of pressure that was placed on South Africa to abandon its policy of apartheid, an internal policy, serves as an example that compliance is not wholly dependent on opposing direct state interest.

Sceptics of IHRL and IHL are quick to cite the massive failures of these regimes, such as the 1994 Rwandan genocide, the Bosnian genocide that followed soon thereafter and more recently the killing of tens of thousands of civilians during the closing phases of the civil war in Sri Lanka.[88] The visibility of these failures is matched by the invisibility of the potential successes of these regimes. What these sceptics fail to appreciate is that efforts directed at the protection of human rights and those in armed conflict do not take much, if anything, away from any other field or discipline. While IHRL and IHL are less effective than one would hope, their pursuits are worthy and they do not have direct negative consequences.[89] Kuper has stated that 'it is arguable that the relevant law serves its purpose if it enables even one child to escape death or injury in armed conflict situations, and clearly it has succeeded in that respect'.[90] She has, however, also questioned 'why, with so much law, it

---

[85] SM Schwebel, 'Commentary' in MK Bulterman and M Kuijer (eds), *Compliance with Judgments of International Courts* (Leiden, Martinus Nijhoff, 1996) 39.

[86] Hathaway, n 84 above, 1937–38.

[87] L Henkin, *How Nations Behave* (New York City, Columbia University Press, 1979) 47 and 235.

[88] The mass atrocities committed in Rwanda and Bosnia during 1994 and 1995, respectively, are well documented and often referenced. However, the atrocities committed in Sri Lanka during 2009 are only just beginning to be brought to light. See especially the 'Report of the Secretary-General's Panel of Experts on Accountability in Sri Lanka' (31 March 2011).

[89] Against: D Kennedy, 'The International Human Rights Movement: Part of the Problem?' (2002) 15 *Harvard Human Rights Journal* 101, see generally; D Kennedy, *The Dark Sides of Virtue: Reassessing International Humanitarianism* (Princeton, NJ, Princeton University Press, 2004) 3; WH Simon, 'Solving Problems vs Claiming Rights: The Pragmatist Challenge to Legal Liberalism' (200405) 46 *William and Mary Law Review* 127, see generally.

[90] J Kuper, 'Children and Armed Conflict: Some Issues of Law and Policy' in D Fottrell,

seems generally so ineffective'.[91] Indeed, this study is aimed at achieving an era of application by materialising the relevant law.

Hathaway and others have attempted to gauge compliance with human rights norms quantitatively.[92] In her extensive study, Hathaway relied 'on a database encompassing the experiences of 166 nations over a nearly forty-year period in five areas of human rights law: genocide, torture, fair and public trials, civil liberties, and political representation of women'.[93] The aims of this study were to:

> examine two separate but intimately related questions. First, do countries comply with or adhere to the requirements of the human rights treaties they have joined? Second, do these human rights treaties appear to be effective in improving countries' human rights practices—that is, are countries more likely to comply with a treaty's requirements if they have joined the treaty than would otherwise be expected?[94]

The conclusions reached in this empirical study suggests that countries do not adhere to their IHRL treaty obligations on a significant scale and states are also not significantly more likely to comply with treaty requirements incumbent upon them as a result of the ratification of an IHRL treaty.[95] Nevertheless, on a qualitative level, Hathaway concludes:

> we must not jump to conclusions about the worth of human rights treaties based solely on the quantitative analysis above. Even if accurate, the results do not preclude the possibility that human rights treaties have a favourable impact on human rights.[96]

These findings are valuable and play an important role in the ongoing debate as to the efficacy of IHRL treaties. However, such a broad-based empirical study also has severe shortcomings, which may prove fatal to the veracity of the results.[97] The five treaty norms incorporated in the study all form part, in some way, of customary international law.[98] As such, the states that are not party to the relevant treaties have

---

*Revisiting Children's Rights: 10 Years of the UN Convention on the Rights of the Child* (Leiden, Brill, 2000).

[91] J Kuper, *International Law Concerning Child Civilians in Armed Conflict* (Oxford, Oxford University Press, 1997) 216; J Kuper, 'International Law Concerning Child Civilians in Armed Conflict', PhD Thesis (University of Oxford, 1996) 308.

[92] Hathaway, n 84 above, generally. See also E. Neumayer, 'Do International Human Rights Treaties Improve Respect for Human Rights?' (December 2005) 49(6) *The Journal of Conflict Resolution* 925, see generally.

[93] Hathaway, n 84 above, 1936.

[94] Ibid, 1939.

[95] Ibid, 2002–20.

[96] Ibid, 2020.

[97] The first shortcoming of such a quantitative study, as Hathaway admits, is flaws in the data relied upon. Ibid, 1967.

[98] The prohibitions against genocide and torture are not only norms of customary international law; there is general consensus that these norms have attained the status of *jus cogens*. In the case of genocide, see especially *Prosecutor v Zoran Kupreškić et al*, Trial

comparable obligations incumbent upon them by virtue of customary international law. The most extreme example among the norms used in the study is genocide. No state would dare argue that they are not under an international law obligation not to commit genocide, regardless of whether that state has ratified any treaty prohibiting such conduct and regardless of the fact that the relevant state engages in the commission of genocide. Therefore, if states do not adhere more to their treaty obligations than they do to their customary international law obligations, the nominal variance between treaty norm observance by states who are subject to the relevant treaty norm vis-à-vis those who are not may be explained.

This study also largely fails to take account of the individual circumstances of the relevant state. For example, the US is not a state party to the CRC, whereas the DRC is.[99] However, the level of compliance by the US to the CRC is significantly higher than that of the DRC. Nevertheless, the CRC may have already had an impact on the rights of children in the DRC, whereas this is not, of course, the case with the US.

Quantitative studies, by definition, are limited to treaty norms. In analysing the weaknesses of Hathaway's study I am not attempting to argue that such statistical analysis is irrelevant, but that such findings are not conclusive. The point of convergence between quantitative and

---

Chamber II, ICTY-IT-95-16 (14 January 2000), para 520; J Wouters and S Verhoeven, 'The Prohibition of Genocide as a Norm of *Ius Cogens* and its Implications for the Enforcement of the Law of Genocide' (2005) 5 *International Criminal Law Review* 401, see generally. In the case of torture see especially *Prosecutor v Anto Furundžija*, Trial Chamber II, ICTY-IT-95-17/1-T10 (10 December 1998), paras 155–57; E De Wet, 'The Prohibition of Torture as an International Norm of *Jus Cogens* and Its Implications for National and Customary Law' (2004) 15 *European Journal of International Law* 97, see generally. Fair and public trial is a broad concept including various individual rights from a human rights perspective. Some of the most fundamental of these rights have been identified as having crystallised into rules of customary international law. CJF Doebbler, and MP Scharf, 'Will Saddam Hussein Get a Fair Trial' (2005-2006) 37 *Case Western Reserve Journal of International Law* 21, see generally; CJF Doebbler, *Introduction to International Human Rights Law* (CD Publishing, 2007) 108. In her study Hathaway defined civil liberties as 'freedom of expression and belief, association and organisational rights, rule of law and human rights, and personal autonomy and economic rights' (Hathaway, n 84 above, 1975). This definition is also very broad, incorporating various rights, most of which undoubtedly form part of customary international law. Political representation of women was measured 'using the percentage of men in each country's legislature' (ibid). There is wide support for the principle of non-discrimination being a *jus cogens* norm; some argue that the *jus cogens* dimensions are limited to racial discrimination: J Dugard, *International Law: a South African Perspective* (Cape Town, Juta, 2011) 39; while others argue that it is broader and includes discrimination based on sex: T Makkonen (revised and updated by J Kortteinen) ,'The Principle of Non-Discrimination in International Human Rights Law and EU Law' (Erik Castrén Institute, University of Helsinki, August 2005) 3. Nevertheless, non-discrimination based on sex undoubtedly forms part of customary international law.

[99] Convention on the Rights of the Child (entered into force 2 September 1990) 1577 UNTS 3.

qualitative data presents a good starting point from which to assess the ability of IHRL and IHL to achieve social change.

The results of Neumayer's quantitative study on whether the ratification of international human rights treaties increases respect for human rights indicate that, in general, for human rights treaty ratification to result in compliance, 'there must be conditions for domestic groups, parties, and individuals and for civil society to persuade, convince, and perhaps pressure governments into translating the formal promise of better human rights protection into actual reality'.[100] This finding is consistent with Cassel's hypothesis of IHRL, which includes IHL in his use of the term,[101] as a rope:

> Where rights have been strengthened the cause is usually not so much individual factors acting independently—whether in law, politics, technology, economics, or consciousness—but a complex interweaving of mutually reinforcing processes. What pulls human rights forward is not a series of separate, parallel cords, but a 'rope' of multiple, interwoven strands. Remove one strand, and the entire rope is weakened. International human rights law is a strand woven throughout the length of the rope. Its main value is not in how much rights protection it can pull as a single strand, but in how it strengthens the entire rope.[102]

Law, politics, technology, economics and consciousness are referenced. They, among innumerable others, also form strands in this rope. In adhering to an instrumentalist view of law, my approach to child soldier prevention in this study accords with Cassel's metaphor of human rights as a rope. Indeed, the norms and enforcement mechanisms of IHL and ICL also form strands in this rope. In order to achieve an era of application in the battle against the use and recruitment of child soldiers, it is necessary to continuously strengthen and refine each of the myriad of mechanisms that have a contribution to make in putting the law into action.

## VI. SUMMARY

Even if one is committed to the prevention of the use and recruitment of child soldiers, it remains important to understand that the issue is a complex one, and that there is no agreement on exactly what the parameters of such prohibition should be—or, indeed, on whether there should be so much focus on child soldier prevention. This chapter has introduced concepts and arguments surrounding the what, why and

---

[100] Neumayer, n 92 above, 952.
[101] Cassel, n 31 above, 126.
[102] Ibid, 123. See also J Tacsan, 'The Effectiveness of International Law: An Alternative Approach' (1996) 2(1) *International Legal Theory* 3, see generally.

how of child soldier prevention. For the most part, the remainder of this work will expand on these concepts.

The distribution, use and causes of child soldiering in contemporary armed conflict are discussed in Chapter 2—informing the reader of child soldiering as a social reality. The distribution of child soldiers is relevant to the prevention of child soldiering in that reliance is placed in this regard on international machinery on a geospecific basis. The capacity in which child soldiers are used in armed conflict is similarly relevant to child soldier prevention, as different legal instruments prohibit only specific degrees of participation in armed conflict by children. Finally, understanding the causes of child soldiering potentially allows for the identification of strategies aimed at child soldier prevention addressing the root causes of the problem, not only its symptoms.

Chapters 3 and 4 addresses child soldiering from the vantage point of IHL and IHRL, respectively. Chapter 4 commences with an analysis of the relationship between IHL and IHRL. This relationship is particularly important in the context of child soldier prevention, as there is probably a larger degree of overlap between the IHL and IHRL prohibitive norms in this regard than any other proscribed conduct. The prohibition of the use and recruitment of child soldiers in terms of legal instruments forming part of IHL and IHRL is then discussed. Lastly, the customary law nature of the prohibition of child soldiering is also discussed.

Chapter 5 is aimed at the war crime of the use and recruitment of child soldiers. The primary contributions of this chapter are, first, an analysis of this war crime as formulated under the Rome Statute, and the scope for prosecution by the ICC; and secondly, the role the ICC can potentially play to prevent the use and recruitment of child soldiers.

The contribution of mechanisms forming part of the UN and the African Union (AU) to the prevention of child soldiering is analysed in Chapter 6. These UN mechanisms represent the core of the international communities' response to child soldiering. Therefore, this chapter presents a critical analysis of those UN mechanism best suited to the prevention of child soldiering, with particular attention being paid to areas of potential improvement to the effectiveness of these mechanisms. Conversely, a descriptive account of mechanisms forming part of the AU is also presented, as these mechanisms have never before been used in response to child soldiering, but have the potential to contribute to the prevention of the use and recruitment of child soldiers.

Chapter 7 is a case study on the prevention of child soldiering in the DRC, one of the countries in which children have been greatly affected by this issue for several decades. The conclusions reached in previous chapters are compared to the practical situation in the DRC in order to establish the accuracy of these conclusions in relation to a concrete situation.

The central thesis of the study is that, in order to enter an era of application in preventing child soldiering, focus must be shifted from norm creation to norm enforcement. In conclusion, Chapter 8 takes stock of key findings regarding international law's contribution to the fight against child soldiering.

# 2

# *Contemporary Child Soldiering: Distribution, Use and Causes*

C HILD SOLDIERING IS a reality in many societies. However, speaking of the prevention of this phenomenon is, for those who have never dealt with child soldiering directly during armed conflict, an abstract concept. Child soldiering is a social phenomenon that I argue can be addressed—and prevented—through the instrumentality of international law. However, to achieve this, international law must address the social reality and not the prevailing perceptions of the reality, which are often determined by popular culture and strategic advocacy, amongst other factors. This chapter analyses the distribution, the nature of the use and the causes of child soldiering—in other words, where, when and why child soldiers are recruited and used in hostilities.

The distribution of child soldiers is analysed in order to indicate the scope and geographical spread of the child soldier problem. This is important in the context of this study, as the mobilisation of international machinery, such as the United Nations Security Council, is dependent on the scope of a problem. Furthermore, the geographical location of the problem is material in the application of international law. Regional legal regimes, such as the African Court on Human and Peoples' Rights, are limited to specific geographical regions. As the era of application occurs within limited resources and capacity, such resources and capacity must be allocated to regions that are most affected by the phenomenon.

The contemporary use of child soldiers is an issue central to the social reality of what the international community wants to address when referring to 'child soldiering'. Yet the definition of 'child soldiering' is problematic for a number of reasons. In many conflicts in developing states, non-state armed groups often take the form of extended networks of people that operate on a nomadic basis. In other words, a combatant's entire family travels with the armed group. Children perform domestic chores, which directly benefits the armed group. Are they child soldiers, or is a more proximate role to hostilities required? While the positive law in this regard is discussed in Chapters 3–5, this chapter offers insight into this facet of the social reality.

Finally, the causes of child soldiering may provide an entry point for addressing the phenomenon through the instrumentality of international law. If clear causes can be identified, the strategies for the enforcement of international law can be focused on addressing such causes. As these questions are often anthropological and socio-geographical in nature, I have set rather modest aims for this chapter. This chapter accordingly provides context to the subsequent chapters that aims at addressing these social realities specifically.

## I. DISTRIBUTION OF CHILD SOLDIERS

During the mid-1990s it was estimated that there were 300,000 child soldiers internationally. Brett and McCallin have been credited with first citing this figure.[1] In 1998, these authors acknowledged that 'the total number of child soldiers in each country, let alone the global figure, is not only unknown but unknowable'.[2] From the outset, this figure was nothing more than guesswork. Nevertheless, a majority of the academic contributions and reports by non- and inter-governmental organisations (NGOs and IGOs) to date indicate that there are approximately 300,000 child soldiers.[3] There is no reliable quantitative data that support this figure and, moreover, the term 'child soldier' lacks definitional precision to categorise a given number of people to that genus. The continuous use of this figure without any revision has led many commentators to conclude that the number of child soldiers has been very stable for close to twenty years.[4] The conclusion may possibly be correct, but the manner

---

[1] J Hart, 'The Politics of Child Soldiers' (2006–07) 13 *Brown Journal of World Affairs* 217, 217.

[2] R Brett and M McCallin, *Children: The Invisible Soldiers* (Stockholm, Rädda Barnen, 1998) 31.

[3] The International Committee for the Red Cross has committed to a figure of 300,000 (www.icrc.org/Web/eng/siteeng0.nsf/html/p0824). The Coalition to Stop the Use of Child Soldiers, '2001 Global Report on Child Soldiers' (2001) 10 and 13 (2001 Global Report) states that there are 300,000 child soldiers, with 120,000 in Sub Saharan Africa. The Coalition moved away from committing to specific figures in its subsequent 2004 Global Report on Child Soldiers (2004) (2004 Global Report), where it was stated that, regardless of the coming to an end of some of the worst conflicts in Africa during the reporting period, there were still in the region of 100,000 active child soldiers in Sub-Saharan Africa. In a recent publication, Singer still adhered to the figure of 300,000 child soldiers globally: PW Singer, 'The Enablers of War: Causal Factors Behind the Child Soldier Phenomenon' in S Gates and S Reich, (eds), *Child Soldiers in the Age of Fractured States* (Pittsburgh, PA, Pittsburgh University Press, 2009) 93.

[4] Some organisations have, however, adapted their figures. Human Rights Watch correctly indicates that no exact figures exist; however, until recently they nevertheless committed to a figure of 200,000. They further state that in some conflicts, such as Sri Lanka, more than a third of all child soldiers were female (www.hrw.org/campaigns/

in which the conclusion is reached is certainly not. Nevertheless, civil society is the primary architect and driving force behind the humanitarian narrative, which paints children as innocent, passive victims who fall pray to evil adults within the context of ever more brutal armed conflict. Utilising a consistent of figure of 300,000 over the course of two decades reinforces this narrative.

Indicating the distribution of child soldiers within acceptable parameters of accuracy is challenging enough, not to mention speculating on the number of child soldiers globally. Nevertheless, in order to obtain a sense of the extent of the child soldier problem, the distribution of child soldiers needs to be taken into account as well as their number. Focusing solely on the distribution of child soldiers has the effect that the extent of the problem in a state with a very small number of child soldiers may be equated with that of a state utilising a significant number of child soldiers. Conversely, focusing solely on the numbers of child soldiers may have the effect that states in which there are not many child soldiers receive little or no attention. Children are not used or recruited in equal measure, by the same methods or for the same reasons across all of these countries. A myriad of human rights violations are committed against child soldiers. Nevertheless, the treatment of children and the roles they perform within military structures also differ widely. For example, one of the particularly egregious problems associated with child soldiering is the sexual abuse of children, particularly, though not exclusively, girls. The sexual misuse of children was the norm in Sierra Leone, whereas in Sri Lanka this practice was apparently unheard of.[5]

A study by Reich and Achvarina indicates that the ratio of child participants in armed groups in different conflicts that overlap temporally and are close in geographic proximity to one another is often very differ-

---

crp/fact_sheet.html). The United Nations Children's Fund (UNICEF) holds that there are 250,000 active child soldiers internationally (www.unicef.org/protection/files/Armed_Groups.pdf). UNICEF cites Otunnu, former United Nations Special Representative to the Secretary-General on Children and Armed Conflict as authority: see OA Otunnu, '"Era of Application": Instituting a Compliance and Enforcement Regime for CAAC', Statement before the Security Council, New York, 23 February 2005, 3. The Coalition to Stop the Use of Child Soldiers, '2008 Global Report on Child Soldiers' (2008) (2008 Global Report) did not commit to exact figures.

[5] CL Hogg, 'The Liberation Tigers of Tamil Eelam (LTTE) and Child Recruitment', Coalition to Stop the Use of Child Soldiers forum on armed groups and the involvement of children in armed conflict, Chateau de Bossey, Switzerland (4–7 July 2006) 13; E Restoy, 'The Revolutionary United Front (RUF): Trying to Influence an Army of Children', Ibid, 5 et seq. More recent evidence suggests that government forces raped Tamil women in the final stages of the conflict. However, the sexual abuse of child soldiers by the Liberation Tigers for Tamil Eelam has not been indicated. See 'Report of the Secretary-General's Panel of Experts on Accountability in Sri Lanka' (31 March 2011), 152–53 and 176.

ent.[6] Again, the accuracy of the figures relied on is highly questionable.[7] Various single-country studies have been conducted on child soldiering. Often these studies include estimates of the number of children who participate or have participated in armed conflict in the relevant conflict. The numbers in any one of these studies are estimates at best, as no vigorous quantitative study into the number of child soldiers in any conflict has been conducted. Relying on these various studies to inform a more global figure of child soldiers is very problematic. The methodologies of these studies differ largely and the definition accorded to concepts such as 'child soldier' and 'armed conflict' also differ among them. However, I do not dispute that children are used militarily and recruited on a massive scale.

The geographical distribution and numbers of active child soldiers are factual questions bound by temporal constraints. Presenting a one-dimensional account of the distribution and numbers of child soldiers in a single time frame yields results of little analytical value. The dynamics of modern conflict are such that many conflicts are short-lived, with high casualty rates, eg the 1994 Rwandan genocide.[8] The 1990s are testament to the fact that the laws of probability do not exclude the occurrence of many brutal conflicts in a single short time-frame.[9] For instance, using the period 1994–95 to ascertain the civilian death rate in conflicts the world over will result in grossly unrepresentative results, as this period includes the genocides in Rwanda and Bosnia.[10] Similarly, the effective-

[6] SF Reich and A Achvarina, 'Why Do Children Fight? Explaining Child Soldier Ratios in African Intra-State Conflicts' (Ford Institute, 2005). For example, this study indicates that in armed conflict in Sierra Leone (1991–2000) children represented 25% of total combatants, whereas in armed conflict in neighbouring Liberia (1999–2003) children represented 53% of all combatants. However, some caution is called for in relying on these figures. The study is not based on fieldwork conducted by the authors, and includes figure on the number of child soldiers who participated in twelve countries. Never before have there been reliable figures on the number of child soldiers in any of these countries, not to mention, for example, the Angolan conflict (1975–95), in which the study claims children made up 10–15% of the combatants, and that a total of 8,000 child soldiers were used. In this study the definitions accorded to the concepts 'child soldier' and 'armed conflict' do not accord with those definitions as used in law.

[7] Ibid. In fairness to Reich and Achvarina, their quantitative analysis on the causes of child soldiering is of immense value. Although their 'N' was limited, this is defensible.

[8] The Rwandan Genocide lasted for approximately 100 days (from 6 April to mid-July 1994), and it is widely considered that at least 500,000 people were killed during this short period (although this is the most conservative estimate). Statistics generally put the death count between 800,000 and 1 million. See A Des Forges, 'Leave None to Tell the Story: Genocide in Rwanda' (Human Rights Watch, 1999); 'Rwanda: How the Genocide Happened' (BBC, 1 April 2004)—this publication subscribes to a figure of 800,000 deaths; and the 'OAU Inquiry into Rwanda Genocide' (August 1998) 12(1) *Africa Recovery* 4—this report subscribes to a figure of 1 million deaths.

[9] 'Human Security Report 2005: War and Peace in the 21st Century' (Human Security Centre, Lui Centre for Global Issues, University of British Columbia, 2005).

[10] The Rwandan genocide took place between 6 April and mid-June 1994, n 8 above). The term 'Bosnian genocide' can refer to two separate occurrences. The first and most general is the Srebrenica genocide (or Srebrenica massacre), during which, in July 1995,

ness of the campaign against child soldiering cannot be gauged without taking account of the post-1990s decline in civil wars.

## A. The 'Child Soldier Global Reports'

Between 2001 and 2008, the Coalition to Stop the Use of Child Soldiers (CSUCS) released 'Child Soldier Global Reports' at three-year intervals. In total, three such reports were released, covering the periods June 1998 to April 2001, April 2001 to March 2004 and April 2004 to October 2007 (see Tables 1–3). These studies are the only studies that produce a global account of the geographical and temporal distribution of child soldiers. Each of these reports addresses child soldiering on a country-by-country basis, and includes a country summary of all countries internationally, detailing the specific countries situation regarding child soldiering. The significance of these reports is not only that they represent the only comprehensive data source on the distribution of child soldiers, but also that a single entity is responsible for all three reports, resulting in a high degree of consistency in the methodologies employed across the reports. During 2011, the CSUCS transitioned from being a coalition of different NGOs to becoming an NGO in its own right. With this came a change in name, to Child Soldiers International, and, it seems, a change in approach and research focus. Following the 2008 Global Report, Child Soldiers International has not yet issued a Global Report of similar scope. The organisation did, however, issue a Global Report entitled 'Louder Than Words: An Agenda to End State Use of Child Soldiers'.[11] This report focuses only on state recruitment and use, and is thus less useful when considering the use of child soldiers generally, over a period of time.

approximately 8000 Bosniak (Bosnian Muslim) men and boys were killed. The second usage of the term 'Bosnian genocide' refers to the ethnic cleansing that took place during the Bosnian War (1992–95). Both these occurrences overlap with the time period 1994–95.

[11] 'Louder Than Words: An Agenda to End State Use of Child Soldiers' (Child Soldiers International, 2012).

**Table 1: The 2001 Global Report: Countries that Used Child Soldiers between June 1998 and April 2001**

|    | Americas and Caribbean | 19 | Yugoslavia (former) |
|----|------------------------|----|---------------------|
| 1  | Colombia               |    | **Middle East & North Africa** |
| 2  | Mexico                 | 20 | Algeria |
| 3  | Peru                   | 21 | Iran |
|    | **Asia/Pacific**       | 22 | Iraq |
| 4  | Afghanistan            | 23 | Israel/Occupied Palestinian Territories |
| 5  | East Timor             | 24 | Lebanon |
| 6  | India                  |    | **Sub-Saharan Africa** |
| 7  | Indonesia              | 25 | Angola |
| 8  | Myanmar                | 26 | Burundi |
| 9  | Nepal                  | 27 | Chad |
| 10 | Pakistan               | 28 | Democratic Republic of the Congo |
| 11 | Papua New Guinea       | 29 | Eritrea |
| 12 | Philippines            | 30 | Ethiopia |
| 13 | Solomon Islands        | 31 | Republic of the Congo |
| 14 | Sri Lanka              | 32 | Rwanda |
| 15 | Tajikistan             | 33 | Sierra Leone |
| 16 | Uzbekistan             | 34 | Somalia |
|    | **Europe and Eurasia** | 35 | Sudan |
| 17 | Russia                 | 36 | Uganda |
| 18 | Turkey                 |    |  |

**Table 2: The 2004 Global Report: Countries that Used Child Soldiers between April 2001 and March 2004**

|    | Americas and Caribbean | 13 | Yemen |
|----|------------------------|----|-------|
| 1  | Colombia               |    | **Sub-Saharan Africa** |
|    | **Asia/Pacific**       | 14 | Angola |
| 2  | Afghanistan            | 15 | Burundi |
| 3  | India                  | 16 | Central African Republic |
| 4  | Indonesia              | 17 | Chad |
| 5  | Myanmar                | 18 | Côte d'Ivoire |

| 6 | Nepal | 19 | Democratic Republic of the Congo |
|---|---|---|---|
| 7 | Philippines | 20 | Guinea |
| 8 | Sri Lanka | 21 | Liberia |
| | Europe and Eurasia | 22 | Republic of the Congo |
| 9 | Russia | 23 | Rwanda |
| | **Middle East & North Africa** | 24 | Sierra Leone |
| 10 | Iran | 25 | Somalia |
| 11 | Iraq | 26 | Sudan |
| 12 | Israel/Occupied Palestinian Territories | 27 | Uganda |

**Table 3: The 2008 Global Report: Countries that Used Child Soldiers between April 2004 and October 2007**

| | Americas and Caribbean | | Middle East & North Africa |
|---|---|---|---|
| 1 | Colombia | 10 | Iraq |
| | **Asia/Pacific** | 11 | Israel/Occupied Palestinian Territories |
| 2 | Afghanistan | | **Sub-Saharan Africa** |
| 3 | India | 12 | Burundi |
| 4 | Indonesia | 13 | Central African Republic |
| 5 | Myanmar | 14 | Chad |
| 6 | Nepal | 15 | Côte d'Ivoire |
| 7 | Philippines | 16 | Democratic Republic of the Congo |
| 8 | Sri Lanka | 17 | Somalia |
| 9 | Thailand | 18 | Sudan |
| | | 19 | Uganda |

Valuable as these studies are, it is important to be aware of their limitations. The 2008 Global Report contained individual country reports for 197 countries.[12] These country studies are based on desk research. Methodologically, the data on the distribution of child soldiers are more reliable than the statistical figures on the number of child soldiers in each country. Quite simply, it is much easier for NGOs, IGOs and international organisations (IOs) to obtain verifiable information that there

---

[12] 2008 Global Report, above n 4, 7.

are child soldiers in an area than to establish how many child soldiers there are. Furthermore, when compiling these reports, the CSUCS relies on an expansive definition of 'child soldier', which uses eighteen as the age threshold and does not require direct participation in hostilities as the majority of legal instruments do.[13] Thus, some countries that are indicated by CSUCS as using or recruiting child soldiers do so without violating any international legal obligation.

The 2001 Global Report indicated that children were used in armed conflict in thirty-six countries and recruited in 'more than 85'.[14] For the 2004 reporting period, twenty-seven countries used child soldiers and 'at least 60 countries' recruited children.[15] Most recently, during the 2008 reporting period, children were used in nineteen countries and recruited in 'at least 86 countries'.[16]

A noticeable decline in the number of countries where child soldiers are used is apparent, whereas the number of countries where children are recruited is more erratic. Nevertheless, no available data supports the inference that this decline is primarily due to international law's prohibition of the use and recruitment of child soldiers. There are many variables involved. Most relevantly, the number of armed conflicts has drastically declined since the mid- to late 1990s.[17] If there are fewer wars, there will be fewer wars in which children are used as combatants. While the ideal will be a reduction in conflict altogether, from a child soldier preventative point of view, the aim is a reduction in the use and recruitment of child soldiers despite the occurrence of armed conflict. The end of the cold war has changed the dynamics of civil war in developing countries for good. States engaged in such conflicts no longer have the backing (financial and otherwise) of opposing superpowers to sustain their internal conflict and war economies. On the positive side, this has led to a reduction in civil wars altogether.[18] On the negative side, this has rendered the face of such civil wars more profit-oriented and criminalised.[19]

In particular, many of the armed conflicts that were specifically known for the prevalence of child combatants have ended. These include Liberia and Sierra Leone, and since the 2008 Global Report the conflict in Sri Lanka has also ended. The anecdotal decline in areas where child soldiers are actively used in hostilities corresponds loosely to such decline in armed conflicts. This alone may possibly account for the greatest reduction in child soldiers. This contention is further substantiated by

---

[13] 2004 Global Report, above n 3, 15.
[14] 2001 Global Report, above n 3, 10 and 27–28.
[15] 2004 Global Report, above n 3, 2–3 and 14.
[16] 2008 Global Report, above n 4, 2–3 and 12.
[17] 'Human Security Report', above n 9.
[18] Ibid, 150–58.
[19] PW Singer, *Children at War* (Oakland, CA, University of California Press, 2006) 49–52.

the less pronounced decline in the number of countries which are not at war but which nevertheless recruit child soldiers. A further effect of the 'new' perception that the use of child soldiers is unacceptable is that offending parties now better hide their use of child soldiers.[20] Given the late response to child soldiering by international law, it is simply too early to draw any conclusions on the long-term effect of these measures.

*i. Child Soldier Distribution Trends: the 'Global Reports'*

The countries that used child soldiers in each of the Global Reports are named and categorised according to region in Tables 1, 2 and 3.

Early modern warfare marked a turning point in the utility of child soldiers; this period is characterised by the emergence of gunpowder weapons on the battlefield. Before firearms were used in armed conflict, younger children were often used in combat support roles, as opposed to direct combat.[21] In the age of slashing and stabbing weapons, younger children would have been vulnerable to older, more experienced soldiers. However, a bullet fired by a child is as deadly as one fired by an adult.

This further substantiates the well-supported argument that the technological advancement of weaponry, specifically the efficient and user-friendly nature of modern weapons, and the proliferation of weapons have had an effect on the number of child soldiers.[22] The

---

[20] A Pollar (member of the United Nations Committee on the Rights of the Child and former child soldier). I interviewed Mr Pollar on 1 February 2011 in Geneva, Switzerland. See also, Singer, ibid, 143–45; 'Children and Armed Conflict', *Watchlist on Children and Armed Conflict Newsletter*, November 2001; J Mamou, 'Soldier Boys and Girls', *Le Monde diplomatique*, November 2001.

[21] See DM Rosen, *Armies of the Young: Child Soldiers in War and Terrorism* (New Brunswick, NJ, Rutgers University Press, 2005) 5–6, who cites DB Parker and A Freeman, 'David Bailey Freeman', *Cartersville Magazine*, 2001, about the boy soldier David Bailey Freeman, who enlisted at age 11, initially as an aide-de-camp; MD Banks, 'Avery Brown (1852–1904), Musician: America's Youngest Civil War Soldier', *America's Shrine to Music Newsletter*, February 2001, about the boy soldier Avery Brown, who enlisted aged eight (stating he was 12 upon enlistment) as a drummer boy; R Talmadge, 'John Lincoln Clem', *The Handbook of Texas Online*, 12 June 2001, about the boy soldier John Lincoln Clem, who enlisted aged 10 as a drummer boy—he was known as the Drummer Boy of Shiloh; R Thompson, 'Village Honor It's Boy Soldier', *Cincinnati Enquirer*, 6 November 1999, about the boy soldier Gilbert van Zandt, who enlisted aged 10.

[22] Singer, n 19 above, 137; PW Singer, 'Talk is Cheap: Getting Serious About Preventing Child Soldiers' (2004) 37 *Cornell International Law Journal* 561, 565; R Stohl, 'Targeting Children: Small Arms and Children in Conflict' (2002–03) 9 *Brown Journal of World Affairs* 281, 288; J Dhanapala, 'Multilateral Cooperation on Small Arms and Light Weapons: From Crisis to Collective Response' (2002–03) 9 *Brown Journal of World Affairs* 163, generally; J Becker, 'Small Arms and Child Soldiers', presentation at the workshop 'Putting Children First: Building a Framework for International Action to Address the Impact of Small Arms', New York, 20 March 2001; V Gamba and R Cornwell, 'Arms, Elites, and Resources in the Angolan Civil War' in M Berdal and DM Malone (eds), *Greed and Grievance—Economic Agendas in Civil Wars* (Boulder, CO, Lynne Rienner Publishers, 2000) 160; AF Musah, 'Small Arms: A Time Bomb under West Africa's Democratization Process' (2002–03) 9 *Brown*

development of gunpowder weapons is one of the key developments in this regard. However, the weapons used during early modern warfare—black powder muskets—were crude and hard to work with. The Kalashnikov of 1947 (AK47) is often seen as the weapon that gave birth to the modern child soldier. Indeed, this is the weapon with which by far the most child soldiers are armed. However, it is important to note that children are armed with a wide range of weapons, from machetes to rocket-propelled grenades. Boys are also instructed to use rape as a weapon of war. Thus, child soldiering came into its own with the advent of modern warfare. This period coincides with the release of modern automatic small arms, including the AK47, and the early emergence of 'fourth generation' or 'post-modern' conflict, as discussed below.[23]

The distinction between the military recruitment on the one hand and the use of children in armed conflict on the other is very important to maintain, yet it is seriously under-recognised by the NGO, IGO and IO sectors and in academia. In less developed states, separate statistics on the military use and recruitment of children are non-existent. This is not true of more developed states that use or recruit children.

The 2001 Global Report indicated that the UK 'routinely sends 17-year-olds into combat'.[24] British soldiers under the age of eighteen were killed in combat in the Gulf War, as well as in the Falkland Islands conflict.[25] Between 1982 and 1999, ninety-two soldiers aged seventeen and sixteen died during military service with the British Armed Forces.[26] It was also reported that, between March 1998 and March 1999, 36.38 per cent of all new recruits into the British Armed Forces were younger than eighteen.[27] Similarly, in the US, children younger than eighteen served in combat units in the Gulf War, Somalia and Bosnia.[28] By 1999, the Pentagon reported that less than 100 soldiers younger than eighteen were serving with combat units.[29] The recruitment practices of the UK and US have remained the same to date. Nevertheless, both states have ratified the Optional Protocol to the Convention on the Rights of the Child on the Involvement of Children in Armed Conflict (the CIAC Protocol) and no longer use children in armed conflict, as opposed to recruiting children younger than eighteen.[30]

---

*Journal of World Affairs* 239; R Stohl, 'Reality Check—The Danger of Small Arms Proliferation' (2005) 6 *Georgetown Journal of International Affairs* 71.

[23] The AK47 became commercially available during 1949.
[24] 2001 Global Report, above n 3, 19.
[25] Ibid.
[26] Ibid, 13.
[27] Ibid, 19.
[28] Ibid.
[29] Ibid.
[30] Optional Protocol to the Convention on the Rights of the Child on the Involvement of Children in Armed Conflict (entered into force 12 February 2002) 2173 UNTS 222.

In some respects, the child soldiering problem is more far-reaching than the Global Reports suggest. Many adult soldiers started out as child soldiers and the psychological wounds sustained by many children who have since been demobilised will take years to heal, if they ever do.

Very often, child soldiering is seen as a uniquely African phenomenon, which is a false and misleading characterisation. It is true that the greatest number of child soldiers was found on the African continent during all three of the reporting periods, and this remains true today. However, it is apparent that, during the reporting period 2001–04, children in more countries were actively used in conflicts in Asia than Africa.[31] It has also been suggested that the child soldier problem was bigger in Latin America and Asia during the 1980s than in Africa.[32]

## B. The United Nations Secretary-General's List of Parties Who Use and Recruit Child Soldiers

In 2001, the Security Council called upon the Secretary-General of the United Nations to

> attach to his report a list of parties to armed conflict that recruit or use children in violation of the international obligations applicable to them, in situations that are on the Security Council's agenda or that may be brought to the attention of the Security Council by the Secretary-General, in accordance with Article 99 of the Charter of the United Nations, which in his opinion may threaten the maintenance of international peace and security.[33]

In 2009, the Security Council amended the Secretary-General's mandate to list groups that use and recruit child soldiers, by also requiring the Secretary-General to include in his report

> those parties to armed conflict that engage, in contravention of applicable international law, in patterns of killing and maiming of children and/or rape and other sexual violence against children, in situations of armed conflict, bearing in mind all other violations and abuses against children.[34]

This resolution further expressly requires that the Secretary-General now appends two annexes to his reports, the first dealing with situations on the agenda of the Security Council and the second with situations

---

[31] 2004 Global Report, above n 3. Children were actively used in thirteen countries in Asia and twelve in Sub-Saharan Africa. Children were also used in Algeria, North Africa.

[32] 2001 Global Report, above n 3, 10.

[33] Security Council Resolution 1379 of 2001, operative para 16. Art 99 of the Charter of the United Nations provides that 'the Secretary-General may bring to the attention of the Security Council any matter which in his opinion may threaten the maintenance of international peace and security'.

[34] Security Council Resolution 1882, operative para 3.

not on the agenda of the Security Council.[35] The Secretary-General has, however, been doing so on his own initiative since 2003.

The focus of the Secretary-General's reports is on naming armed groups that use or recruit child soldiers, including national armed forces, but not states as such, as is indicated by the words 'parties to armed conflict' and 'parties in situations of armed conflict' used in the relevant Security Council resolutions.[36] Indeed, it has been expressly stated in relevant reports that the focus is not on listing states as such, but parties to armed conflict.[37] In Table 4 I indicate in which states these armed groups are active. To date, ten reports have been filed containing such annexes,[38] yet there have been seven different sets of criteria for inclusion on the list.

**Table 4: The Criteria in the Different Reports of the UN Secretary-General**

| 2002 | Annex: 'Parties to armed conflict that recruit or use child soldiers.' |
|------|------------------------------------------------------------------------|
| 2003 | Annex 1: 'Updated list of parties to armed conflict that recruit or use children in situations of armed conflict on the agenda of the Security Council.' |
|      | Annex 2: 'Other parties to armed conflict that recruit or use children in armed conflict.' |

---

[35] Ibid, operative para 19(a).

[36] See Security Council Resolutions 1379 and 1882, operative paras 16 and 19(a), respectively.

[37] See, eg 'Report of the Secretary-General on Children and Armed Conflict' Security Council (26 April 2012) A/66/782, S/2012/261 (2012 Secretary-General's Report) 47.

[38] 'Report of the Secretary-General on Children and Armed Conflict' Security Council (26 November 2002) S/2002/1299 (Secretary-General's Report 2002) 14; 'Report of the Secretary-General on Children and Armed Conflict' Security Council (10 November 2003) A/58/546, S/2003/1053 (Secretary-General's Report 2003) 20–23; 'Report of the Secretary-General on Children and Armed Conflict' Security Council (9 February 2005) A/59/695, S/2005/72 (Secretary-General's Report 2005) 36–39; 'Report of the Secretary-General on Children and Armed Conflict' Security Council (26 October 2006) A/61/529, S/2006/826 (Secretary-General's Report 2006) 34–38; 'Report of the Secretary-General on Children and Armed Conflict' Security Council (21 December 2007) A/62/609, S/2007/757 (Secretary-General's Report 2007) 40–45; 'Report of the Secretary-General on Children and Armed Conflict' Security Council (26 March 2009) A/63/785, S/2009/158 (Secretary-General's Report 2009) 47–51; 'Report of the Secretary-General on Children and Armed Conflict' Security Council (13 April 2010) A/64/742, S/2010/181 (Secretary-General's Report 2010) 48–51; 'Report of the Secretary-General on Children and Armed Conflict' Security Council (23 April 2011) A/65/820, S/2011/250 (Secretary-General's Report 2011) 52–55; 'Report of the Secretary-General on Children and Armed Conflict' Security Council (26 April 2012) A/66/782, S/2012/261 (Secretary-General's Report 2012) 48–51; 'Report of the Secretary-General on Children and Armed Conflict' Security Council (15 May 2013) A/67/845, S/2013/245 (Secretary-General's Report 2013) 48–51.

| 2005 | Annex 1: 'List of parties that recruit or use children in situations of armed conflict on the agenda of the Security Council, bearing in mind other violations and abuses committed against children.' |
|---|---|
| | Annex 2: 'List of parties that recruit or use children either in situations of armed conflict not on the agenda of the Security Council or in other situations of concern, bearing in mind other violations and abuses committed against children.' |
| 2006 2007 | Annex 1: 'List of parties that recruit or use children in situations of armed conflict on the agenda of the Security Council, bearing in mind other violations and abuses committed against children.' |
| 2009 | Annex 2: 'List of parties that recruit or use children in situations of armed conflict not on the agenda of the Security Council, or in other situations of concern, bearing in mind other violations and abuses committed against children.' |
| 2010 2011 | Annex 1: 'List of parties that recruit or use children, kill or maim children and/or commit rape and other forms of sexual violence against children in situations of armed conflict on the agenda of the Security Council, bearing in mind other violations and abuses committed against children.' |
| | Annex 2: 'List of parties that recruit or use children, kill or maim children and/or commit rape and other forms of sexual violence against children in situations of armed conflict not on the agenda of the Security Council, or in other situations of concern, bearing in mind other violations and abuses committed against children.' |
| 2012 | Annex 1: 'List of parties that recruit or use children, kill or maim children, commit rape and other forms of sexual violence against children, or engage in attacks on schools and/or hospitals in situations of armed conflict on the agenda of the Security Council, bearing in mind other violations and abuses committed against children.' |
| | Annex 2: 'List of parties that recruit or use children, kill or maim children, commit rape and other forms of sexual violence against children, or engage in attacks on schools and/or hospitals in situations of armed conflict not on the agenda of the Security Council, or in other situations, bearing in mind other violations and abuses committed against children.' |
| 2013 | Annex 1: 'List of parties that recruit or use children, kill or maim children, commit rape and other forms of sexual violence against children, or engage in attacks on schools and/or hospitals in situations of armed conflict on the agenda of the Security Council.' |
| | Annex 2: 'List of parties that recruit or use children, kill or maim children, commit rape and other forms of sexual violence against children, or engage in attacks on schools and/or hospitals in situations of armed conflict not on the agenda of the Security Council, or in other situations.' |

I do not rely on the Secretary-General's reports to present a global account of the geographical distribution of child soldiers for a number of reasons. The reports name offending groups but not states as such. Because the categories have changed six times over the course of ten reports, no reliable comparison can be made between the reports. Most importantly, the Secretary-General is not tasked with listing all offending parties, but rather those on the agenda of the Security Council or those that the Secretary-General deems necessary to bring to the attention of the Security Council. This is rather arbitrary, as is indicated, for example,  by the inclusion of a group in Northern Ireland in the 2003 report and the exclusion of armed groups in the Central African Republic in the same report. It is nevertheless of value to note that groups in twenty-two countries have been included at least once in ten of the Secretary-General's reports to date. Excluding the first report, on average, groups in thirteen countries are represented in each report. Thus, even when comparing the results of these reports, there is no indication of either a decline or increase in the number of countries where child soldiers are used or recruited.

These reports do, however, provide a valuable data source to triangulate the data contained in the Global Reports. The 2003 and 2004 Secretary-General's reports loosely overlap with the 2004 Global Report. Similarly, the 2006 and 2007 Secretary-General's reports loosely overlap with the 2008 Global Report. All the states listed in the Secretary-General's reports are also listed in the corresponding Global Reports, except for the inclusion of Northern Ireland in the 2003 Secretary-General's report. However, the Secretary-General's reports are much more conservative than the Global Reports, save for the inclusion of Northern Ireland in the 2003 report, which was questionable at the time. Accordingly, the Global Reports list many more states than the Secretary-General's reports.

## C. Summary

It is to be expected that, from a regional perspective, the less developed regions of the world will represent the greatest number of child soldiers. At the beginning of this section I stated that, in order to obtain a sense of the extent of the child soldier problem, one should take into account the distribution as well as the number of child soldiers. However, the numbers that are available are not reliable. Nevertheless, it is clear that, even in terms of the most conservative estimates, hundreds of thousands of children have served, or are serving, in armed forces or groups the world over. It is further apparent that countries where children are actively used in conflict are generally clustered together: for example, there were clear clusters in Central Africa, West Africa, East Africa and

South-East Asia during the different reporting periods.[39] From a regional perspective, child soldiering is by far most prolific in Africa, followed by Asia.


## II. THE CONTEMPORARY USE OF CHILD SOLDIERS

Children perform many different roles in conflict, such as combatants, porters, spies, bodyguards, cooks, domestic servants and sex slaves. This creates problems in assessing when a child is unlawfully used or recruited in terms of the positive law and when a child is used as a child soldier as opposed to a child labourer. In this regard, there is a disconnect between most international law standards which proscribe child soldier use and recruitment and the broader, soft law definitions used by NGOs.[40] The hard law standards generally require direct or active participation in hostilities, whereas indirect participation in hostilities is sufficient in terms of soft law standards.[41]


## A. Child Soldier Use as an Asymmetric Conflict Structure

'Asymmetric warfare' denotes an armed conflict in which at least two opposing belligerents are engaged with a significant disparity in their military strength.[42] Where such a conflict exists, both sides cannot be committed to traditional tactics of war. The side with the severe military disadvantage will inevitably lose. 'Asymmetric conflict structures' refers to strategies and tactics used by one side to a conflict to level this uneven playing field.[43] The classic example is the use of guerrilla tactics by the Boers during the two Anglo-Boer Wars. Today, terrorism is most closely associated with the term 'asymmetric conflict structures'.[44]

Ancker and Burke speak of asymmetric conflict structures as a classic action–reaction–counteraction cycle.[45] What this denotes is that asym-

---

[39] A Honwana, *Child Soldiers in Africa* (Philadelphia, PA, University of Pennsylvania Press, 2005) 45, applies the concept 'war-scapes' to account for the influence armed conflicts exert on other conflicts in close proximity.

[40] See generally Chapter 1.IV above.

[41] See Chapters 4 and 5 generally for an analysis of the legal prohibition of the use and recruitment of child soldiers.

[42] See generally, E Benvenisti, 'The Legal Battle to Define the Law on Transnational Asymmetric Warfare' (2009–2010) 20 *Duke Journal of Comparative and International Law* 339.

[43] R Geiß, 'Asymmetric Conflict Structures' (2006) 88(864) *International Review of the Red Cross* 757. Recently 'asymmetric warfare' has been used more broadly so as to include specific strategies and tactics. Thus in the broad sense 'asymmetric warfare' can include 'asymmetric conflict structures'.

[44] Ibid, 758.

[45] CJ Ancker III and MD Burke, 'Doctrine for Asymmetric Warfare' [July–August 2003] *Military Review* 18.

metric tactics by definition encompass a large degree of uncertainty, thus one only knows how to react after the initial action, and the same holds true of any counteraction. For example, the armed conflict between the US and Al Quaeda and associated forces in Afghanistan is very much an asymmetric armed conflict. The US has vastly superior military strength. Al Quaeda and associated forces therefore employ civilian suicide bombings as an asymmetric conflict structure in reaction. In counteraction, the US escalates targeted killings by unmanned aerial vehicles. However, this is not necessarily how all such conflicts will play out. Should every reaction to an opposite action merely meet the threshold of the initial action, then there is no asymmetry to speak of.

Again, guerrilla tactics serve as an apt example. During the two Anglo-Boer Wars, such tactics were novel and were used only by one side to the conflict, hence it being asymmetric. However, guerrilla tactics during warfare are seen as standard today and completely acceptable. Thus, once all sides began to benefit from these tactics, they were no longer asymmetrical. Military strategists have developed war tactics and strategies to the extent that most armed forces will use conflict tactics to the very edge of permissibility in terms of IHL, ie military necessity versus humanitarian considerations. Thus, should an inferior force wish to employ asymmetric tactics, ie those not used by its opposition, such tactics, almost without exception, will be in violation of IHL.[46] The party that employs such tactics does so relying on an assumption that its opposition will refrain from doing so. A symmetric landscape will once again be established if the opposition does employ such tactics. Of course, the exception hereto is if the asymmetry is created as a result of the superior capacity of one participant to the armed conflict, for example, in technology in the case of the US in the so-called 'war on terror', or in vastly superior manpower, as was the case with Ethiopia in the Ethiopian/Eritrean war.

Traditionally, the use of child soldiers was explained by simply stating that the bigger the age range, the more people there are to replenish the ranks. Today, children are often recruited not because they are soldiers that increase the force numbers, but specifically because they are children. Thus, the use of child soldiers, like terrorism, is an asymmetric conflict structure. The most common illustration of the contribution the unique physical attributes of a child can make to a war effort is the common use of children for intelligence gathering, ie as spies.[47]

Beyond intelligence gathering, there are further asymmetries involved in the use of children on the battlefield. Good military strategists and

---

[46] See Geiß generally, n 43 above.

[47] Between April 2004 and October 2007 the government armed forces of Burundi, Colombia, the Democratic Republic of the Congo, India, Indonesia, Israel, Nepal and Uganda used children as spies, informants and messengers.

tacticians use their personnel's individual characteristics to their greatest benefit. For example, in Sri Lanka the Liberation Tigers of Tamil Elam used female child soldiers to execute suicide bombings in urban environments. The reason for specifically using female child soldiers was that they were less subject to thorough body searches by the police.[48] The most high-profile example was the assassination, by suicide bomb, of former Indian Prime Minister Rajiv Gandhi. Thenmozhi Rajaratnam is believed to have been younger than eighteen years old when she detonated the bomb.[49]

A further example of the advantages children carry onto the battlefield is that adult soldiers often find it difficult to fire on children, accounting for the title of Dallaire's book on child soldiering *They Fight Like Soldiers, They Die Like Children*.[50] The first American military casualty in the US/ Afghan war was US Army Special Forces Sergeant Nathan R Chapman, who was gunned down by a fourteen-year-old boy.[51]

The use of children as an asymmetrical conflict structure has received almost no academic attention and further research into this phenomenon is of great importance. Such use of children adds to the demand for child soldiers, and is thus relevant to the prevention of the recruitment and use of child soldiers.

## B. Modern Armed Conflict, National Armed Forces and the Use and Recruitment of Child Soldiers

It is often said that during the era of modern warfare—the emergence of the 'Kalashnikov generation'—the dynamics of conflict worldwide have shifted from the old position (pre-World War II), where the targets of conflict were military personnel and wars were fought between nations, to the new position (post-World War II), where civilians are the primary targets and non-international armed conflict represents the great majority of modern conflicts. According to UNICEF, before 1900 civilians represented 5 per cent of all conflict deaths, whereas during the 1990s civilians represented 90 per cent of all war-related fatalities.[52] Whether this is indeed true is questionable. Pinker and others have argued very

---

[48] D Ganguly, 'Female Assassins Seen in Sri Lanka' (Associated Press, 5 January 2000); D Ganguly, 'Female Fighters Used in Sri Lanka' (Associated Press, 10 January 2000); Hogg, n 5 above, 13.

[49] See, eg RJ Frey, *Fundamentalism* (New York, Facts on File, 2007) 365.

[50] R Dallaire, *They Fight Like Soldiers, They Die Like Children* (London, Random House, 2010).

[51] DE Sanger, 'Bush, On Offense, Says He Will Fight to Keep Tax Cuts', *New York Times*, 6 January 2002.

[52] 'The State of the World's Children' (UNICEF, 2005) 40.

convincingly that in bygone eras violence and armed conflict was more rampant and more violent than today.[53]

Nevertheless, there are significant differences between the manner in which conflicts are fought today and how they were fought in the past. A number of models to account for this changing nature of conflict have been developed, such as the 'fourth generation conflict' model.[54] In the context of child soldiering, Singer speaks of 'post-modern warfare'.[55] Breaking war down into generations can be misleading: as Echevarria argues, 'the generational model is an ineffective way to depict changes in warfare. Simple displacement rarely takes place, significant developments typically occur in parallel.'[56] Such theories deal with war on a linear basis and, as such, Singer's open-ended designation of post-modern warfare is to be preferred. More often than not, wars in which children are used as soldiers are fought on battlefields in developing countries; the strategies and tactics used are more brutal and, on an increasing basis, legitimate ideology is being replaced with criminal and profit motives. For example, many theorists are of the view that the Revolutionary United Front's (RUF) real motivation in fighting the Sierra Leonean civil war was profit based.[57] This is purportedly the reason why they used Kono, the diamond-mining district, as their base. In Afghanistan and Colombia, a vicious circle has emerged where poppy fields (for heroin production) and coca plantations (for cocaine production), respectively, are kept to fund the war and the war is perpetuated to protect the drug trade.[58] In essence, the profitability of the drug trade has resulted in a situation where the arguably once defensible ideologies for the initiation of war have been replaced by a desire to protect the various groups' interests in a multi-billion dollar industry. Similarly, in the DRC, a great emphasis in recent conflict has been placed on the control of coltan (columbite–tantalite) mining areas.[59]

In all these countries mentioned, child soldiering is a problem.[60] Asymmetrical tactics are premised on an assumption that one's enemies

[53] See, eg S Pinker, *The Better Angels of our Nature: Why Violence has Declined* (New York, Penguin Books, 2011).

[54] WS Lind et al, 'The Changing Face of War: Into the Fourth Generation' [October 1989] *Marine Corps Gazette* 22.

[55] Singer, n 19 above, 49–52.

[56] AJ Echevarria II, *Fourth Generation War and Other Myths* (US Army Strategic Studies Institute, November 2005) 10.

[57] Restoy, n 5 above, 2; N Florquin and EG Berman (eds), *Armed and Aimless: Armed Groups, Guns and Human Security in the ECOWAS Region* (Small Arms Survey, Geneva, May 2005) 370.

[58] Singer, n 19 above, 50–51; S Wilson, 'Columbian Fighters Drug Trade is Detailed', *Washington Post*, 25 June 2003; M Kaldor, *New and Old Wars* (Cambridge, Polity Press, 1999), 102; J Dao, 'The War on Terrorism Takes an Aim at Crime', *New York Times*, 7 April 2002.

[59] J Lasker, 'Inside Africa's PlayStation War' (8 July 2008), available at www.toward-freedom.com.

[60] See Tables 1, 2 and 3.

will not follow suit. Recent experience has shown that this assumption frequently proves false in the context of child soldiering. Very often, the use of child soldiers by one party to an armed conflict results in their opposition also using child soldiers. The Sierra Leonean government forces had no answer to the military superiority of the RUF, a group infamous for their use of child soldiers. Ultimately, the Sierra Leonean government forces also resorted to child soldier use and recruitment.[61]

With the advent of globalisation, governments and aspiring governments in developing states have had to protect their status as 'legitimate' to a greater extent than in the past. The use of child soldiers by government forces is often seen as bad publicity, as it may hamper investment cooperation and foreign aid from developed states. This has led such forces to hide their use of child soldiers or to use intermediary groups that use child soldiers—so-called proxies. The use of proxies enables governments to maintain the benefits of having children among their ranks while still maintaining their position as legitimate. In some cases, however, these aims of legitimacy have led to the abandonment of the use or recruiting of child soldiers.[62]

Between April 2001 and March 2004, the national armed forces of Burundi, the DRC, Côte d'Ivoire, Guinea, Liberia, Myanmar, Rwanda, Sudan, Uganda and the US all used children younger than eighteen in armed conflict (as direct or indirect participants).[63] Furthermore, government-backed militias (proxies) in Colombia, Somalia, Sudan and Zimbabwe also used such children in hostilities.[64] Between April 2004 and October 2007, the national armed forces of Chad, the DRC, Israel, Myanmar, Somalia, Sudan and Southern Sudan, Uganda, Yemen and the UK used children in armed conflict.[65] During this period, the governments of Chad, Colombia, Côte d'Ivoire, the DRC, India, Iran, Libya, Myanmar, Peru, Philippines, Sri Lanka, Sudan and Uganda supported militias that used child soldiers.[66]

Today, armed conflict in developing states can generally be divided into those conflicts that are profit driven and criminalised, as discussed above, and the more traditional conflicts aimed at regime change. In the case of the former, few entry points exist to engage directly with belligerents to prevent child soldiering. Other avenues of prevention may be more appropriate. However, in the context of the second group, a greater premium is placed on the legitimacy of regimes in international politics than was the case during the cold war. As such, direct engagement with

---

[61] See *Prosecutor v Fofana and Kondewa*, SCSL-04-14-T.
[62] See generally Chapter 3.B below.
[63] 2004 Global Report, above n 3, 13.
[64] Ibid.
[65] 2008 Global Report, above n 4, 16.
[66] Ibid.

such regimes provides a very strong and viable entry point. The same holds true for engagement with governments where the national armed forces of a state uses and recruits child soldiers. This is evident in the increasing propensity among states not to use and recruit child soldiers in their national armed forces, but instead to support armed groups that do so. By so doing, states evade the negative implications of child soldier use and recruitment while still enjoying the benefits thereof. It is important that preventative efforts be aimed specifically at proxy forces that use or recruit child soldiers.

### III. CAUSES OF CHILD SOLDIERING

There are two facets to the causes of child soldiering. First, there are overarching causes of the phenomenon, which include social constructions like age thresholds and the actual ability of children to make decisions versus the social perception of not only a child's ability to make decisions, but also the role of a child in society. Secondly, there are the more proximate causes of child soldiering, eg poverty.

There are two dimensions in relation to the causes of child soldiering. There are those factors that cause a child to volunteer to join an armed group and those factors that lead to the members of an armed group enlisting or conscripting a child. In this regard, Andvig and Gates speak of the 'demand and supply' of child soldiers.[67] The factors that enhance the supply of child soldiers, ie that make children join armed forces and groups, like poverty and fear, are part of a systemic problem more deeply entrenched even than the child soldier phenomenon itself.

### A. Overarching Causes of the Child Soldier Phenomenon

On a daily basis, child soldiers aged seven to seventeen are recruited and used in armed conflict. Some are abducted at gunpoint, others volunteer, yet others take up arms by their own accord without any adult interference.[68] Nevertheless, there is a tendency to classify all such children generically as child soldiers.

The extreme disparity between these situations has divided theorists on the causes of child soldiering. The first group argues that universal causes of child soldiering can be identified and highlight the similari-

---

[67] JC Andvig and S Gates, 'Recruiting Children for Armed Conflict' in Gates and Reich, above n 3, 77–78. See also I Cohn and GS Goodwin-Gill, *Child Soldiers: The Role of Children in Armed Conflict* (Oxford, Oxford University Press, 1994) 23–43 for a similar approach.

[68] Situations have occurred where adults tried to stop children from engaging in conflict, but failed, ibid, 30.

ties between contemporary conflicts.[69] The second group highlights the *sui generis* nature of each situation and argues that such common causes cannot be identified across the board.[70] Accordingly, these are referred to as the 'common causes approach' and the '*sui generis* approach', respectively. This division is one that generally coincides with the narrative to which the particular commentator subscribes regarding her/his view of the child soldier phenomenon in broad terms. The 'humanitarian narrative' is dominant in this regard and paints the picture of child soldiers as innocent victims of adult manipulation and exploitation, whereas the conflicting narrative, the 'conscious actor narrative', holds that children are conscious decision-makers who exercise a choice to participate in conflict and, moreover, deserve recognition for their accomplishments as soldiers.

Essentially, those subscribing to the 'humanitarian narrative' focus on an aspect that ties children in conflict together: their vulnerability and susceptibility to exploitation. It therefore makes sense for them also to subscribe to the common causes approach. Conversely, those subscribing to the *sui generis* approach by definition focus on the unique attributes and situation of each child, and accordingly this view lends itself to the conscious decision narrative.

Some commentators argue that both narratives are present and applicable to varying degrees across many conflicts.[71] This group's position is best suited to play a meaningful role in assessing the causes of child soldiering for purposes of preventing the phenomenon. This is so due to the flexibility and adaptability of this approach. It is factually incorrect to equate the surrounding circumstances of all conflicts in which children act as soldiers with each other. It is equally incorrect to argue that there are no root causes that affect a majority of child soldiers and specifically their recruitment into conflict.

### i. The Common Causes versus Sui Generis Approach

Rosen is a champion of the *sui generis* approach. He argues that 'the specifics of history and culture shape the lives of children and youth during peace and war, creating many different kinds of childhood and many different kinds of child soldier'.[72] The proponents of the common causes approach do not suggest that the factors they have identified can account for the presence of each and every child soldier in conflict. For

---

[69] Singer, n 19 above, 46; R Brett and I Specht, *Young Soldiers: Why They Choose to Fight* (Boulder, CO, Lynne Rienner Publishing, 2004); M Wessells, *Child Soldiers: From Violence to Protection* (Boston, MA, Harvard University Press, 2006).

[70] Rosen, n 21 above, 132.

[71] Wessells, n 69 above, 31–32; Cohn and Goodwin-Gill, n 67 above, 23–43.

[72] Rosen, n 21 above, 132.

example, as root causes, force and poverty have received a great deal of focus, yet it has been noted that in specific instances, such as in Liberia, children were the first eager volunteers in recruitment queues,[73] and in El-Salvador upper-middle-class children volunteered at young ages.[74] Both approaches are present and applicable to varying degrees across many conflicts. As Wessells states, 'children become soldiers through different channels and for different reasons', in essence agreeing with Rosen.[75] However, Wessells goes on to state that each narrative forms part of the bigger picture.[76]

In adhering to specific narratives to account for child soldiering, a ripple effect is created that will ultimately affect issues such as the individual criminal responsibility of the child soldier, should the relevant child soldier have committed crimes while being a child soldier. In stating that the historical and cultural effects on the child are different on a case-by-case basis, Rosen also challenges the dominant view that the great majority of these children are victims of adult manipulation.[77] Child soldiers, he argues, deserve more credit for their participation in conflict, as in some instances fighting is the lesser evil as opposed to not fighting.[78] The converse of this argument is that children, as conscious participants, are less deserving of protection and should be treated as having individual responsibility for their deeds, in contrast with the dominant view, which focuses on the child as victim.

Wessells has acknowledged the multiplicity of contributory factors to the child soldier phenomenon, while still being able to identify areas of concern or factors regarding the causes of child soldiering.[79] He states that even within one conflict child recruitment may vary greatly according to context.[80] An interesting paradoxical relationship exists in that the circumstances in one conflict can differ so much that two children can take part without sharing any common motivational factor, whilst two different conflicts can influence each other to the extent that the

---

[73] Cohn and Goodwin-Gill, n 67 above, 23.

[74] Ibid, 30.

[75] Wessells, n 69 above, 32.

[76] Ibid. Wessells also explicitly identifies a third narrative: that children's sense of patriotic duty accounts for their presence on the battlefield. This narrative is said to be favoured by particular governments—obviously those which employ the use of child soldiers.

[77] Rosen, n 21 above, 132.

[78] This statement seems to have two levels of applicability. The first is in the mind of the child, ie she/he should fight to make a difference. It is thus a putative application. The second is in the form of objective necessity—if the child does not fight, she/he will perish. Rosen presents this in his case study of Jewish Partisan children during the Second World War. Rosen, n 21 above, 19–56.

[79] Wessells, n 68 above, 31.

[80] Ibid, 32.

use of child soldiers in the one can account for this phenomenon in the other[81]—what Nordstrom calls 'war-scapes'.[82]

## ii. Forced versus Voluntary Recruitment

The very high proportion of child members in some groups, like the Lord's Resistance Army (LRA), can be explained by the lack of appeal the group holds for voluntary recruits. The LRA has no clear political objective or ideology, and is seen by the communities in the areas where they operate as a threat.[83] There is not much appeal for voluntary recruits to join the LRA. As such, the LRA has relied very heavily on abduction and forced recruitment tactics. Children are much easier to recruit in this manner than adults. This goes a long way towards accounting for this group's extreme reliance on child soldiers.

The degree to which a young person can exercise an unfettered discretion in joining armed groups is disputed. In the most extreme cases, like the LRA, children abducted and forced to be child soldiers. Yet, in a majority of cases, children join voluntarily. In fact, many children who speak of their participation in conflict after demobilisation, even years after demobilisation, still hold the view that it was a wise choice they exercised to join and that it benefited their lives greatly.[84] In some instances, the survival rate of child soldiers was higher than that of child civilians.[85]

The question which then arises is whether children have the capacity to join an armed group truly voluntarily. Many argue that social factors, such as violent environments, poverty or starvation, force the hand of children to the extent that exercising the choice to become a soldier was really never a choice. Yet others argue that adults too are influenced by the same factors,[86] so the question posed is whether anybody exercises free choice in such circumstances. This argument must fail due to its treatment of children and adults as having the same decision-making and cognitive abilities and its failure to take into account the best interests of the child principle, which, by definition, does not apply to adults.

---

[81] Honwana, n 41 above, 45.

[82] Ibid.

[83] G Waschefort, 'Child Soldiers: The Legacy of East African Conflict' [July/August 2009] *De Kat* 70.

[84] K Peters and P Richards, 'Why We Fight: The Voices of Youth Combatants in Sierra Leone' (1998) 68 *Africa* 2; H West, 'Girls with Guns: Narrating the Experience of War of FRELIMO's "Female Detachment"' (2000) 73 *Anthropolgical Quarterly* 4; A Veale, 'From Child Soldier to Ex-Fighter, Female Fighters, Demobilisation and Reintegration in Ethiopia', Monograph 85 (Institute for Security Studies, 2003).

[85] Rosen, n 21 above, 19–56.

[86] G Van Bueren, *The International Law on the Rights of the Child* (Amsterdam, Kluwer, 1998) 335–36.

In an interview I conducted with Radhika Coomaraswamy, Under-Secretary-General of the United Nations and Special Representative to the Secretary-General for Children and Armed Conflict (as she then was), she argued that children younger than eighteen generally do not have a 'death concept', and that therefore the recruitment and use of such children remains exploitative even if one is sensitive to the participatory rights of children.[87] This is the preferred construction. In essence, Coomaraswamy argues, children are unable to give informed consent.

### iii. The Cognitive Development of Children

Psychiatric and psychologically identified stages of development have been used to determine the cognitive development of a child, most notably Piaget's theory of cognitive ability.[88] This involves drawing concrete lines between age groups based on general findings.[89] In fact, both international and municipal law in general rely on such categorisation of age groups to, for instance, determine criminal responsibility.[90]

This approach has been challenged by some social scientists arguing that children are more capable in many respects than the theory of cognitive development would suggest, their findings being based on ethnography.[91] Rosen sides with the new social-scientific side of this debate, arguing for the voluntary nature of children's decisions.[92] Those arguing for the decisional abilities of children place a further emphasis on greater participatory rights for children.[93] Freedom of association

---

[87] I interviewed Ms Coomaraswamy on 7 February 2011 in New York, USA. I have the interview notes on file.

[88] See specifically Piaget's work: J Piaget and B Inhelder, *The Growth of Logical Thinking from Childhood to Adolescence* (London, Routledge & Kegan Paul, 1958); J Piaget and B Inhelder, *The Early Growth of Logic in the Child: Classification and Seriation* (New York, Norton & Co, 1964); J Piaget, *The Child's Conception of the World* (London, Routledge & Kegan Paul, 1928); J Piaget, *The Moral Judgment of the Child* (London, Kegan Paul, Trench, Trubner & Co, 1932); J Piaget, *The Child's Construction of Reality* (London, Routledge & Kegan Paul, 1955).

[89] Piaget identified the following categories: sensorimotor stage (birth to age 2); preoperational stage (ages 2–7); concrete operational stage (ages 7–11); and formal operational stage (age 11 onwards).

[90] For example, Art 26 of the Rome Statute of the International Criminal Court (Rome Statute) (entered into force 1 July 2002) 2187 UNTS 90 excludes the criminal jurisdiction of the International Criminal Court (ICC) over persons younger than 18. Every municipal criminal justice system also used such age delineations to determine the age of criminal responsibility. To use one example: in terms of s 34 of the Crime and Disorder Act 1998, British municipal criminal law provides that age 10 is the minimum age for criminal responsibility. Preceding the Crime and Disorder Act a rebuttable presumption existed in British common law, presuming that children between the ages 10 and 14 were *doli incapax*.

[91] A Prout and A James, 'A New Paradigm for the Sociology of Childhood' in A Prout and A James *Constructing and Reconstructing Childhood* (London, Falmer Press, 1990) 8.

[92] Rosen, n 21 above, 133.

[93] Van Bueren, n 86 above, 335; Children of War, 'Report from the Conference on Children in War', Raoul Wallenberg Institute Report No 10 (1991).

and freedom of expression are also used to argue for the autonomy of the child.[94] Yet Van Bueren states that 'to regard the issue as only that of protection versus participation is too simplistic as some children will not survive unless taken into the armed forces'.[95] When I interviewed Zermatten, deputy chair (now chair) of the Committee on the Rights of the Child, he emphasised that the paradigm shift from child protection to child rights has not yet been completed.[96]

If it is true that all theorists will agree that at some developmental stage a child cannot make the informed decision to participate freely in conflict, there will be no pragmatic option but to apply the theory of cognitive development. This necessitates determining a yardstick age, to be used to determine whether a child has the ability to exercise free choice to join an armed force or group. This will be the case regardless of the fact that some children develop faster than others.

Clearly, international law cannot function without determining a cut-off age. However, that cut-off age is subject to criticism on the grounds that neither the fifteen- nor the eighteen-year-old yardsticks were established in terms of age parameters based upon psychiatric developmental data. Instead, these yardsticks were developed arbitrarily in terms of societal constructs of age and corresponding social roles. However, the best interest of the child is a trite principle of international law. It calls for a higher threshold that includes individuals with the decision-making competencies to voluntarily join armed forces or groups. This is so in order to protect those who do not possess comparable decision-making competencies.

## B. Proximate Causes of Child Soldiering

With reference to the causes of child soldiering, Singer speaks of 'enablers of war',[97] whereas Ames breaks these causes up into four categories.[98] 'Grievance factors' include poverty, loss of parents, ethnicity and political beliefs. 'Inducement factors' include pay, glory and future material gain. 'Solidarity factors' include group cohesion, village networks and friends. 'Accessibility factors' include presence and vulnerability of refugee camps. These factors are focused more on the supply than the demand of child soldiers.

[94] Van Bueren, n 86 above, 335.
[95] Ibid.
[96] I interviewed Mr Zermatten on 2 February 2011 in Geneva, Switzerland. I have the interview notes on file.
[97] Singer, n 3 above, 93–107.
[98] B Ames, 'Methodological Problems in the Study of Child Soldiers' in Gates and Reich, above n 3 15.

In employing Andvig and Gates's 'supply and demand' terminology, a distinction is created between the factors that influence the decision to join an armed group, the supply, and the factors that influence the decision to enlist children, the demand. In abduction cases it is only the recruiter's actions and decisions that are relevant. Nevertheless, with voluntary enlistment, factors associated with the decision of the adult actor to accept the enlistment of the child is still very relevant—particularly from an international law point of view, as international law only concerns itself with the decisions and actions of the adult, not the child.

The low cost, convenience and added value of child soldiers, coupled with the impunity of commanders, results in broad-based child recruitment. As Singer states, 'the costs are outweighed by the benefits'.[99] In the field, commanders have difficulty in replenishing their ranks and commanders are well aware of the actual or perceived benefits the use and recruitment of child soldiers hold. Therefore it happens that lower-level field commanders recruit children even where the leaders of the group denounce the use of child soldiers. This creates many obstacles for effective prevention.[100] It is also often argued that children are easily programmable to execute the most horrible attacks.[101] Commentators have paid little attention to the strategic use of child soldiers as an asymmetrical conflict structure. As I have previously argued, this presents the second dimension to the demand for child soldiers.

A multitude of factors have been identified as causes of child soldiering. These include poverty, the need for shelter and the need for 'family'. There is no use in listing each of the factors that have been identified by theorists, as there is no systematic model that presents these factors in any specific order or even data that supports the contention that they do contribute to child soldiering. No existing model adequately takes into account the proximity of specific causes to the problem, nor is the interplay acknowledged between these seemingly independent causes.

In their empirical study, Reich and Achvarina argue that 'while poverty may remain a necessary condition for the advent of child soldiers, and thus may possibly have a threshold effect, it certainly does not offer an effective causal explanation for child soldier rates'.[102] Similarly, these authors dismiss the suggested link between large pools of orphans and child soldiers.[103] They do, however, find that there is a strong link

---

[99] Singer, n 19 above, 52.
[100] Pollar, n 20 above; Wessells, n 68 above, 32.
[101] J Briggs, *Innocents Lost* (New York, Basic Books, 2005) xi; Singer, n 19 above, 87. quotes a former Liberian militia commander as saying 'Children make the best and bravest . . . Don't overlook them. They can fight more than we people. It is hard for them to just retreat.'
[102] SF Reich and A Achvarina, above n 6, 40.
[103] Ibid.

between the access that these armed groups have to internally displaced person (IDP) and refugee camps and child soldiering.[104]

Further similar research can be very beneficial to child soldier preventative strategies, as identifying poverty as a root cause of child soldiering has little effect. One cannot tackle global poverty as a child soldier preventative strategy. It is much more realistic for peacekeeping missions to provide greater protection to refugee camps. However, more research is called for in this regard as there seems to be a disjuncture in Reich and Achvarina's reasoning. First, people in refugee and IDP camps are, virtually without exception, poor. Those with means have the mobility to flee the area in which they are being persecuted and take refuge further afield. As such, one cannot dismiss poverty as a root cause of child soldiering. Indeed, in dismissing poverty as a key cause, Reich and Achvarina state that 'richer countries may not have child soldiers in intrastate conflict. But neither do child soldiers serve in all poor ones.'[105] This reasoning leaves much to be desired as, by the same token, neither were all child soldiers refugees/IDPs nor are all refugee/IDP camps in conflict affected areas plagued by child soldier recruitment. Virtually all children who become child soldiers live in extreme poverty.

This is not the entire picture. The specific causes of child soldiering cannot be considered without considering the contextual matrix within which they exert their various influences. Singer employs a more contextual approach by breaking the causes up into three critical factors, which, he argues, form a causal chain:

1) Social disruptions and failures of development caused by globalization, war and disease that have led not only to a greater global conflict and instability, but also to generational disconnections;
2) Technological improvements to small weapons now permit these child recruits to be effective participants in war fare; and
3) There has been a rise in a new type of conflict that is far more brutal and criminalized ('post-modern conflict').[106]

These factors form part of the greater context that facilitates the use of child soldiers, but are not the root causes. Thus, this contextual approach is applicable to both forced and voluntary recruitment. Similarly, Honwana's application of the 'war-scapes' concept to child soldiering also finds application.[107]

---

[104] Ibid.
[105] Ibid.
[106] Singer, n 19 above, 37–38.
[107] Honwana, n 41 above, 42.

## IV. SUMMARY

Investigating the distribution of child soldiers serves two purposes: it indicates the scope of the problem and suggests where preventative efforts should be focused geographically. I have argued that the extent of the problem cannot be indicated quantitatively, as there is no reliable data. Nevertheless, it is clear that, geographically, child soldiering is a problem of global proportions, affecting hundreds of thousands of children. Works such as Becker's are telling in this regard: 'although precise figures are impossible to establish, the number of child soldiers in the region [Asia] is likely to exceed 75 000'.[108]

Children function in a range of different capacities during armed conflict. Some participate in hostilities directly and others indirectly; yet others are recruited during peacetime. The use of child soldiers as an asymmetrical conflict structure indicates that the rationale for the use of child soldiers is not as one-dimensional as traditionally thought. There are more entry points in engaging with governments to end the use and recruitment of child soldiers than with non-state entities. Governments are still among the principal violators of the prohibition against the use and recruitment of child soldiers, whether the national armed forces directly engage in child use or recruitment, or the government supports a proxy force that does so. This creates a valuable entry point for the enforcement and application of international law rules prohibiting child soldiering that should be pursued in the era of application.

Finally, the causes of child soldiering are a contested domain. Unfortunately, there is a strong argument to be made that many children join armed groups in their legitimate pursuit of self-preservation. Undoubtedly, there are many children who have survived because they joined armed forces or groups. For this reason alone, the supply of child soldiers in many regions remains very strong. This speaks to an even deeper systemic problem than child soldiering. Nevertheless, international law does not prohibit a child from being a soldier; it prohibits the use and recruitment of children. As such, the law is aimed not at the supply of child soldiers, but at the demand for child soldiers.

[108] J Becker, 'Child Recruitment in Burma, Sri Lanka and Nepal' in Gates and Reich, above n 3, 108.

# 3

# International Humanitarian Law and the Prevention of Child Soldiering

T HE FACT THAT child soldiering was first directly prohibited by the Additional Protocols to the Geneva Conventions of 1977 perhaps indicates that the 'humanization of humanitarian law', as Meron terms it, was a more gradual process than generally believed.[1] This humanisation process is an ongoing one and had achieved a greater level of maturity by 1977 than in 1949, when the Geneva Conventions were adopted. Also relevant to this is the idea that international humanitarian law (IHL) is by and large a reactive regime of international law—that is to say, developments within IHL are often moulded by major preceding events, such as World War II (WWII). Children did participate directly in hostilities during WWII on a large scale, but at the close of the war this was not one of the issues deemed important enough to be included in the Geneva Conventions.[2] Norms prohibiting child soldiering are perhaps some of the best examples of the shift within IHL from military necessity/efficiency to humanitarianism. While humanity has always been a consideration in the 'laws and customs of war', over time the balance between military necessity and humanity has shifted. In IHL of old, military necessity/efficiency enjoyed primacy and humanitarianism played a secondary role. However, the Geneva Conventions of 1949 finally shifted this balance.[3] Child soldiers increase the

---

[1] T Meron, 'The Humanization of Humanitarian Law' (2000) 94 *American Journal of International Law* 239, 239; Art 77(2) of Protocol I Additional to the Geneva Conventions of 12 August 1949, and relating to the Protection of Victims of International Armed Conflicts, adopted 8 June 1977 (entered into force 7 December 1978) 1125 UNTS 17512; Art 4(3)(c) of Protocol II Additional to the Geneva Conventions of 12 August 1949, and relating to the Protection of Victims of Non-International Armed Conflicts, adopted 8 June 1977 (entered into force 7 December 1978) 1125 UNTS 609.

[2] See, eg DM Rosen *Armies of the Young: Child Soldiers in War and Terrorism* (New Brunswick, NJ, Rutgers University Press, 2005) 19–56.

[3] Meron, n 1 above; although this trend to 'humanise' the law of armed conflict was first identified during the early 1960s, G Schwarzenberger, *The Frontiers of International Law* (London, Stevens & Sons, 1962) 256–73; MC Bassiouni, 'Repression of Breaches of the Geneva Conventions under the Draft Additional Protocol to the Geneva Conventions of August 12, 1949' (1976–77) 8 *Rutgers-Camden Law Journal* 185.

military capacity of a given armed force or group, thus military necessity/efficiency provides no basis for prohibiting such conduct, yet the humanitarian considerations at play have come to counterbalance the military advantage of child soldiering to such an extent that there is no longer any legal or political arguments in support of the general use and recruitment of child soldiers.[4]

Although Geneva Convention IV has limited value from a child soldier prevention point of view, the two Additional Protocols to the Geneva Conventions of 1977 form the basis of international law's response to child soldiering. While legal development within IHL is rather stagnant, associated fields of international law have proven more agile. Today, international human rights law (IHRL) and international criminal law (ICL) are as important to the prohibition of child soldiering as IHL. Indeed, developments within ICL are the most recent, and this branch of law is most active in relation to prohibiting child soldiering.[5] The Rome Statute of the International Criminal Court criminalises child soldiering both in non-international and international armed conflict.[6] War crimes are essentially IHL norms, the violation of which results in criminal responsibility on the international plane. Nevertheless, ICL has expanded into a vast legal regime in its own right. Thus, in taking an 'issues-based approach' to child soldier prevention, it is imperative not to view the contribution of a single sub-regime of international law, such as IHL, in isolation.[7] The present chapter presents a meticulous, yet sterile analysis of the child soldiering prohibitions from within IHL. This is inevitable, as the law in action cannot be discussed in isolation from IHRL and ICL. Chapter 4 considers the role of IHRL in combating child soldiering; the co-application of IHL and IHRL forms a substantial part of this chapter. The war crimes of child soldier enlistment, conscription and use, as well as associated developments within ICL, are discussed in detail in Chapter 5.

---

[4] There are commentators such as Rosen who challenge the underpinnings of much of the humanitarian narrative that opposes child soldiering. Many of these critiques are well founded; however, this does not change the fact that no state or non-state group defends their use of child soldiers by way of legal argumentation or politically. See Rosen, n 2 above, 1.

[5] See Chapter 5 below generally.

[6] Arts 8(2)(b)(xxvi) and 8(2)(e)(vii) of the Rome Statute of the International Criminal Court (Rome Statute) (entered into force 1 July 2002) 2187 UNTS 90, relevant to international and non-international armed conflict respectively.

[7] See G Waschefort, 'Beyond Fragmentation: An Issues-Based Approach to "Human Rights"' (2012) 37 *South African Yearbook of International Law* 61.

## I. THE GENEVA CONVENTIONS

Only in a limited number of cases does Geneva Convention IV relate to protecting children from military recruitment, and does so indirectly.[8] The terms 'children', 'protected persons' and 'protected persons . . . over eighteen years of age' are distinguished by these provisions. It has been argued that, for the purposes of Geneva Convention IV, 'child' or 'children' denotes a person (or persons) under fifteen.[9] Geneva Convention IV in fact creates many different categories according to age: children; young children; children under seven; children under twelve; children under fifteen; children and young people; protected persons over eighteen years of age; and protected persons under eighteen years of age.

Like 'children under seven' and 'children under twelve', 'children under fifteen' creates a sub-genus of 'children'. The concept 'children' is used elsewhere in Geneva Convention IV. Interpretively, this indicates that 'children' is a broader concept than 'children under fifteen'. The category 'protected persons over eighteen years of age' may be interpreted to mean that all people below eighteen years of age are protected persons by virtue of their age. The category 'protected persons under eighteen years of age' also exists and, prima facie, may oppose the former argument, as it may be suggested that there are also unprotected persons under eighteen. However, this category of person only appears once in Geneva Convention IV in the following context: 'In any case, the death penalty may not be pronounced on a protected person who was under eighteen years of age at the time of the offence'.[10] A viable and reasonable interpretation is that this provision only offers protection to persons who were 'protected persons' by virtue of their young age (under eighteen) at the time of commission of the crime. According to the Rapporteur, 'there should be no precise definition of the term children'.[11] This is a problematic position. The Geneva Conventions provide protection to people in various circumstances based solely on their age up to persons under eighteen.[12] It is thus suggested that, where the Geneva Conventions use the unqualified term 'children', depending on the circumstances, such children should include people under the age of eighteen.

[8] Arts 50 and 51 of Geneva Convention (IV) Relative to the Protection of Civilian Persons in Time of War (entered into force 21 October 1950) 75 UNTS 287.

[9] J Pictet (ed), *Commentary, IV Geneva Conventions Relative to the Protection of Civilian Persons in Time of War* (Geneva, ICRC, 1958) 395; M Happold, *Child Soldiers in International Law* (Manchester, Manchester University Press, 2005) 56.

[10] Art 68 of Geneva Convention IV.

[11] OR XV 465, CDDH/407/Rev 1, para 63.

[12] Of course reference is made here to measures aimed at protecting persons due to their young age, not old.

Academic commentators are quick to dismiss the relevance of Geneva Convention IV to child soldier prevention.[13] It is generally argued that this Convention was drafted in response to WWII and child soldiering was not viewed as an IHL concern at the time.[14] The provisions of the Geneva Conventions are disassociated from child soldier prevention, as these provisions are generally not framed as 'child soldier prohibitive norms'. A specific example is that all of the provisions of Geneva Convention IV that relate, albeit indirectly, to child soldier prohibition are limited to occupied territories. This is a significant limitation, and reflects the post-WWII thinking. There are no situations at present where an occupying power is recruiting or using child soldiers from within the occupied community.

Article 50 of Geneva Convention IV holds that:

> The Occupying Power shall take all necessary steps to facilitate the identification of children and the registration of their parentage. It may not, in any case, change their personal status, nor enlist them in formations or organizations subordinate to it.[15]

This provision has been explained as referring specifically to ideology-based youth movements, such as those established in many countries of Europe under Nazi occupation, and not to child soldier prevention.[16] The protected class is 'children'. Children are only protected from the occupying power. Thus, their own forces, and forces not hostile to them, can enlist them in such movements. It is true that this article was intended to prohibit enlistment in ideology-based youth movements; however, the terminology employed by the article is 'formations or organizations subordinate to it [the occupying power]'. Should it be established that armed forces of an occupying power fall within the broad scope of such subordinate formations or organisations, this article will prohibit the occupying power from enlisting children from within occupied territories into its armed forces.

Article 51 of Geneva Convention IV holds that: 'The Occupying Power may not compel protected persons to serve in its armed or auxiliary forces. No pressure or propaganda which aims at securing voluntary enlistment is permitted.'[17] This article's relevance to child soldiering is often explained away through the broadness of its scope of applica-

---

[13] For example, neither Rosen nor Wessells mention a single article of the Geneva Conventions as relevant to child soldier prevention in their work: M Wessells, *Child Soldiers: From Violence to Protection* (Boston, MA, Harvard University Press, 2006) 233; Rosen, n 2 above, 139.

[14] A Honwana, *Child Soldiers in Africa* (Philadelphia, PA, Pennsylvania University Press, 2006) 31.

[15] Art 50 of the Geneva Convention IV.

[16] Happold, n 9 above, 56.

[17] Art 51 of the Geneva Convention IV.

tion.[18] It is more specifically aimed at prohibiting the conscription of 'protected persons' in general, as opposed to children in particular. Pictet and Happold both point out that this article not only provides protection to protected individual persons, but 'is also concerned with the duties that those individuals have to the states of which they are nationals'.[19] It should be noted that the protection of an individual's duty towards his state of nationality remains the protection of the individual person. Happold further points out that both Articles 50 and 51 are reaffirmations of the Hague Regulations of 1907.[20] 'Children' are protected persons in terms of the Geneva Conventions; it is thus unconvincing to argue that this provision does not protect children from military recruitment merely because it also protects other classes of protected persons from such recruitment. However, the protection afforded is once again limited in that it only extends to protection from the occupying power. In child soldier preventative terms. the provision is also unique in using the term 'serve in its armed or auxiliary forces' instead of enlistment, recruitment or conscription.

Article 51 of Geneva Convention IV further holds that:

> The Occupying Power may not compel protected persons to work unless they are over eighteen years of age . . . In no case shall requisition of labour lead to a mobilization of workers in an organization of a military or semi-military character.[21]

Protected persons may thus be compelled to work, but not in organisations of a military or semi-military character. However, protected persons younger than eighteen years of age may not be compelled to work in any capacity. From a child rights/protection point of view, this is a significant extension of the Hague Regulations of 1907. Lastly, by employing the language 'an organization of a military or semi-military character', this article, more directly, also prohibits the occupying power from forcing such protected persons from serving in paramilitary groups distinct from, but in cohort with, the occupying power.

The three major shortcomings of Geneva Convention IV's actual protection of child soldiers are, first and foremost, that it only protects the occupied people from an occupying power. Secondly, this also means that protection is limited to international armed conflict (IAC). Thirdly, there is a distinct lack of specificity in the provisions[22] since commentators

---

[18] Happold, n 9 above, 56.

[19] Ibid; J Pictet, *Commentary on the Geneva Conventions of 12 August 1949* (Geneva, ICRC, 1955) Vol IV, 46.

[20] Happold, n 9 above, 56; Art 45 of The Hague Regulations Concerning the Laws and Customs of War on Land (1907).

[21] Art 51 of the Geneva Convention IV.

[22] However, had they been more specific it may well have been that 'child soldiering' would positively have fallen outside the scope of these provisions and as such Geneva Convention IV.

have long argued that the fact that none of the Geneva Convention provisions are aimed specifically at child soldiering relegates the Geneva Conventions to a position of irrelevance. Geneva Convention IV finds very limited application to child soldier prevention. Because reference is never made to child soldiers, awareness of the problem is not promoted at all and such an application of Geneva Convention IV requires more judicial initiative. The provisions of the Additional Protocols to the Geneva Conventions are in every way more suited to child soldier prevention. Thus, since the emergence of these provisions, the application of Geneva Convention IV is hardly at issue.

## II. ADDITIONAL PROTOCOL I TO THE GENEVA CONVENTIONS

What sets IHL apart from IHRL is the fact that it must be triggered by armed conflict and so applies to regulate the conduct of the related hostilities and the protection of people, both civilian and military, during such conflict. The argument has been made that some provisions of the Geneva Conventions and Additional Protocols apply during peacetime, and that if any provision should so apply, the child soldier prohibition should. This argument is ill-conceived both with regard to the Geneva Conventions and the Additional Protocols in general, and with regard to the child soldier prohibitions specifically. Common Article 2 to the Geneva Conventions states:

> In addition to the provisions which shall be implemented in peace-time, the present Convention shall apply to all cases of declared war or of any other armed conflict which may arise between two or more of the High Contracting Parties, even if the state of war is not recognized by one of them.

Obviously, the argument is founded on the reference to peacetime, and in fact there are numerous provisions within the Geneva Conventions and Additional Protocol II that are applicable to times of peace.[23] No modern treaty can function without provisions applicable during times of peace. For example, denouncing the Conventions will only take effect once peace has been attained, should the denouncing state be at war at the time of the denouncement.[24] However, there is not a single provision applicable to peacetime that regulates either the conduct of hostilities or the protection of victims of war. The fallacy in an argument that

---

[23] Arts 23, 26, 44, 47, 63 and Annex 1, Art 7 of Geneva Convention I; Arts 44, 48 and 62 of Geneva Convention II; Arts 127 and 142 of Geneva Convention III; Arts 14, 38, 70, 144, 158 and Annex 1, Art 7 of Geneva Convention IV; Arts 6, 18, 60, 66 and 83 of Additional Protocol I; Additional Protocol II makes no reference to 'peace'.

[24] Art 63 of Geneva Convention I; Art 62 of Geneva Convention II; Art 143 of Geneva Convention III; Art 158 of Geneva Convention IV.

any substantive and proper IHL provision of the Geneva Conventions applies during peacetime is well illustrated by attempting to determine the nature of the armed conflict in deciding which Protocol to apply and whether Common Article 3 is applicable. If there is no armed conflict, it cannot be international in nature, as such, the whole of the Geneva Conventions, save for Common Article 3, will not be applicable. Furthermore, Common Article 3 will also not be applicable as it expressly only applies to 'armed conflict not of an international character'. Furthermore, the last part of the provisions, 'even if the state of war is not recognized by one of them', was designed to make it implementable during times when de facto conflict exists but the relevant states deny the existence of an armed conflict—as was the case during the conflict between China and Japan preceding WWII.[25] As regards the argument that the child soldier prohibitive norms in particular should apply to times of peace, Article 77(2) of Additional Protocol I expressly refers to 'parties to the conflict'. Additional Protocol II's roughly corresponding provision makes no such reference, but Additional Protocol II stands alone as the only instrument out of all the Geneva Conventions and Additional Protocols that makes no reference to peacetime whatsoever. Thus, the child soldier prohibitive norms in Additional Protocol I/ Additional Protocol II only apply during times of armed conflict. An enquiry into the existence of armed conflict aims primarily to determine whether the degree of hostilities/force/violence meets the threshold to amount to an 'armed conflict', and whether this armed conflict is international or non-international in character.[26]

Prior to the coming into force of Additional Protocol II, the Geneva Conventions made no specific provision for non-international armed conflict (NIAC) save for Common Article 3, which in turn made no specific reference to children or the regulation of participation in armed groups or forces. This is what sets Additional Protocols I and II apart from each other: the first is applicable to IAC and the second to NIAC. Both Protocols make reference to 'children' and 'children who have not attained the age of fifteen years'. Strictly speaking, where the term 'children' is unqualified, the possibility exists that such protection extends to all those over fifteen but under eighteen as well. This is based on the same argument as in relation to the Geneva Conventions above. Furthermore, in recruiting among people older than fifteen but younger than

---

[25] JAC Gutteridge, 'The Geneva Conventions of 1949' (1949) 26 *British Year Book of International Law* 298, 298–99.

[26] For more information on establishing the threshold of armed conflict see the Inter-American Commission on Human Rights communication, *Juan Carlos Abella v Argentina*, Case No 11, 137, Annual Report 1997, OAS Doc OAE/Ser.L/V/II.98 Doc 7 rev (13 April 1998); for more information on the nature of an armed conflict see the ICTY Appeals Decision in *Prosecutor v Dusko Tadić*, Case No IT-94-1-AR72, App.Ch (2 October 1995), para 70.

eighteen, Additional Protocol I endeavours to grant more protection to people the younger they are, and this protection is afforded in the section dealing with 'protection of children',[27] thus giving further credence to the argument that those aged between fifteen and eighteen are still deemed children.

With regard to the prevention of child soldiering in the context of IAC, Additional Protocol I holds:

> The Parties to the conflict shall *take all feasible measures* in order that children who have not attained the age of *fifteen years* do not take a *direct part in hostilities* and, in particular, they shall refrain from recruiting them into their armed forces. In recruiting among those persons who have attained the age of fifteen years but who have not attained the age of eighteen years the Parties to the conflict shall endeavour to give priority to those who are oldest.[28]

It is often argued that this provision is relatively weak in its protection of children, and for legal-analytical purposes it is divided in two parts: first, the prohibition of using and recruiting children younger than fifteen; and secondly, the provision stating that, when recruiting children between fifteen and eighteen, preference should be given to older children.

The language used in the second part of the provision is not contentious and needs little further explanation; it is therefore dealt with first. It is almost impossible to hold an armed force or group to account for a violation of this provision. Where the actual prohibition of the use and recruitment of child soldiers can be seen as a direct child protection measure, this provision is indirect. Should a group use or recruit children under fifteen, they will be in contravention of the Protocol as long as the child remains part of the group and younger than fifteen; this is what is called a 'continuing crime' in criminal law terms. This provision thus aims at the demobilisation of child soldiers, which amounts to direct protection. However, where a group fails to give priority to older children when recruiting among those aged between fifteen and eighteen, such a remedy will not be available. It is not unlawful for the group to recruit and use children between fifteen and eighteen; it is 'merely' the group's recruitment practice that violates Additional Protocol I. Thus, it is not so much who is recruited but more the context in which they are recruited that is central to this provision. This part of the provision therefore offers very little protection to children.

In the first part of the child soldier prevention provision, two distinct forms of conduct are prohibited: first, 'the Parties to the conflict shall take all feasible measures to ensure that children who have not attained the age of fifteen years do not take a direct part in hostilities', and secondly, 'in particular, they shall refrain from recruiting them into their

---

[27] Art 77 of Additional Protocol I.
[28] Art 77(2) of Additional Protocol I (emphasis added).

armed forces'. It is clear that the age of the protected children is below fifteen. With regard to the 'use' of children in hostilities, the obligation of the parties (to the conflict) is limited to taking 'all feasible measures' to ensure that children do not take a 'direct part in hostilities'. The prohibition on recruitment (as opposed to use) is not subject to either the 'direct part in hostilities' qualifier or the 'all feasible measures' qualifier. Children are thus better protected from recruitment into armed forces than they are from being used in direct hostilities. It is important to note that children can be used in armed conflict without having been recruited for purposes of the Additional Protocols (this is discussed further below).

The more contentious elements of the child soldier prohibition in Additional Protocol I are analysed below. Although this analysis is undertaken under the heading 'Additional Protocol I', they apply *mutatis mutandis* to all other relevant provisions that contain the same elements.

## A. Take all Feasible Measures

Earlier drafts of Article 77(2) of the Additional Protocol I contained the standard 'all necessary measures'. The word 'necessary' was only replaced with 'feasible' in the final drafts of the provision. The feasibility of a measure in a given circumstance is a subjective determination when compared to determining what may be 'necessary' within the same circumstances. Bothe et al argue that the 'feasible' standard is a determination of what is practically possible or practicable, taking account of all circumstances at the time including the military success of the operations.[29] Sandoz et al argue that the provision should be interpreted in line with the standard dictionary meaning of the word 'feasible'.[30] The dictionary definition they provide is 'capable of being done, accomplished or carried out, possible or practicable'. Bothe's understanding of the standard incorporates this definition, but goes further in holding that circumstances at the time must be taken into account when determining what is practically possible or practicable. The source of this understanding is statements made by various countries in relation to the adoption of Article 57 at the Diplomatic Conference.[31] The feasibility standard in this article relates to precautions during attack, not child soldiering. The question remains whether the success of military

[29] See also M Bothe, K Partch and W Solf, *New Rules for Victims of Armed Conflicts* (The Hague, Martinus Nijhoff Publishers, 1982) 372–73.

[30] Y Sandoz, C Swinarski and B Zimmermann (eds), *Commentary on the Additional Protocols of 8 June 1977 to the Geneva Conventions of 12 August 1949* (Geneva, ICRC, 1987) 681–82.

[31] These countries were Algeria, Belgium, Canada, Italy, the Netherlands and Spain. See Happold, n 9 above, 61, note 26 ; LS Boudreault, 'Les reserves apportees au Protocole additionnel 1 aux Conventions de Geneve sur le droit humanitaire' (198990) 6 *Revue quebecoise de droit international* 105.

operation, should be a factor in determining what is practically possible or practicable when taking account of the circumstances at the time. Both Mann and Kuper have adopted this definition in relation to child soldiering.[32]

If the success of military operations is indeed a factor that should properly be taken into account when determining what is feasible, it may often not be feasible to demobilise children before military engagement during armed conflict. Thus, ideally, this standard is what is practically possible or practicable when taking account of the circumstances at the time, but not including the success of military operations. It appears, however, that the inclusion of military necessity has taken hold in the definition of what is 'feasible'. This understanding is further supported by the declarations made by some states in relation to the Optional Protocol to the Convention on the Rights of the Child on the Involvement of Children in Armed Conflict (the CIAC Protocol) that also contains this standard.[33]

This qualification is not ideal by any measure. However, the actual impact this qualification is likely to have on the prohibition of the use and recruitment of child soldiers is less severe than it may seem. The use and recruitment of child soldiers constitutes a continuing violation, or continuing offence in the ICL sense. Armed forces and groups obliged to take all feasible measures that children do not participate in hostilities are therefore obliged to do so in relation to each military engagement children participate in. The systematic use of children in armed conflict can never be justified on the basis that all feasible measures had been taken to prevent such participation.

## B. Take a Direct Part in Hostilities

This standard forms the basis of one of the central tenets of IHL: the principle of distinction. This customary law principle holds that parties to a conflict must distinguish between civilian and military targets unless the civilian directly participates in hostilities.[34] Reference to either active or direct part in hostilities is made only once in each of the Geneva Conventions, and that is in Common Article 3, where the term 'persons taking no active part in the hostilities' is used. By the time the Additional Protocols to the Geneva Conventions came about, a shift in language

---

[32] H Mann, 'International Law and the Child Soldier' (1987) 36 *International & Comparative Law Quarterly* 32, 46; J Kuper, *International Law Concerning Child Civilians in Armed Conflict* (Oxford, Oxford University Press, 1997) 102.

[33] Optional Protocol to the Convention on the Rights of the Child on the Involvement of Children in Armed Conflict (entered into force 12 February 2002) 2173 UNTS 222.

[34] JM Henckaerts, L Doswald-Beck and C Alvermann, *Customary International Humanitarian Law: Rules* (Cambridge, Cambridge University Press, 2007) 2–8.

had occurred—and the notion of 'active part in the hostilities' did not feature at all; instead, the term 'take a direct part in hostilities' was used. Interestingly, the war crime of child soldier use and recruitment, as proscribed by the Statute of the Special Court for Sierra Leone (SCSL) and the Rome Statute of the International Criminal Court, reverted to the language of the Geneva Conventions: that of 'active' part in hostilities.[35]

These shifts in language have given rise to considerable debate as to whether the standards 'direct' and 'active' part in hostilities are the same or different. There is a lack of consistency between the approaches of the international tribunals. The International Criminal Tribunal for Rwanda has, for example, held that they do indeed amount to the same standard,[36] whereas the International Criminal Court (ICC) has determined that they are different standards. Chapter 5 addresses these concepts in the context of international criminal law, and aims to give meaning to the concept 'active participation' as this is the concept relevant to ICL. The present discussion relates to the interpretation of 'direct' and 'active' part in hostilities only in relation to IHL.

From a linguistic perspective, there is certainly an argument that direct and active denote different standards if they serve to qualify one's participation in conduct. Direct would speak to the proximity of one's contribution to the conduct in question, whereas active would speak to the intensity of one's participation in the conduct in question. This notwithstanding, it is very instructive to note that, where the English texts of the Geneva Convention on the one hand use the descriptor 'active' and the Additional Protocols on the other hand use the descriptor 'direct', the equally authoritative French texts of all six instruments uses the term *'participent directemen'* consistently. Thus, as is argued more comprehensively in Chapter 5, 'direct' and 'active' should be deemed the same. Nevertheless, there exists much authority that supports the opposite position, not least among which is the emerging ICC jurisprudence.

'Acts of war which by their nature or purpose are likely to cause actual harm to the personnel and equipment of the enemy armed forces' has long been the standard definition of 'direct participation'.[37] This definition certainly also lacks clarity, but until recently no authoritative source made any attempt at such clarity. The Supreme Court of Israel, hearing the *Targeted Killings* case in 2005, was the first to do so.[38] More recently, the ICRC published 'Interpretive Guidance on the Notion of

---

[35] Statue of the Special Court for Sierra Leone (SCSL) (entered into force 12 April 2002) 2178 UNTS 138 Rome Statute of the International Criminal Court (Rome Statute) (entered into force 1 July 2002) 2187 UNTS 90.

[36] See generally Chapter 5.II.B.ii below.

[37] Sandoz et al, n 30 above, 681–82, para 1944.

[38] *The Public Committee against Torture in Israel v Government of Israel et al* HCJ 769/02 (11 December 2005) (*Targeted Killings* case).

Direct Participation in Hostilities under International Humanitarian Law' (DPH Study).[39]

Perhaps expectedly so, the Israeli Supreme Court was very broad in its interpretation of direct participation. In this instance, the Court considered the notion of direct participation in the context of the principle of distinction. The Court cited Schmitt, stating that grey areas should be interpreted in favour of direct participation.[40] Schmitt argues that:

> One of the seminal purposes of the law is to make possible a clear distinction between civilians and combatants. Suggesting that civilians retain their immunity even when they are intricately involved in a conflict is to engender disrespect for the law by combatants endangered by their activities. Moreover, a liberal approach creates an incentive for civilians to remain as distant from the conflict as possible—in doing so they can better avoid being charged with participation in the conflict and are less liable to being directly targeted.[41]

From a child soldier preventative point of view, a liberal interpretation in favour of direct participation would be preferable. The further the child is removed from hostilities while still being deemed to directly participate, the more protection she/he receives. For example, where a child acts as a cook to the armed forces, a more strict interpretation of 'direct participation' will likely find that the child is not participating directly. Therefore, her/his use in hostilities will not be unlawful. A more liberal approach would likely have found that she/he is directly participating and, as such, her/his use in hostilities is unlawful. However, Schmitt's position is nevertheless strongly contested.

This standard is not used solely in the context of child soldiering, but in the protection of civilians as a whole. A liberal interpretation in favour of greater protection of child soldiers (which was not Schmitt's rationale) will correspondingly place more civilians in harm's way as direct participants. This distinction between civilians and fighters is not an end in itself, but a necessary determination to allow the law to protect civilians and allow armed forces to target combatants. It is this very balance that forms the basis of any argument over whether a 'liberal' or 'conservative' interpretation should be afforded to 'direct'. Lastly, one would expect that the possibility of harm is a greater deterrent to civilians from becoming involved in hostilities than 'being charged with participation in the conflict'; thus this argument is not convincing.

This gives rise to the question whether the standard implied by direct/active participation in hostilities should be interpreted as the same stand-

---

[39] N Melzer, *Interpretive Guidance on the Notion of Direct Participation in Hostilities under International Humanitarian Law* (Geneva, ICRC, 2009).

[40] MN Schmitt, 'Direct Participation in Hostilities and 21st Century Armed Conflict' in H Fischer, *Crisis Management and Humanitarian Projection: Festschrift für Dieter Fleck* (Berlin, Berliner Wissenschafts-Verlag, 2004) 505–09.

[41] Ibid.

ard when the purpose is to distinguish between military and civilian targets, and when determining the lawfulness of the use of a child in armed conflict. First, it is important to note that, among different instruments, both 'direct' and 'active' are used in the context of distinction and both standards are used in the context of child soldier prevention. As such, the answer cannot be found in the language itself. Instead, one will have to rely on interpretive devices, such as the 'most favourable' principle in human rights law, which was given content to by the Inter-American Court of Human Rights in the following terms: 'when interpreting the Convention it is always necessary to choose the alternative that is most favorable to protection of the rights enshrined in said treaty, based on the principle of the rule most favorable to the human being'.[42] Applied to the present context, this principle may lead to a narrower construction of direct/active participation in hostilities in the context of the principle of distinction and a broader construction in the context of child soldier prohibition.[43] Other similar interpretive devices exist that may yield similar results. The maxim *in favorem vitae, libertatis, et innocentiae omnia praesumuntur* may be applied as a general principle of law. This interpretive device provides for a presumption in favour of life, liberty and innocence when applying a substantive norm of law. Again, applied to the present context, the likely result of this principle will be that what is direct/active participation in hostilities in the context of the principle of distinction will be interpreted so as to best safeguard the lives and wellbeing of civilians, and what is direct/active participation in hostilities in the context of the child soldier prohibition will be interpreted to best safeguard the wellbeing of children used or potentially used in armed conflict.

The results such interpretive devices may yield are appealing. Nevertheless, they are not necessarily consonant with IHL as a regime of international law. In the context of the principle of distinction, for instance, the counterbalancing factors in determining which interests are to prevail through interpretation is not clear at all. While the protection of civilian life is an incredibly important factor in this equation, so too is the basic notion that combatants or fighters may target their enemy on the battlefield. In a human rights context, the conclusion will likely be reached that the protection of civilian life is the determining factor; however, in IHL, where loss of life is a given, this will likely not be the

---

[42] '*Mapiripdn Massacre*' *v Colombia*, 2005c, § 106.

[43] The 'most favoured' principle is also discussed in Chapter 4.I.C.i below. See further A Lindroos, 'Addressing Norm Conflicts in a Fragmented Legal System: The Doctrine of Lex Specialis' (2005) 74 *Nordic Journal of International Law* 27, 41; H Krieger, 'A Conflict of Norms: The Relationship between Humanitarian Law and Human Rights Law in the ICRC Customary Law Study' (2006) 11 *Journal of Conflict and Security Law* 265, 274; M Killander, 'Interpreting Regional Human Rights Treaties' (2010) 13 *Sur — International Journal on Human Rights* 145, 147.

case. As such, the standards of direct/active participation in armed conflict should be interpreted to be the same standard as regards both the principle of distinction and the child soldier prohibition.

The Supreme Court of Israel in the *Targeted Killings* case endeavoured to provide examples of what direct participation is, but at the same time it acknowledged that a case-by-case determination is called for.[44] In line with the Court's acceptance of Schmitt's liberal interpretation, the Court's only example of direct participation is 'a person who . . . provides service to them [weapons], be the distance from the battlefield as it may'.[45] This application is unacceptably broad in all circumstances, but its unacceptability becomes more apparent when considering the more extreme scenarios. For example, modern weapons are often very technical in nature and technologically advanced. In terms of this view, should such a weapon be shipped a thousand miles from the battlefield for calibration by a civilian expert, the opposing armed forces will be acting within their rights if they target this civilian technician.

There is an ongoing debate as to whether the application of IHL is limited geographically. One camp essentially argues that there is a 'hot zone' of operations and that the legality of the targeting of enemy forces is to be determined in relation to the geographical proximity of the military engagement to this hot zone.[46] The other camp essentially argues that there are no limiting geographical factors in the application of IHL; rather, the lawfulness, in IHL, of the targeting of enemy forces is determined functionally or by status, as the case may be. That is to say, an individual becomes targetable due to either his/her status as a combatant or member of an armed group or his/her function at the relevant time — that of a direct participant in hostilities. Thus, geographical location is not a limiting factor insofar as the application of IHL is concerned, though other branches of international law, such as the law of inter-state use of force and sovereignty, may limit the geographical scope of operations. However, these are factors extraneous to IHL. The *Targeted Killings* case endorsed the second argument, which I am also a proponent of, but the Court's interpretation of what direct participation in hostilities is, in my view, is too broad.

The ICRC has expanded on the definition of 'direct participation' originally contained in the commentary to Additional Protocol I:

> In order to qualify as direct participation in hostilities, a specific act must meet the following cumulative criteria:

---

[44] *Targeted Killings* case, n 38 above, para 34.
[45] Ibid, para 35.
[46] See, eg JC Daskal, 'The Geography of the Battlefield: A Framework for Detention and Targeting Outside the 'Hot' Conflict Zone', (2013) 161 *University of Pennsylvania Law Review* 1165.

1. The act must be likely to adversely affect the military operations or military capacity of a party to an armed conflict or, alternatively, to inflict death, injury, or destruction on persons or objects protected against direct attack (threshold of harm), and
2. there must be a direct causal link between the act and the harm likely to result either from that act, or from a coordinated military operation of which that act constitutes an integral part (direct causation), and
3. the act must be specifically designed to directly cause the required threshold of harm in support of a party to the conflict and to the detriment of another (belligerent nexus).[47]

The example presented by the Supreme Court of Israel does not meet any of the three threshold requirements stated by the ICRC. Direct participation is not necessarily limited to the execution phase of an act meeting the threshold criteria. Measures in preparation of the execution phase are also included in 'direct participation'. Deployment to and return from the location forms part of such preparatory measures, if it constitutes an integral part of such a specific act or operation.[48]

It is worth noting that the DPH Study has generated significant criticism, including from a number of experts that were invited to form part of the study. The spring 2010 issue of the *NYU Journal of International Law and Politics* was dedicated to discussion of this interpretive guidance. This special edition of the journal contains critical contributions by Watkin, Schmitt, Boothby and Parks,[49] as well as a detailed response to these critical contributions by the principal architect of the DPH Study, Melzer.[50] The primary criticisms levelled at the DPH study are the creation of the so-called 'continuous combat function' (CCF)[51] and recommendation IX, which is charged with importing human rights standards into IHL.

Direct participation in hostilities is a question of function, not status. The CCF category determines direct participation in hostilities on the basis of status, and as such is unsupported in the positive law. Signifi-

---

[47] N Melzer, 'Keeping the Balance between Military Necessity and Humanity: A Response to Four Critiques of the ICRC's Interpretive Guidance on the Notion of Direct Participation in Hostilities' (2009–10) 42 *New York University Journal of International Law & Politics* 831, 46.

[48] Ibid, 65.

[49] K Watkin, 'Opportunity Lost: Organized Armed Groups and the ICRC Direct Participation in Hostilities Interpretive Guidance' (2009–10) 42 *New York University Journal of International Law & Politics* 641; B Boothby, 'And for Such Time as: The Time Dimension to Direct Participation in Hostilities' (2009–10) 42 *New York University Journal of International Law & Politics* 741; MN Schmitt, 'Deconstructing Direct Participation in Hostilities: The Constitutive Elements' (2009–10) 42 *New York University Journal of International Law & Politics* 697; WH Parks, 'Part IX of the ICRC Direct Participation in Hostilities Study: No Mandate, No Expertise, and Legally Incorrect' (2009–10) 42 *New York University Journal of International Law & Politics* 769.

[50] Melzer, n 47 above.

[51] Ibid, 46.

cantly, Alston points out that the relevant treaty language limits direct participation in hostilities to 'for such time' and not 'all the time'.[52] As with the broad interpretation Schmitt affords to direct participation, the CCF category can enhance protection of child soldiers, as the protection will not be limited to the actual time that the child directly participates. However, this category may lead to the targeting of people outside of the parameters provided for by IHL and should thus not be supported.

Recommendation IX of the DPH Study deals with 'restraints on the use of force in direct attack', and provides:

> In addition to the restraints imposed by international humanitarian law on specific means and methods of warfare, and without prejudice to further restrictions that may arise under other applicable branches of international law, the kind and degree of force which is permissible against persons not entitled to protection against direct attack must not exceed what is actually necessary to accomplish a legitimate military purpose in the prevailing circumstances.[53]

This provision, too, may be seen as advantageous from a child protection perspective. As was discussed before, the use and recruitment of child soldiers is unlawful, but, once a child participates directly in armed conflict, or by virtue of his/her status, such as combatant status, he/she will be a legitimate target. Recommendation IX, it could be argued, may restrict the amount of force employed during battle against child participants, and so serve to protect children. However, this recommendation imports a human rights law style of proportionality that calls for force to be escalated only in direct relation to the situation at hand. There is virtually no support for such proportionality standard within IHL sources of law. Recommendation IX is thus fatally flawed.

In the context of child soldiering, to meet the threshold of direct/active participation, the act performed by the child must meet the threshold of harm, direct causation and the belligerent nexus; there is no *numerus clausus* of acts that constitute direct participation in hostilities.[54] It is unfortunate that only children directly participating in hostilities enjoy the protection of instruments such as Additional Protocol I. While it is tempting to embrace concepts such as the CCF category to DPH created by the ICRC, and in so doing extend that protection a little more, this should not be done as it has the potential to create deep structural damage to the IHL regime. Instead, the fact that only those children directly participating in hostilities are protected should be addressed through the development of international law.

---

[52] P Alston, 'Report of the Special Rapporteur on Extrajudicial, Summary or Arbitrary Executions' A/HRC/14/24/Add.6 (2010), para 65.

[53] Melzer, n 47 above, 77.

[54] See Chapter 5.II.B.ii below for an example of direct participation in hostilities specifically in relation to child soldiering as an international crime.

## C. Shall Refrain from Recruiting Them

The words 'accepting their voluntary enlistment' was deleted from an earlier draft of Article 77(2) of Additional Protocol I. This begs the questions whether the provision is weakened by the deletion of these words, ie does 'recruitment' encapsulate 'enlistment'. In terms of the preparatory work on Additional Protocols I and II the prohibition against 'recruitment' contained therein does not prohibit voluntary enlistment. The commentary to Article 77(2) of Additional Protocol I also foresees the possibility of enlistment not prohibited by this provision.[55] Furthermore, the Rapporteur of Committee III stated that in some instances it is not realistic to absolutely prohibit 'voluntary participation' of children younger than fifteen.[56] However, saying that 'enlistment' is not prohibited is not the same as saying 'voluntary recruitment' is not prohibited. Schabas states that the replacement of the word 'recruiting' in an earlier draft of the Rome Statute with 'conscripting or enlisting' 'suggests something more passive, such as putting the name of a person on a list'.[57] In other words, he holds the word 'recruitment' to include 'voluntary recruitment', but voluntary recruitment is not as passive as enlistment. A similar view was adopted by the Secretary-General of the United Nations in his report to the Security Council on the establishment of the SCSL.[58] Van Bueren argues that, as Geneva Convention IV explicitly refers to 'voluntary enlistment',[59] the use of the word 'recruitment' in Additional Protocols I and II would suggest it has a different meaning, ie recruitment is less passive.[60] Finally, in the *Recruitment* case, Justice Robertson, in his dissent, also held that enlistment is more passive than recruitment.[61]

The substitution of the word 'recruitment' used in earlier instruments such as Additional Protocols I and II with the words 'conscription or enlistment' used in more recent instruments such as the Rome Statute and the Statute of the SCSL suggests a development of the law. This would mean that recruitment, while overlapping with enlistment, is not as passive as enlistment. Should this view be upheld, it would mean that

---

[55] Sandoz et al, n 30 above, 900 para 3184.

[56] OR XV, p 465, CDDH/407/Rev.1, para 63.

[57] W Schabas, *An Introduction to the International Criminal Court* (Cambridge, Cambridge University of Press, 2001) 50.

[58] 'Report of the Secretary-General on the establishment of a Special Court for Sierra Leone' UN S/2000/915 (4 October 2000), para 17–18.

[59] Art 51 of Geneva Convention IV. It should be noted that 'voluntary enlistment' is used here in the context of an occupying power compelling protected persons from working in its armed or auxiliary forces.

[60] G van Bueren, *The International Law on the Rights of the Child* (Amsterdam, Kluwer, 1998) 337.

[61] *Prosecutor v Sam Hinga Norman Decision on Preliminary Motion Based on Lack of Jurisdiction* SCSL-2004–14-AR72(E) (31 May 2004) (*Child Recruitment* decision), para 27.

the presence of children under fifteen in armed forces is not unlawful per se in terms of Additional Protocol I. Thus, as was alluded to earlier, the fact that a child participates in hostilities does not necessarily mean that that child was recruited unlawfully. What is more, this would have the implication that, when an armed force uses a child enlistee of ten to participate indirectly in an IAC, that armed force would not be acting in violation of IHL.

The commentary to Article 4(3)(c) of Additional Protocol II holds that this article also prohibits recruitment where force is not present. In fact, it states that a child cannot enlist himself.[62] Although this commentary relates to Additional Protocol II, which applies to NIAC, both Protocols use the word 'recruit' with reference to child soldier prevention. The meaning of the word cannot differ between the two instruments. It is not unheard of for children to eagerly volunteer their services to armed groups.[63] Unfortunately, legal authority is stacked against the interpretation presented by the commentary to Additional Protocol II, and, indeed, if the 'recruiting force' merely included these children's names on their list of soldiers with the relevant child eagerly volunteering, it is foreseeable that such acquisition of soldiers would not be prohibited by this provision.

## D. Their Armed Forces

The concept 'armed forces' is generally defined as 'a country's army, navy and air force'.[64] As such, this concept excludes armed groups that do not represent the force of a nation. Within the ambit of Additional Protocol I there are a number of groups, distinct from state armed forces, that can be a party to a conflict over which Additional Protocol I enjoys application. These include, for example, non-state armed groups which participate in an IAC, and peoples fighting against colonial domination, alien occupation or racist regimes in the exercise of their right of self-determination.[65]

Aware of this problem, the drafters of Additional Protocol I set out to resolve it:

> The armed forces of a Party to a conflict consist of all organized armed forces, groups and units which are under a command responsible to that Party for the conduct or its subordinates, even if that Party is represented by a government or an authority not recognized by an adverse Party. Such armed forces shall be subject to an internal disciplinary system which, inter

---

[62] Sandoz et al, n 30 above, para 3184 and 4557.
[63] See generally Chapter 2.III.A.ii above.
[64] See, eg *Concise Oxford English Dictionary* (Oxford, Oxford University Press, 2004).
[65] Art 1(4) of the Additional Protocol I.

alia, shall enforce compliance with the rules of international law applicable in armed conflict.[66]

Thus non-state armed groups can be deemed 'armed forces' if they are organised; under a command responsible to a party to the conflict; and are subject to an internal disciplinary system. Non-state entities can be party to an IAC and are bound by the rules of IHL, including the prohibition of the use and recruitment of child soldiers. Of course, the degree of organisation and the quality of the command and disciplinary systems can differ greatly. 'Armed forces' are construed relatively broadly.[67] Non-state entities are thus deemed parties to the armed conflict in their own right and not by virtue of a relationship to a party to the conflict that is a state.

In summary, Additional Protocol I's treatment of child soldiering is twofold, prohibiting 'use' and prohibiting 'recruitment'. Both the prohibition of use and the prohibition of recruitment are subject to their own limitations. The terms 'all feasible measures' and 'direct participation in hostilities' limit the degree of protection afforded in relation to the 'use' of child soldiers. Furthermore, the words 'refrain from recruit[ing]' and 'armed forces' limits the extent of the protection offered in relation to the 'recruitment' of child soldiers. The fifteen-year-old yardstick is regrettable, as the two Protocols set the scene for instruments to come and the development of customary international law. Be that as it may, this limitation affects both use and recruitment and is unambiguous.

## III. ADDITIONAL PROTOCOL II TO
## THE GENEVA CONVENTIONS

Armed conflicts of a non-international character have long been deemed matters of internal concern to the state within which the conflict occurred. As such, consistent with the doctrine of state sovereignty, such states were left to their own devices in dealing with such conflicts and those who participated therein. Theoretically, IHRL was to be applicable in lieu of IHL; however, in practice, a vacuum existed as no IHL rules outside of Common Article 3 to the Geneva Conventions were applicable, and a large body of human rights law could be derogated from. What is more, IHRL as an international law regime was normatively still very much in the process of development prior to 1977.

By the early 1970s, when the need for the Additional Protocols was recognised, it had become apparent that IHL should take a greater

---

[66] Art 43 of the Additional Protocol I.

[67] See P Verri, 'Combattants armés ne pouvant se distinguer de la population civile' (1982) 21(No 1–4) *Revue de droit pénal militare et de droit de la guerre* 345.

interest in NIAC. However, by no means were such conflicts deemed deserving of treatment equal to that of IAC, as they were still largely seen as matters of internal concern. For this reason, Additional Protocol II consists of only twenty-eight articles, the provisions of which are generally much less onerous than their corresponding provisions in Additional Protocol I and the Geneva Conventions. Child soldiering is possibly the only exception to this rule, and is an extreme one at that. Additional Protocol II offers a great deal more protection to children from military use and recruitment than Additional Protocol I. Indeed, as is clear when considering the comparable human rights provisions, this provision — one of the first child soldier prohibitive provisions — still represents the nearest to an absolute prohibition of child soldiering.

The concept of NIAC differs between Additional Protocol II and Common Article 3, and the threshold of violence required to activate the operation of Additional Protocol II exceeds that of Additional Protocol I and the Geneva Conventions in general.[68] Additional Protocol II is not applicable to situations of internal disturbances and tensions, such as riots or isolated and sporadic acts of violence. With regard to child soldiers, Additional Protocol II holds:

> Children shall be provided with the care and aid they require, and in particular:
>
> ...
>
> (c) children who have not attained the age of fifteen years shall neither be recruited in the armed forces or groups nor allowed to take part in hostilities;
>
> (d) the special protection provided by this Article to children who have not attained the age of fifteen years shall remain applicable to them if they take a direct part in hostilities despite the provisions of subparagraph (c) and are captured;[69]

Again, the provision is divided into 'recruitment' and 'use', and the threshold age is set at younger than fifteen. However, no part of this provision serves to limit the degree of protection offered to children younger than fifteen insofar as prohibiting their recruitment and use in hostilities is concerned.

The words 'shall neither be recruited . . . nor allowed' are prescriptive. This provision is applicable to 'armed forces or groups' compared to 'armed forces' as used in Additional Protocol I. It is further prohibited to use a child to 'take part in hostilities' compared to 'take a direct part

---

[68] States often deny the existence of armed conflict, specifically in the context of internal armed conflict. For example, they are able to enforce a greater level of municipal criminal law on their adversary. Thus, in practical terms, often neither Additional Protocol I nor Additional Protocol II finds application in a situation that meets the threshold criteria as being an armed conflict.

[69] Art 4(3) of the Additional Protocol II.

in hostilities'. This provision amounts to a near-absolute prohibition of the use and recruitment of children younger than fifteen. The 'all feasible measures' standard was also done away with.[70]

This does not mean that there are no weaknesses in this provision. Most commentators will undoubtedly first point to the retention of the younger than fifteen age standard. However, perhaps more important is the retention of the word 'recruit'. As has been argued with reference to Additional Protocol I, recruit is not a broad enough concept to cover all means and methods by which children can become associated with and even members of armed groups. Most notably, enlistment is a broader concept, requiring a more passive involvement on the part of the armed group in securing the services of the child. Thus, if the manner in which the child becomes part of the armed group falls short of 'recruitment', the enlistment of the child will be lawful. However, under Additional Protocol I such an enlisted child would lawfully be subject to indirect participation in conflict, whereas in NIAC such a child may not even be used to take part in hostilities indirectly. Non-state entities incur IHL obligations on the international plane in the contexts of both IAC and NIAC, and are thus equally bound to IHL child soldier prohibitions.[71]

## IV. CONCLUSION

The two Additional Protocols were the first international law instruments to prohibit the use and recruitment of child soldiers. As such, among regimes of international law, IHL pioneered this important endeavour. Nevertheless, as will be discussed in the next chapter, these prohibitions within IHL created virtually no traction up to the point, during the mid-1990s, when the IHRL movement took up the cause of child soldier prevention. The child soldier prohibition contained in Additional Protocol I, and relevant to IAC, leaves much to be desired. Some elements to the definition, such as the requirement that all feasible measures be taken that a child does not participate in hostilities, have much less of an impact in practice than many may imagine. Yet, other elements to the definition, such as the direct participation in hostilities element, indeed exclude a great number of children from legal protection. However, notwithstanding the fact that the minimum age threshold of younger than fifteen was retained, Additional Protocol II, relevant to NIAC, contained what is probably still the most absolute prohibition of child soldiering to date.

---

[70] See the discussion of 'all feasible measures' above.
[71] G Waschefort, 'The Pseudo Legal Personality of Non-State Armed Groups in International Law' (2011) 36 *South African Yearbook of International Law* 226.

Due to the lack of enforcement mechanisms within IHL, the jurisprudence on child soldier prevention has only been generated in the
dimensions of ICL and, to a much more limited extent, IHRL. Moreover, while the prohibition of the use and recruitment of child soldiers
within IHL is rather straightforward, the IHL dimension to the problem
accounts for only one contributing regime. As a brand of crisis law,[72]
IHL enjoys a limited scope of application and as such leaves significant
gaps that need to be filled for the effective prevention of child soldiering. The contributions of IHRL and ICL follow in the subsequent two
chapters. Central to an effective legal framework for the prohibition of
child soldiering is a holistic understanding of the contributing regimes
of law. This implies knowing and understanding not only the contributions of regimes such as IHL, IHRL and ICL to the problem at hand, but
also knowing and understanding the interaction of these regimes *inter se.*

---

[72] IHL applies only during armed conflict, once the expected modes of conflict resolution such as dialogue and political engagement has deteriorated into violence, that is to
say as a last resort.

# 4

# International Human Rights Law and International Humanitarian Law: An Integrated International Law Response to the Prevention of Child Soldiering

T HE HISTORY OF international humanitarian law (IHL) is vastly different from that of international human rights law (IHRL). Modern IHL's first written incarnations appeared in the form of the Lieber Code and the first Geneva Convention, of 1863 and 1864, respectively.[1] By that time, the law of war, as it then was, had enjoyed a very long history in customary practice.[2] Indeed, custom has always dictated practice during armed conflict, and by 2000 BC the Egyptians and Sumerians had treaties in place regulating the initiation and conduct of armed conflict.[3] The law of war aimed at balancing military necessity and prevailing considerations of humanity. By the turn of the century, with the adoption of the Hague Conventions of 1899 and 1907, a slow but steady movement was initiated, progressively shifting this balance towards prevailing considerations of humanity. Conversely, in the case of IHRL, a much more recent legal phenomenon, custom followed treaty obligations. The internationalisation of human rights law emerged after the First World War and was only mainstreamed after the Second World War in the form of the Charter of the United Nations of

---

[1] Lieber Code, Instructions for the Government of Armies of the United States in the Field (1863); Convention for the Amelioration of the Condition of the Wounded in Armies in the Field, Geneva (22 August 1864).

[2] R Bernhardt, *Encyclopaedia of Public International Law Volume 2* (Amsterdam, Elsevier, 1992) 933–36; J Ober, 'Classical Greek Times' in M Howard, GJ Andreopoulos and MR Shulman (eds), *The Laws of War: Constraints on Warfare in the Western World* (New Haven, Yale University Press, 1994).

[3] L Friedman (ed), *The Law of War* (New York, Random House, 1972) 3; MC Bassiouni, 'Repression of Breaches of the Geneva Conventions under the Draft Additional Protocol to the Geneva Conventions of August 12, 1949' (1976–77) 8 *Rutgers-Cam Law Journal* 185.

1945 and the Universal Declaration of Human Rights of 1948.[4] Thereafter, state practice followed suit, resulting in a large body of customary international law.

Today, child soldiering is prohibited by various transnational and municipal legal regimes, among which IHL, IHRL and international criminal law (ICL) are most important. This chapter commences by analysing the relationship between IHL and IHRL, which has only recently begun receiving the attention it deserves, and no proper analysis of this relationship has previously been undertaken in relation to child soldier prevention. I anticipate that a thorough understanding of this relationship and the corresponding application of norms belonging to these regimes may assist greatly those who occupy functions aimed at preventing child soldiering. Next, the proscriptive content of child soldier prohibitive norms belonging to IHRL are assessed separately. Finally, customary international law norms prohibiting child soldiering are assessed.

## I. THE CO-APPLICATION OF IHRL AND IHL IN THE PREVENTION OF THE USE AND RECRUITMENT OF CHILD SOLDIERS

Child soldier prohibitive rules are 'hybrid' in nature, spanning the divide between IHL and IHRL.[5] Prohibiting the use of children in armed conflict is, by definition, dependent on the existence of armed conflict, and as such relates more to IHL. Yet the recruitment of child soldiers is also prohibited during times of peace, when IHL is not applicable at all, and thus IHRL is responsible for prohibiting recruitment during such times. However, it is not just the characteristics of a specific norm that determine whether the norm belongs to IHL or IHRL, but also the nature of the instrument to which the norm belongs.

The child soldier prohibition in the Convention on the Rights of the Child (CRC) is almost a verbatim restatement of the corresponding norm in Additional Protocol I to the Geneva Conventions.[6] Even though these norms are materially the same, the CRC norm, as an IHRL norm, creates

---

[4] Universal Declaration of Human Rights, GA res 217A (III), UN Doc A/810 (1948).

[5] WA Schabas, 'Lex Specialis? Belt and Suspenders? The Parallel Operation of Human Rights Law and the Law of Armed Conflict, and the Conundrum of Jus ad Bellum' (2007) 40 *Israel Law Review* 592, 603. It is difficult to classify child soldier prohibitive norms as either IHL or IHRL norms. The prohibition of the use of child soldiers is more akin to the IHL regime, whereas the prohibition of the recruitment of children is more akin to the IHRL regime. Schabas contends that these norms are hybrid in nature.

[6] Art 38 of the Convention on the Rights of the Child (entered into force 2 September 1990) 1577 UNTS 3; Art 77(2) of Protocol I Additional to the Geneva Conventions of 12 August 1949, relating to the Protection of Victims of International Armed Conflicts, adopted 8 June 1977 (entered into force 7 December 1978) 1125 UNTS 17512.

obligations only on states parties and applies during peace and armed conflict, whereas the Additional Protocol I norm, an IHL norm, creates obligations on all parties to an armed conflict and applies only during the armed conflict.[7] Assessing the relationship between IHL and IHRL in the context of child soldiering is thus very important, as there is potential for norm conflict between the IHL and IHRL regimes as they pertain to child soldier prohibition. The large majority of this section relates to the relationship between IHL and IHRL in general, and not child soldiering specifically. This assessment is necessary in order to address potential norm conflict in the context of the child soldier prohibition.

It is trite law that IHL is reserved for the exclusive domain of armed conflict. In the early days of IHRL this led many to believe that IHRL is reserved for the exclusive domain of times of peace.[8] Time has proven this assumption to be false.[9] Nevertheless, IHRL instruments and state practice of that era were often premised on the inapplicability of IHRL during times of armed conflict. By 1968, a shift had begun to occur towards the recognition of the applicability of IHRL during times of armed conflict and so began the growth of substantive IHRL to cover situations of armed conflict.[10] However, it was only during 1996 that the International Court of Justice (ICJ) formally found that IHRL continues to apply during armed conflict.[11]

After the emergence of IHRL, beginning in the inter-war period and really gaining momentum post-WWII, commentators began drawing parallels between IHL and IHRL.[12] Over time, these parallels resulted in a two-dimensional narrative along the lines that the influence of IHRL is progressively 'humanising' IHL;[13] and that these two bodies of law are developing towards a 'convergence' or 'fusion'.[14] However, some com-

---

[7] IHL also applies during situations of belligerent occupation. However, such situations do not have a direct bearing on child soldiering.

[8] See, eg GIAD Draper, 'Human Rights and the Law of War' (1971–72) 12 *Virginia Journal of International Law* 326 332 and 338.

[9] *Legality of the Threat or Use of Nuclear Weapons*, ICJ Reports 1996, para 25 (*Nuclear Weapons* case).

[10] 'Human Rights in Armed Conflicts' Resolution XXIII adopted by the International Conference on Human Rights, Teheran (12 May 1968).

[11] *Nuclear Weapons* case, n 9 above, para 25.

[12] Early commentators included GIAD Draper, 'Humanitarian Law and Human Rights' [1979] *Acta Juridica* 193, 199 and 205; JL Kuntz, 'The Laws of War' (1956) 50 *American Journal of International Law* 313 322; T Meron, 'A Report on the NYU Conference on Teaching International Protection of Human Rights' (1980–81) 13 *New York University Journal of International Law & Politics* 881, 914–39. More recent commentators include A Orakhelashvili, 'The Interaction between Human Rights and Humanitarian Law: Fragmentation, Conflict, Parallelism, or Convergence?' 19 *European Journal of International Law* (2008) 161; R Arnold and N Quenivet (eds), *International Humanitarian Law and Human Rights Law: Towards a New Merger in International Law* (The Hague, Brill, 2008).

[13] T Meron, 'The Humanization of Humanitarian Law' (2000) 94 *American Journal of International Law* 239 239–278.

[14] Draper, n 12 above.

mentators were weary of these arguments—in 1967, Bassiouni wrote that 'the humanization of armed conflict has been the object of regulation and concern by every civilization for centuries';[15] and in 1979, Draper warned against this new movement towards the 'fusion' of these legal regimes, saying that IHRL and IHL are 'diametrically opposed'.[16]

Arguing that IHRL is humanising IHL speaks to the substantive content of IHL, whereas the convergence of these regimes speaks not only to the substantive content, but also the formal nature of these regimes, which includes their respective objectives.

## A. The 'Humanisation' of IHL

IHL is the older of the two regimes and, like IHRL, its existence is dependent on the promotion of principles of humanity—the name 'international *humanitarian* law' is telling. As Meron states:

> Chivalry and principles of humanity created a counterbalance to military necessity, serving as a competing inspiration for the law of armed conflict. Indeed, tension between military necessity and restraint on the conduct of belligerents is the hallmark of that law.[17]

Meron goes on to argue that the balance between these two competing interests has shifted over time: whereas the bias used to be in favour of military necessity, that bias is now in favour of principles of humanity.[18]

Nevertheless, there is a cause/effect problem, with the broad-based argument that it is primarily the human rights legal regime that inspired or effected the change in this balance. Even though international law has become more focused on individuals, it is still for the most part states that 'create' international law. As such, it is the interests, motives and principles of states that dictate the trends within new law and practice. If principles of humanity become more aligned with state interests, this development will trickle through to virtually all state actions, including the creation and new interpretation of law. Placing the IHRL regime firmly on the agenda is as much an expression of states' values as is the progressive reform of IHL from a system stacked in favour of military necessity to one stacked in favour of humanitarianism.

Nevertheless, the parallel development of these branches of law, which are clearly interrelated, has resulted in a situation where one branch can be influenced by the other. As the parameters of IHL are more restrictive—indeed, it is generally considered to be the *lex specialis*

---

[15] Bassiouni, n 3 above, 185.
[16] Draper, n 12 above, 199 and 205.
[17] Meron, n 13 above, 243.
[18] Ibid, 243–244.

of the two regimes[19]—IHL will be influenced by IHRL far more often than vice versa. There are nevertheless examples of IHL provisions that have been included in IHRL instruments.

One further area where IHRL directly influences IHL is through the interpretation of IHL by bodies created by human rights instruments.[20] The only judicial bodies tasked with the interpretation and application of IHL are the international criminal tribunals, and this function accounts for only part of their duties.[21] Moreover, they interpret and apply IHL in the guise of war crimes, which have developed in the context of ICL and have taken on a character of their own.

## B. The Convergence of IHL and IHRL

While the substantive content of the two regimes largely overlap, the *raisons d'être* for their existence are different. IHL aims to regulate the conduct of hostilities and protect the victims of war, whereas IHRL aims to provide protection to individuals from the abuse of power by states (this includes the obligation to promote, protect, respect and fulfil fundamental rights). As function dictates form, the structure of each regime is tailored to achieve its specific goals.

While the *ius in bello* realm of law concerns itself not with the lawfulness of conflict, but with its conduct and effects, there are developments within IHRL that view the existence of conflict a violation per se. Schabas, for instance, is of the view that there is a right to peace, albeit one that is underdeveloped.[22] This is affirmed by one of the resolutions adopted at the 1968 UN Conference of Human Rights, entitled 'Human Rights in Armed Conflict' which holds: 'considering that peace is the underlying condition for the full observance of human rights and war is their negation'.[23]

The neutral approach of IHL as regards the unlawfulness of any party to a conflict's acts *ius ad bellum* is dependent on the principle of equality of belligerents. This principle is central to the enforcement of IHL. The equality of belligerents means 'the rules of international humanitarian law apply with equal force to both sides to the conflict, irrespective of

---

[19] *Nuclear Weapons* case, n 9 above, para 25.
[20] See, eg *'Mapiripán Massacre' v Colombia* Inter-American Court of Human Rights (15 September 2005), para 114.
[21] See generally Chapter 5.I below.
[22] Schabas, n 5 above, 593; see also M Sassòli, AA Bouvier and A Quintin, *How Does Law Protect in War: Cases, Documents and Teaching Materials on Contemporary Practice in International Humanitarian Law* (Geneva, ICRC, 1999) 266.
[23] Human Rights in Armed Conflicts, n 10 above.

who is the aggressor'.[24] One of the primary effects of this rule is that all parties to a conflict governed by IHL will be bound by IHL, including non-state actors. There is no general agreement on the theoretical basis for such obligations on non-state actors, and it is worth noting that this is a feature unique to IHL.[25]

Sassòli has identified two primary constructions that account for this phenomenon. First and foremost, when states ratify treaties or practise custom, they implicitly confer the necessary legal capacity on such non-state groups to incur obligations under IHL.[26] Secondly, such obligations will also be founded on municipal law through municipal implementation.[27] However, obligations founded on the second construction are municipal law obligations, not international ones, and even the first construction is not wholly satisfactory. My approach is founded on the recognition of a limited legal capacity on the part of non-state groups within IHL.[28] Be that as it may, it is well recognised that non-states parties incur such obligations. IHRL, on the other hand, only provides for obligations on states. As is the case with the contrary position within IHL, this can be traced to the fundamental aims of IHRL. Thus, even where IHRL endeavours to dictate the actions of non-state entities, this is attempted through the instrumentality of a state, by creating obligations on the state. In order to comply with such an obligation, a state party will then, for example, enact municipal criminal legislation that aims to direct the behaviour of non-state entities. Furthermore, IHRL is more concerned with vertical power relationships and IHL with horizontal power relationships.[29]

## C. Resolving Norm Conflict

The polar opposite to arguments suggesting the convergence of IHL and IHRL is the conflict of norms within these legal regimes. This problem is only material if two norms apply to the same subject matter and there is an irreconcilable conflict between them;[30] or else both may apply in

---

[24] C Greenwood, 'Historical Development and Legal Basis' in D Fleck (ed), *The Handbook of International Humanitarian Law* (Oxford, Oxford University Press, 2008) 11.

[25] See generally, G Waschefort, 'The Pseudo Legal Personality of Non-state Armed Groups in International Law' (2011) 36 *South African Yearbook of International Law* 226.

[26] Sassòli et al, n 22 above, 214–17. It is well accepted that non-state groups incur such obligations. However, the reasoning is still somewhat unsound.

[27] Ibid.

[28] Waschefort, n 25 above.

[29] B Bowring, 'Fragmentation, Lex Specialis and the Tensions in the Jurisprudence of the European Court of Human Rights' (2009) 14 *Journal of Conflict and Security Law* 485, 490.

[30] G Fitzmaurice, 'The Law and Procedure of the International Court of Justice 1951–4: Treaty Interpretation and other Treaty Points' (1957) 33 *British Yearbook of International Law* 237.

harmony. There are numerous possibilities when there are two or more conflicting rules on the same substantive subject matter in international law.[31] However, two specific methods will be discussed, as contemporary international legal practice prefers the second and international law scholars have recently drawn some attention to the first.[32] The first approach has its roots in the 'more favourable principle' founded in human rights law, in terms of which the rule that provides the best protection must prevail. It has been suggested that this rule must be applied, *mutatis mutandis*, to conflicts between IHL and IHRL.[33] The second approach calls for the application of the maxim *lex specialis derogat legi generali*. The *lex specialis* rule is a rule of interpretation, accepted in international law, which provides that 'where two or more norms deal with the same subject matter, priority should be given to the rule that is more specific'.[34] It should, however, be noted that there are increasing calls that further possibilities for resolving norm conflicts between IHL and IHRL should be explored. Speaking only of the co-application of IHL and IHRL during military operations and armed conflict is an oversimplification of a more complex environment. The International Law Association's study group on 'The Conduct of Hostilities under International Humanitarian Law—Challenges of 21st Century Warfare' correctly warned that

> During the discussions of the Study Group, it was noted that the intersection between IHL and international human right law is only one aspect of the legal pluriverse applicable to armed forces and hence, resolving frictions between the two will not necessarily stop the same frictions appearing in other guises. The activities of the armed forces are subject to a multitude of partly distinct, partly overlapping international legal regimes, including the law governing the jus ad bellum, international humanitarian law, international human rights law, international environmental law, the law of the sea, the law of State jurisdiction and State immunity, the law of State responsibility, but also domestic law of the State to which they belong as well as (potentially) the law of the territorial State in which they are present to name some of the most important ones.[35]

The ICJ advisory opinion in the *Threat or Use of Nuclear Weapons* case is now widely regarded as the *locus classicus* dealing with conflict of

[31] A Lindroos, 'Addressing Norm Conflicts in a Fragmented Legal System: The Doctrine of Lex Specialis' (2005) 74 *Nordic Journal of International Law* 27, 41.

[32] Ibid; Schabas, n 5 above, 593; SA Sadat-Akhavi, *Methods of Resolving Conflicts between Treaties* (Leiden, Martinus Nijhoff, 2003) 213–32.

[33] Schabas, ibid, 593 and 599.

[34] M Koskenniemi, 'Fragmentation of International Law: Difficulties Arising from the Diversification and Expansion of International Law, Report of the Study Group of the International Law Commission', UN Doc A/CN.4/L.682, 13 April 2006; Report of the International Law Commission (ILC), Fifty-sixth Session, UN Doc A/59/10, 408, para 5.

[35] 'The Conduct of Hostilities and International Humanitarian Law' (ILA Study Group, 2014) 6–7.

norms among IHL and IHRL.[36] The case has bearing on both the 'more favourable principle' and the application of the *lex specialis* rule. The Court was called upon by the General Assembly of the United Nations to render an advisory opinion. The General Assembly asked 'is the threat or use of nuclear weapons in any circumstance permitted under international law?'[37] The right to life provision under the International Covenant on Civil and Political Rights (ICCPR) was raised as one of the possible treaty provisions that could render the threat or use of such weapons a violation of international law per se. This provision holds that 'every human being has the inherent right to life. This right shall be protected by law. No one shall be arbitrarily deprived of his life.'[38] The court held that 'the test of what is an arbitrary deprivation of life, however, then falls to be determined by the applicable *lex specialis*, namely, the law applicable in armed conflict which is designed to regulate the conduct of hostilities'.[39]

### i. More Favourable Principle

The more favourable principle is problematic in its application between norms belonging to two different branches of law, as opposed to between two human rights law norms. Within the ambit of human rights law, states' obligations are generally founded on their agreement to be bound to such norms (or through customary international law). Their undertaking to be so bound draws no distinction between the scope of application of different IHRL norms, except for limitations found within treaties. Yet, essentially, states undertake obligations to be applied in the same jurisdiction and to be interpreted and applied within the same formal legal framework that determine such obligations, ie human rights law. The norms within that branch subscribe to the same overarching ratio. Thus, applying the most favoured principle within IHRL makes sense—determining that one rule applies in lieu of another has no bearing on the state's consent to be bound; indeed, the state agreed to bound to the two provisions equally.

Applying the principle to IHRL and IHL *inter se* provides some problems with regard to the *pacta sunt servanda* principle, 'the most basic norm of customary international law'.[40] This principle provides that, once a state has undertaken a commitment, it must be carried out in

---

[36] *Nuclear Weapons* case, n 9 above, para 25.

[37] General Assembly Resolution 49/75K (15 December 1994).

[38] Art 6 of the International Covenant on Civil and Political Rights (entered into force 23 March 1976) 999 UNTS 171.

[39] *Nuclear Weapons* case, n 9 above, para 25.

[40] WP Gormley, 'The Codification of *Pacta Sunt Servanda* by the International Law Commission: The Preservation of Classical Norms of Moral Force and Good Faith' (1969–70) 14 *St Louis University Law Journal* 370 371.

good faith as the state expressly agreed to be so bound.[41] As has been acknowledged with regard to the *lex specialis* principle, treaties must be interpreted to give the best expression to the state's consent.[42] Applying the most favourable principle between IHL and IHRL in a given case might be against the states' wishes. This is illustrated well by the problem the ICJ faced in the *Threat or Use of Nuclear Weapons* case. The application of the most favoured principle would likely have resulted in a finding that the right to life provision under the ICCPR prevails over the conflicting IHL provisions. This would be completely contrary to the basic existence of the law of war.[43] From an individualist perspective, IHRL will almost inevitably provide better protection than IHL in a situation where there is a norm conflict between the two regimes. The 'more favourable principle' is accordingly not useful for determining the outcome of a norm conflict between these two regimes.

*ii.* Lex specialis derogat legi generali

The Court's finding in the *Threat or Use of Nuclear Weapons* advisory opinion that 'the test of what is an arbitrary deprivation of life, . . . then falls to be determined by the applicable *lex specialis*, namely, the law applicable in armed conflict which is designed to regulate the conduct of hostilities',[44] has two very important implications. First, in instances of armed conflict, IHL is always the *lex specialis*. It may be argued that the finding in the *Palestinian Wall* advisory opinion supports this contention.[45] Secondly, the *lex specialis* does not supplant IHRL *in toto*. The ICCPR remains applicable, as does the right to life, but arbitrary deprivation is then determined in terms of the prevailing *lex specialis*. As Koskenniemi states, this is in keeping with the principle of harmonisation.[46] The ICJ had further opportunity to consider these matters in the *Legal Consequences of the Construction of a Wall in the Occupied Palestinian Territory* advisory opinion (*Palestinian Wall* advisory opinion) and the *Armed Activities on the Territories of the Congo (DRC v Uganda)* case.[47] In the *Palestinian Wall* advisory opinion the Court held:

> the protection offered by human rights conventions does not cease in case of armed conflict, save through the effect of provisions for derogation . . .

---

[41] Ibid.

[42] M Akehurst, 'The Hierarchy of the Sources of International Law' (1974–75) XLVII *British Yearbook of International Law* 273; Lindroos, n 31 above, 36–37.

[43] C Garraway, '"To Kill or Not to Kill?" Dilemmas on the Use of Force' (2009) 14 *Journal of Conflict & Security Law* 500.

[44] *Nuclear Weapons* case, n 9 above, para 25.

[45] *Legal Consequences of the Construction of a Wall in the Occupied Palestinian Territory*, ICJ Reports 2004, para 106.

[46] Koskenniemi, n 34 above, para 9.

[47] *Armed Activities on the Territories of the Congo (DRC v Uganda)*, ICJ Reports 2004.

> As regards the relationship between international humanitarian law and human rights law, there are thus three possible situations: some rights may be exclusively matters of international humanitarian law; others may be exclusively matters of human rights law; yet others may be matters of both these branches of international law. In order to answer the question put to it, the Court will have to take into consideration both these branches of international law, namely human rights law and, as *lex specialis*, international humanitarian law.[48]

Schabas contends that this formulation is incorrect in law. His argument is based on his own paraphrased version of the Court's dicta: 'three scenarios are possible, namely the application of international human rights law, the application of international humanitarian law, and the application of both branches of law'.[49] The Court found that the case at hand fell into the last category. Schabas states that *lex specialis* is not invoked if both branches apply, and that more properly *lex specialis* relates to the second category. His formulation of the three options is strictly speaking not correct. The Court did not speak of the possible application of the branches of law, but instead the relevant rights being '"exclusively matters of" the specific branches of law'. For instance, IHL is silent on freedom of the press during belligerent occupation; this implies that this is an issue exclusively a matter of human rights law. Similarly, IHRL is silent on the need and obligation to wear a distinctive uniform. Again, this implies that the issue is exclusively a matter of IHL. Finally, the use of lethal force is the prime example of an issue that is a matter of both IHL and IHRL.

Schabas is correct that in option two the *lex specialis*, being IHL, is applicable. However, the basis for its application in option two is not its nature as being *lex specialis*, but instead the fact that it is the only branch that finds application with regard to the specific issue at hand—there is no conflict of norms as IHRL is not applicable and no rule of interpretation is required to decide the applicability of a regime. Schabas goes on to state that where both systems apply simultaneously the construction will only work if the bodies of law are perfectly compatible.[50] This is not correct. They will arguably never be perfectly compatible, as the two bodies create obligations for different groups, ie IHL creates obligations on non-state groups and IHRL does not. In the final sentence of the quote from the Court's judgment, it is stated that the Court will consider both branches of law, namely 'human rights law and, as *lex specialis*, international humanitarian law'.[51] This brings this judgment completely in line with the *Nuclear Weapons* case. In the *DRC v Uganda* case the Court

---

[48] *Palestinian Wall* case, n 45 above, para 106.
[49] Schabas, n 5 above, 597.
[50] Ibid, 598.
[51] *Palestinian Wall* case, n 45 above, para 106.

dealt with violations of both IHL and IHRL, but did not deal with the clash between these branches of law. As such, that judgment is of less relevance and has led some commentators to suggest that the Court is moving away from the *lex specialis* approach to resolving norm conflict.[52] However, this is pure speculation. By virtue of the Court not expressly dealing with the *lex specialis* approach, it can equally be interpreted as the Court viewing the matter as having been dealt with. No alternative approach was used or implemented. Indeed, the opinion in the *Palestinian Wall* matter was rendered on 9 July 2004, whereas judgment in the *DRC v Uganda* case was rendered on 19 December 2005. It is unlikely that, in the Court's interpretation, the law had developed to that extent in a mere 18 months. It is more likely that the court did not refer to the *lex specialis* approach as there was no irreconcilable norm conflict in that case. As such, Bethlehem's approach is to be preferred: he argues that the *Nuclear Weapons* advisory opinion engages with the issue at a more nuanced level, and should thus be the primary point of departure for an analysis of the co-application of these regimes.[53]

Some commentators suggest that IHL supplants IHRL completely during armed conflict, and whether IHL will always be the *lex specialis* vis-à-vis IHRL remains a point of contention.[54] The real distinguishing feature of this argument from that rendered by the ICJ is that the ICJ in effect categorised IHL as an independent 'norm system'[55] or 'self-contained regime',[56] thus justifying that IHL as a whole is *lex specialis* and not the specific relevant norm. Proponents of this second approach postulate that this is incorrect. According to them, one must not look at the nature of the self-contained regime to determine which of two contesting, but overlapping, rules will prevail. Instead, one must look at the relevant specific rules to determine which one is the *lex specialis* vis-à-vis the other. This implies that the analysis must take place on a case-by-case basis. This interpretation is sound, as *lex specialis* is not a substantive rule of international law, but instead a more mechanical con-

---

[52] I Scobbie, 'Principle or Pragmatics? The Relationship between Human Rights Law and the Law of Armed Conflict' (2009) 14 *Journal of Conflict and Security Law* 449, 453. N Prud'homme, '*Lex Specialis*: Oversimplifying a More Complex and Multifaceted Relationship?' (2007) 40 *Israel Law Review* 356, 385.

[53] D Bethlehem 'The Relationship between International Humanitarian Law and International Human Rights Law in Situations of Armed Conflict' (2013) (2)2 *Cambridge Journal of International and Comparative Law* 193.

[54] Some commentators suggest that IHL supplants HRL completely, see MJ Dennis, 'Application of Human Rights Treaties Extraterritorially to Detention of Combatants and Security Internees: Fuzzy Thinking All Around?' (2005–06) 12 *ILSA Journal of International and Comparative Law* 472. Lindroos, n 31 above, 28; M Sassòli and LM Olson, 'The Relationship between International Humanitarian and Human Rights Law Where it Matters: Admissible Killing and Internment of Fighters in Non-international Armed Conflicts' (2008) 90(871) *ICRC Review* 603.

[55] Lindroos, ibid.

[56] Koskenniemi, n 34 above, 410–12.

struction of interpretation that lacks clear content.[57] *Lex specialis* can be used in the contexts of both individual rules and different 'self-contained regimes'. The question thus becomes which approach is appropriate in the case of IHL and IHRL.

The rationale for holding that IHL, as a self-contained regime, is the *lex specialis* vis-à-vis IHRL is that the former is applicable only in the context of regulating the conduct of hostilities and the protection of victims of war. Thus, it is IHL's narrow scope of application that renders it *lex specialis*. There is something of a fallacy in this argument. Only in the event of conflict between two specific norms will the *lex specialis* nature of the one be assessed. Yet, instead of looking at the two relevant norms, the nature of the regime is considered to determine the order of the specific norms. When an IHRL norm is applicable to a matter that is relevant to either the conduct of hostilities or the protection of victims of war and there is no corresponding IHL norm, the nature of the legal regime of IHRL will be immaterial. Thus, the content of the relevant norms should then have an impact on the assessment. The limited scope of application of IHL remains a factor in determining which of two norms is the *lex specialis*, and may well be decisive.

International law, with the exception of *jus cogens* and Article 103 of the UN Charter, is a regime that knows no hierarchy. Nevertheless, situations can and do arise in terms of which two valid, applicable and binding norms that are mutually exclusive, yet hierarchically equal, compete for application. In a strict sense, the primacy of one norm over the other, regardless of the legal reasoning, disposes of this foundational aspect of international law—that there are no hierarchies. However, conflict of norms cannot arise where a hierarchical structure is recognised—there will be no conflict as one norm will take precedence as a matter of law, except if both norms are of the same rank in the hierarchical structure. How, then, can the resolution of norm conflict be achieved without resulting in the recognition of a hierarchical norm structure? The *lex specialis* rule ultimately gives greater effect to state consent—*pacta sunt servanda*. Within treaty law, where a state is bound by two conflicting norms, it is presumed that the state intended for the rule that is more specific to the situation at hand to be applicable. This construction does not necessarily affect the nature of the rule itself regarding hierarchy. For example, Sassòli argues that IHL should not always be the *lex specialis* where both IHL and IHRL are applicable. Thus, in one situation one norm will be dominant and potentially in another the other norm would be dominant. The rules are not inherently hierarchical. However, the ICJ dictum holds that IHL will always be the *lex specialis*. At least in the strict sense, this can be seen as hierarchical preference.

---

[57] Lindroos, n 31 above, 36.

The question then arises if, in theory, IHRL can be the *lex specialis* vis-à-vis IHL, are there practical scenarios in which this can conceivably happen? I argue that this is indeed the case. Take, for example, the question whether a civilian who takes up arms to defend himself against a combatant attacker during armed conflict loses his protection from targeting by the attacker or other combatants as he becomes a direct participant in hostilities. To be clear, the example focuses on an individual, not a group, using force to defend himself from an unlawful attack in a setting that would speak to self-defence in the law enforcement paradigm, where the attacker is a combatant and the situation occurs in an area where there is an ongoing armed conflict. Such attacks on civilians are not uncommon during armed conflict. A mechanical application of IHL renders a finding that the civilian does indeed lose his protection from targeting. However, as IHRL also applies during armed conflict, an irreconcilable norm conflict arises between the civilian's right to life and the permissive rules of IHL which allow lethal targeting. In the circumstances of the *Legality of the Threat or Use of Nuclear Weapons* advisory opinion, the test as to which of these norms are the *lex specialis* was said to tilt in the favour of IHL. However, in the present circumstances, I would argue that the scales tilt in the favour of IHRL—that is, until such time that the attack against the civilian has ceased.

## D. IHL and IHRL: Potential Conflict of Norms

Sadat-Akhavi defines conflict of norms thus:

> A conflict of norms arises when it is impossible to comply with all requirements of two norms. The impossibility of complying with two norms implies that the norms are mutually exclusive; they cannot coexist in a legal order. Compliance with one norm entails non-compliance with the other.[58]

Although different treaties provide for different standards of protection, there is no conflict of norms between two norms prohibiting child soldiering that prevents such norms from applying in harmony. However, the potential for conflict of norms is not limited to the substantive content of the two relevant norms only. The working of the two legal regimes may make the norms mutually exclusive.

The obligations the Protocol to the CRC (the Protocol) creates on non-state actors are stricter than those imposed upon state actors in two material respects. First, non-state actors may not recruit persons younger than eighteen under any circumstances, whereas the Protocol allows for the recruitment of children aged sixteen to eighteen by states parties.

---

[58] Sadat-Akhavi, n 32 above, 1.

Secondly, states parties must take all feasible measures to ensure that persons younger than eighteen do not take a direct part in hostilities, whereas non-state entities may not use children, directly or indirectly, in hostilities under any circumstances.

The equality of belligerents is a foundational principle central to the application of IHL, specifically in the context of non-international armed conflict (NIAC),[59] and provides that 'the rules of international humanitarian law apply with equal force to both sides to the conflict, irrespective of who is the aggressor'.[60] Indeed, the existence of IHL is founded on equal treatment of parties regardless of the causes for the conflict, and specifically who the antagonists are. This, in itself, is an incarnation of the 'equality of belligerents' principle. There is no norm conflict between the different standards of protection created by the Protocol. However, the fact that the Protocol creates different obligations on the basis of the status of the relevant group is in conflict with the IHL principle of the equality of belligerents. The *lex specialis* rule is applicable.[61] In keeping with the dictum in the *Legality of the Use or Threat of Nuclear Weapons* case, the IHRL norms remain applicable even if IHL is the *lex specialis*, but must be interpreted so as not to conflict with the *lex specialis*. In the *Legality of the Use or Threat of Nuclear Weapons* case, the impression was created that the right to life was completely supplanted by the more permissive rules of IHL. This has led many to mistakenly conclude that, during armed conflict, IHL supplants IHRL totally. In relation to the Protocol, the fact that there is conflict of norms does not mean that the Protocol finds no application. Instead, it must be applied in conformity with the *lex specialis*. This means that all parties must take all feasible measures to ensure that children younger than sixteen do not take a direct part in hostilities. This is the lowest common denominator. The continued application of the Protocol is evidenced in that the age threshold is sixteen and not fifteen, as is the case with all IHL child soldier prohibitive norms.

The IHRL nature of the Protocol dictates that the obligation to enforce this stricter obligation on non-state groups lies with the state itself, as IHRL does not create obligations for non-state groups. Thus, it may be argued that the equality of belligerents is not violated, due to the obligation being placed on the state. However, in effect, this creates a

---

[59] Sassòli, n 26 above, 214–17; J Somer, 'Jungle Justice: Passing Sentence on the Equality of Belligerents in Non-international Armed Conflict' (2007) 89(867) *ICRC Review* 655; LM Olson, 'Practical Challenges of Implementing the Complementarity between International Humanitarian and Human Rights Law—Demonstrated by the Procedural Regulation of Internment in Non-International Armed Conflict' (2007–09) 40 *Case Western Reserve Journal of International Law* 437.

[60] Greenwood, n 24 above, 11.

[61] The rule is applicable between treaty and non-treaty standards, as *in casu*, see *INA Corporation v Government of the Islamic Republic of Iran* IRAN-US CTR Vol 8 (1985-I) 378.

further inequality on the part of the non-state group. Not only does the non-state group not receive equal treatment of the law, but the duty to enforce this stricter standard lies in the hands of their opponents on the battlefield, resulting in enforcement invariably remaining problematic.

## II. THE SUBSTANTIVE CONTENT OF CHILD SOLDIER PROHIBITIVE NORMS: HUMAN RIGHTS LAW

### A. Convention on the Rights of the Child

As IHRL traditionally concerns itself with the relationship between the state and its subjects, the international law duties and obligations established by IHRL provisions relevant to child soldiering fall on states. As will be discussed, IHRL instruments are addressed at 'states parties' and not 'parties to the conflict', or any other construction that includes non-state actors. Thus, in order for states to comply with their international law obligations they must enact municipal legislation, both criminal and civil, proscribing the use and recruitment of child soldiers within that state's municipal jurisdiction. IHRL is theoretically applicable at all times, although derogation from some provisions is permitted during states of emergency and, as has been discussed, IHL is generally, though not always, the *lex specialis* during armed conflict. IHRL has developed child protection with regard to prohibiting the recruitment of child soldiers significantly in that child soldier recruitment is prevented during times of peace as well.

The CRC is the IHRL treaty that received the most instruments of ratification and accession at the fastest pace ever. and came into force on 2 September 1990.[62] This is a unique IHRL instrument in that it contains provisions which are more akin to those contained in IHL instruments, specifically with regard to the prohibition of the use of child soldiers.[63] However, this extension of the subject-matter jurisdiction of IHRL does not affect the implementation and nature of IHRL as such. With regard to child soldiering, the CRC holds:

> 2. States Parties shall take all feasible measures to ensure that persons who have not attained the age of fifteen years do not take a direct part in hostilities.
>
> 3. States Parties shall refrain from recruiting any person who has not attained the age of fifteen years into their armed forces. In recruiting among those

---

[62] UN Treaty Collection, available at http://treaties.un.org (last accessed on 2 September 2011).

[63] S Detrick, *A Commentary on the United Nations Convention on the Rights of the Child* (Leiden, Martinus Nijhoff, 1999) 655–56; F Ang, *A Commentary on the United Nations Convention on the Rights of the Child: Article 38 Children in Armed Conflicts* (The Hague, Brill, 2005) 3.

persons who have attained the age of fifteen years but who have not attained the age of eighteen years, States Parties shall endeavour to give priority to those who are oldest.[64]

Unlike the Additional Protocols and Geneva Conventions, the CRC defines a child as 'every human being below the age of eighteen years unless under the law applicable to the child, majority is attained earlier'.[65] However, only with regard to child soldiering does the CRC deviate from this definition and provide for a lower age threshold for protection, being younger than fifteen. Indeed, the *ratio legis* of paragraphs 2 and 3 directly mirror Article 77(2) of Additional Protocol I and as such creates exactly the same obligations as Additional Protocol I save for the scope of application (not limited to armed conflict) and parties bound (states parties only). This is due to the different natures of IHL and IHRL, and is illustrated by the use of 'states parties' in the CRC and 'parties to the conflict' in Additional Protocol I.[66] In the context of IHRL, the parties bound will always be 'states parties'. The language is not a verbatim restatement of Additional Protocol I, but is so similar that there is no legal-technical difference between the obligations created, except for those differences attributable to the nature of the relevant legal regime.[67]

The biggest material difference is that in Additional Protocol I the prohibition on the 'use' of children is separated from the prohibition on 'recruitment' by the words 'in particular'. This may be interpreted as meaning that there is a greater obligation in terms of Additional Protocol I to prohibit 'recruitment' than 'use'—an interpretation that is not mirrored in the CRC. Unfortunately, as the CRC adopted the text of Additional Protocol I, the scope of prohibition of the use of child soldiers has not been extended to situations not amounting to armed conflict. The CRC uses the word 'hostilities' in defining the prohibition of the use of child soldiers. Given the broader scope of application of IHL, this provision had the potential to prohibit the use of children during violent situations falling short of armed conflict, such as uprisings and internal disturbances. Furthermore, again due to the different natures of the IHRL and IHL legal regimes, the CRC places a duty on the state party to take all feasible measures to prevent the use of children younger than fifteen years old from participating directly in hostilities. This includes preventing non-state entities from so using children in conflict. The same is not true of recruitment, where the duty on the

---

[64] Art 38 of the CRC.
[65] Art 1 of the CRC.
[66] See discussion below.
[67] As these provisions materially present the same level of protection, and as the same concepts are used—'all feasible measures', 'direct participation' and 'refrain from recruiting'—the treatment of these concepts relevant to Additional Protocol I as discussed above applies equally to Art 38(2) of the CRC.

state party is solely to take all feasible measures not to recruit children younger than fifteen years old themselves.[68] In other words, textually the CRC does not create an obligation on states party to the Convention to prohibit non-state entities from recruiting children. In my view, this is likely attributable to the direct importation of IHL provisions into IHRL instruments without paying due regard to the formal nature of the different legal regimes. Finally, the incorporation of the 'priority rule' in the CRC—to give priority to older children when recruiting among those aged between fifteen and eighteen—means that this rule is extended to potentially apply to NIAC as well.

As the disarmament, demobilisation and rehabilitation of children is an indirect child soldier preventative measure, Article 39 of the CRC deserves mention, as it states:

> States Parties shall take all appropriate measures to promote physical and psychological recovery and social reintegration of a child victim of . . . or armed conflicts. Such recovery and reintegration shall take place in an environment which fosters the health, self-respect and dignity of the child.

Article 38 was the subject of considerable debate during the drafting of the CRC. Most of this debate revolved around three issues: the threshold age; whether a distinction should be drawn between 'voluntary recruitment' and 'conscription'; and whether the provisions should specifically provide for recruitment for the purposes of training and education.[69] In order to resolve differences between delegates, a text reflecting the provision in Additional Protocol I was agreed upon at the expense of legal development and greater protection to children. What is more, unlike Additional Protocol I, the CRC is not limited to IAC, but may also be applicable during NIAC, and indeed when no armed conflict exists. The CRC's standard, however, falls short of the existing protection offered in such conflicts by Additional Protocol II and even Additional Protocol I considering that the CRC binds states parties only.[70]

## B. Optional Protocol to the Convention on the Rights of the Child

Many states were dissatisfied with the failure of Article 38 of the CRC to develop the law. In 1991, at the first session of the Committee on the Rights of the Child (CRC Committee), it was decided that a day of the

---

[68] This different treatment of 'use' and 'recruitment' is somewhat comparable to the use of the qualifier 'their armed forces' used in Additional Protocol II. However, because IHRL only creates obligations on states parties, these provisions function somewhat differently.

[69] C Breen, 'When Is a Child Not a Child? Child Soldiers in International Law' (2007) 8(2) *Human Rights Review* 83–87

[70] Detrick, n 63 above, 655–56.

session would be dedicated to 'children in armed conflicts'.[71] By 1994, the Commission on Human Rights adopted a resolution establishing an open-ended inter-sessional working group with the aim of drafting an Optional Protocol to the Convention on the Rights of the Child on the Involvement of Children in Armed Conflict.[72] This protocol was duly adopted and came into force on 12 February 2002. Like the CRC, this instrument forms part of IHRL, and as such creates obligations on 'states parties'. Unlike the instruments already discussed, it deals exclusively with children's participation in hostilities. Only the substantive provisions of this instrument are discussed here; the administrative and implementation provisions are discussed elsewhere together with the work of the CRC Committee.[73]

Article 1 of the Optional Protocol to the Convention on the Rights of the Child on the Involvement of Children in Armed Conflict (CIAC Protocol) provides: 'States Parties shall take all feasible measures to ensure that members of their armed forces who have not attained the age of 18 years do not take a direct part in hostilities'. This provision only deals with 'use', not 'recruitment'. The qualifiers 'all feasible measures' and 'direct part in hostilities' have been retained, but the age threshold has been lifted to younger than eighteen. The obligation here does not include an obligation to prevent non-state actors from using children in hostilities; such instances are addressed separately. Thus, insofar as the use of children by states parties is concerned, the only area in which the level of protection afforded to children is increased is by raising the age threshold to below eighteen. In their declarations, states parties have included their interpretations of when they may use children directly in hostilities without being in breach of Article 1. In this regard, the UK stated:

> The United Kingdom understands that Article 1 of the Optional Protocol would not exclude the deployment of members of its armed forces under the age of 18 to take a direct part in hostilities where:-
> a)  there is a genuine military need to deploy their unit or ship to an area in which hostilities are taking place; and
> b)  by reason of the nature and urgency of the situation:-
>     i)   it is not practicable to withdraw such persons before deployment; or
>     ii)  to do so would undermine the operational effectiveness of their ship or unit, and thereby put at risk the successful completion of the military mission and/or the safety of other personnel.[74]

---

[71] Committee on the Rights of the Child, 'Report on the Second Session', UN Doc CRC/C/10, para 61.

[72] Commission on Human Rights Resolution 1994/91.

[73] See generally Chapter 6.B below.

[74] Declaration of the United Kingdom of Great Britain and Northern Ireland, upon ratification (24 June 2003), available at http://treaties.un.org.

Vietnam's declaration states:

> To defend the Homeland is the sacred duty and right of all citizens. Citizens have the obligation to fulfil military service and participate in building the all-people national defence. Under the law of the Socialist Republic of Vietnam, only male citizens at the age of 18 and over shall be recruited in the military service. Those who are under the age of 18 shall not be directly involved in military battles unless there is an urgent need for safeguarding national independence, sovereignty, unity and territorial integrity.[75]

These provisions highlight the margin of appreciation afforded to states parties by utilising the subjective obligation of means that is created by the language 'all feasible measures', together with the high threshold of participation in hostilities, ie 'direct part in hostilities'.

Article 2 of the CIAC Protocol provides: 'States Parties shall ensure that persons who have not attained the age of 18 years are not compulsorily recruited into their armed forces'. This provision is again limited to 'states parties', and lifts the compulsory recruitment age to under eighteen. In previous provisions, the language used is 'shall refrain from recruiting', which creates a negative obligation, whereas Article 2 creates a positive obligation.

'Voluntary recruitment' is addressed separately. According to UNICEF, 'voluntary recruitment is understood to mean that children are under no compulsion to join armed forces and that safeguards are in place to ensure that any voluntary recruitment is genuinely voluntary'.[76] As such, a distinction remains between 'voluntary recruitment' and 'enlistment', and the Protocol failed to extend protection to include enlistment. The Protocol states:

> 1. States Parties shall raise in years the minimum age for the voluntary recruitment of persons into their national armed forces from that set out in Article 38, paragraph 3, of the Convention on the Rights of the Child, taking account of the principles contained in that article and recognizing that under the Convention persons under the age of 18 years are entitled to special protection.
>
> 2. Each State Party shall deposit a binding declaration upon ratification of or accession to the present Protocol that sets forth the minimum age at which it will permit voluntary recruitment into its national armed forces and a

---

[75] Declaration of Vietnam, upon ratification (20 December 2001), available at http://treaties.un.org.

[76] According to UNICEF, 'Voluntary recruitment is understood to mean that children are under no compulsion to join armed forces and that safeguards are in place to ensure that any voluntary recruitment is genuinely voluntary': UNICEF and Coalition to Stop the Use of Child Soldiers, 'Guide to the Optional Protocol on the Involvement of Children in Armed Conflict' (2003), 16.

description of the safeguards it has adopted to ensure that such recruitment is not forced or coerced.[77]

This implies that states parties must lift their voluntary recruitment age by at least one year from that set out in the CRC (younger than fifteen), ie the minimum allowable age is younger than sixteen, but it can range up to younger than eighteen. The minimum age is to be raised by depositing a declaration also setting out safeguards adopted to prevent forced or coerced recruitment.[78] These safeguards must ensure, as a minimum, that: the recruitment is genuinely voluntary; informed consent of the person's parents or legal guardians have been obtained; the candidate is fully informed of the duties involved in such military service; and reliable proof of age is provided by the candidate.[79]

Unlike earlier child soldier prohibitions, this provision is silent on the nature and extent of the obligation owed by states parties. The qualifiers 'states parties', 'voluntary recruitment' and 'their national armed forces' are present, but the provision is silent on the strength of the obligation, eg whether 'all feasible measures' are to be taken or whether states parties 'shall not' do so. Instead, the parameters of the prohibition contained in Article 38 of the CRC are incorporated by reference: 'taking account of the principles contained in that article [Article 38 of the CRC]'. Incorporation by reference is not a new phenomenon in international treaty law, specifically related to IHRL.[80] However, the possibility exists that a state can ratify the CIAC Protocol without having ratified the CRC. This is only possible with regard to the two states which have not ratified the CRC, the US and Somalia—and the US has ratified the CIAC Protocol without being a party to the CRC. Attached to their Article 3 declaration, the US added a section entitled 'Understandings', where it is stated that 'The United States understands that the United States assumes no obligations under the Convention on the Rights of the Child by becoming a party to the Protocol'.[81]

Buergenthal argues that such incorporation by reference is only effective if the law so incorporated binds the relevant state party.[82] However,

---

[77] Art 3 of the CIAC Protocol.

[78] States parties can raise their minimum voluntary recruitment age at any time. Furthermore, the requirement to raise the minimum voluntary recruitment age is not applicable to schools operated by or under the control of the armed forces of the States Parties. Arts 3(4) and 3(5) of the CIAC Protocol.

[79] Art 3(3) of the CIAC Protocol.

[80] See, eg Art 15 of the European Convention on Human Rights and Fundamental Freedoms 213 UNTS 221.

[81] Declaration of the United States of America, upon ratification (23 December 2002), available at http://treaties.un.org.

[82] T Buergenthal, 'International and Regional Human Rights Law and Institutions: Some Examples of Their Interaction' 12 *Tex. International Law Journal* 321 (1977); see also T Meron, 'Norm Making and Supervision in International Human Rights: Reflections on Institutional Order' (1982) 76 *American Journal of International Law* 754.

his argument in this regard is relevant to Article 15 of the European Convention on Human Rights, which incorporates 'other obligations under international law'. This non-specific provision will obviously only refer to such obligations to which the relevant state is bound. In the case at hand, the incorporating law is not only specific with regard to the instrument that is incorporated, but also with regard to the specific provision. As such, *pacta sunt servanda* will dictate that states parties do not assume obligations under other treaties, but that the principles contained in Article 38 becomes part of the CIAC Protocol by reference. Thus, all states parties are subject to this reference;[83] and the 'strength' of the obligation for states parties is to 'refrain from recruiting' such persons. Moreover, the priority rule is also applicable.

Being an IHRL treaty, the CIAC Protocol places obligations on the state. However, it also endeavours to regulate the use and recruitment of children by non-state armed groups. In such instances, the obligation still falls on the state to prevent these groups from using and recruiting children. The standards prescribed for such non-state groups are markedly different to those applicable to the states themselves:

1. Armed groups that are distinct from the armed forces of a State should not, under any circumstances, recruit or use in hostilities persons under the age of 18 years.

2. States Parties shall take all feasible measures to prevent such recruitment and use, including the adoption of legal measures necessary to prohibit and criminalize such practices.[84]

Such 'armed groups' include all non-state armed groups.[85] Non-state armed groups may not recruit persons younger than eighteen voluntarily under any circumstances, although states parties may do so, provided they have entered a declaration to that effect. Moreover, in the prohibition of the use of child soldiers, the qualifiers 'all feasible measures' and 'direct part in hostilities' are omitted. The word 'should' instead of 'shall' in 'armed forces of a State should not' indicates the nature of the IHRL provision in that the obligation falls on the state to enforce the provision and does not create obligations on non-state armed groups comparable to those created by IHL.[86]

The unequal treatment of states parties and non-state armed groups means that states are allowed to recruit persons as young as sixteen

---

[83] Ang, n 63 above, 33.

[84] Art 4, CIAC Protocol.

[85] M Happold, 'The Optional Protocol to the Convention on the Rights of the Child on the involvement of children in armed conflict' [2000] *Yearbook of International Humanitarian Law* 239.

[86] Helle is of the view that this is indicative of a moral obligation instead of a legal obligation in international law: D Helle, 'Optional Protocol on the Involvement of Children in Armed Conflict to the Convention on the Rights of the Child' [2000] *ICRC Review* 839.

on a voluntary basis; non-state groups may only recruit persons aged eighteen or older. In the context of 'use' of children, the obligation on states parties is limited to taking 'all feasible measures' and the degree of hostilities from which children are protected is 'direct part in hostilities'. Non-state groups, however, 'should not, under any circumstances, recruit or use in hostilities persons under the age of 18 years'. This provision does not create an international law obligation on non-state groups (as IHL does), thus the duty lies on the states parties to enforce this grossly unequal standard. What this protocol has done is allow states to create a further power imbalance between themselves and their non-state adversaries. States are in stronger power positions in a great majority of civil conflicts. Increasing this power imbalance places further strain on non-state groups to rely on asymmetrical conflict strategies, of which the use of child soldiers is one example[87] and terrorist tactics is the best example.[88] As was argued earlier, creating different obligations upon parties to hostilities based on status is inconsistent with the equality of belligerents. Therefore, in the context of armed conflict, where IHL is often the *lex specialis*, the lowest standard applicable to all parties to the conflict should be applied.

Article 38(2) of the CRC Protocol indicates well that, regardless of its substantive content, this is an IHRL instrument, as the obligation remains that of the state.[89] The reference to all feasible measures in this instance refers to the state's duty to prevent non-state armed groups from using and recruiting children, and not to the nature of the duty on such armed groups, as there is no international legal duty incumbent upon them.

## C. International Labour Organization Convention 182

The CIAC Protocol was not the first IHRL instrument to increase the threshold age for 'forced or compulsory recruitment' to eighteen.[90] The International Labour Organization Convention 182 came into force on 19 November 2000 and holds that 'Each Member which ratifies this Convention shall take immediate and effective measures to secure the prohibition and elimination of the worst forms of child labour as a matter

---

[87] See generally Chapter 2.A above.
[88] G Waschefort, 'Drawing the Boundaries between Terrorism and Crimes against Humanity' (2007) 22(2) *SA Public Law* 457; R Geib, 'Asymmetric Conflict Structures' (2006) 88(864) *International Review of the Red Cross* 758.
[89] F Grunfeld, 'Child Soldiers' in J Willems (ed), *Developmental and Autonomy Rights of Children. Empowering Children, Caregivers and Communities* (Antwerp, Intersentia, 2002) 285.
[90] MJ Dennis, 'The ILO Convention on the Worst Forms of Child Labor' (1999) 93(4) *American Journal of International Law* 944.

of urgency',[91] a 'child' being all persons under the age of eighteen.[92] The convention goes on to define the worst forms of child labour to include 'forced or compulsory recruitment of children for use in armed conflict'.[93]

## D. African Charter on the Rights and Welfare of the Child

The African Charter on the Rights and Welfare of the Child, also referred to as the African Children's Charter, is the only binding regional human rights law instrument regulating the use and recruitment of children in armed conflict. In many respects the African Children's Charter is revolutionary and in some respects it provides the strongest protection for children in armed conflict;[94] indeed, it generally provides better protection than the CRC.[95] Its child soldier prohibition holds 'States Parties to the present Charter shall take all necessary measures to ensure that no child shall take a direct part in hostilities and refrain in particular, from recruiting any child'.[96] A 'child' is deemed to be every human being below the age of eighteen years.[97]

Although this instrument only came into force on 29 November 1999, it was opened for signature during 1990. As such, in drafting terms, it is much more a peer of the CRC than the CIAC Protocol. Bearing this in mind, this provision prohibits the use and compulsory and voluntary recruitment of children under eighteen. What is more, the obligation on states parties is to 'take all necessary measures'. This is an obligation of result rather than an obligation of means as contained in the corresponding provision of the CRC. This provision also treats 'use' and 'recruitment' on a more equal footing, which is a welcome approach, as in practice this distinction can be somewhat contrived: children are often recruited to be used in direct participation in hostilities.[98] The

---

[91] Art 1 of the International Labour Organization Convention 182 (entered into force 19 November 2000).

[92] Ibid, Art 2.

[93] Ibid, Art 3.

[94] F Viljoen, 'Supra-national Human Rights Instruments for the Protection of Children in Africa: The Convention on the Rights of the Child and the African Charter on the Rights and Welfare of the Child' (1998) 31 *Comparative and International Law Journal of Southern Africa* 199; A Lloyd, 'Evolution of the African Charter on the Rights and Welfare of the Child and the African Committee of Experts: Raising the Gauntlet' (2002) 10 *International Journal of Children's Rights* 179, 184; D Olowu, 'Protecting Children's Rights in Africa: A Critique of the African Charter on the Rights and Welfare of the Child' (2002) 10 *International Journal of Children's Rights* 127, 131.

[95] F Viljoen, 'Why South Africa Should Ratify the African Charter on the Rights and Welfare of the Child' (1999) 116 *South African Law Journal* 660.

[96] Art 22(2) of the African Children's Charter.

[97] Ibid, Art 2.

[98] See generally Chapter 2.II.

African Children's Charter is the only instrument relevant to child soldiering that directly addresses the tension between a universalist and
culturally relative approach to the age of childhood and the associated
protection. The African Children's Charter proclaims its supremacy over
any custom, tradition and cultural or religious practices, insofar as they
may be inconsistent with the rights contained in the African Children's
Charter.[99] However, this is done while still taking account of nuances
peculiar to Africa.[100]

The African Children's Charter has four primary shortcomings insofar
as it relates to the prevention of child soldiering. First, it has retained the
qualifier 'direct part in hostilities' in relation to the 'use' of child soldiers.
Secondly, it prohibits 'recruitment' and not 'enlistment'. Thirdly, it does
not contain a provision similar to Article 39 of the CRC dealing with
physical and psychological recovery and social reintegration for former
child soldiers.[101] Lastly, it does not protect children from 'recruitment'
by non-state armed groups.

The founding of the African Committee of Experts on the Rights and
Welfare of the Child, which monitors compliance with the African Children's Charter, was mandated by the African Children's Charter. This
committee is discussed in Chapter 5.

A majority of the international instruments discussed, including the
CRC, prohibits the use and recruitment of children younger than fifteen.
Every other right enshrined in the CRC is afforded to children, being
persons younger than eighteen. Regardless of the inherent contradiction
hereof, the absurdity of this state of affairs is further illustrated by the
fact that, in practice, child soldiers generally enjoy none of the other
rights afforded to them by virtue of being children, or indeed human,
such as the right to health and education. While this work focuses on
child soldier prevention specifically, it is important not to lose sight of
the plight of child soldiers in relation to all rights children generally
enjoy, but to which child soldiers are denied.

### III. THE SUBSTANTIVE CONTENT OF
### CHILD SOLDIER PROHIBITIVE NORMS:
### CUSTOMARY INTERNATIONAL LAW

Matheson, speaking in 1987 as Deputy Legal Advisor at the US State
Department (*ex officio*), explained that, while the US was not ready

---

[99] DM Chirwa, 'The Merits and Demerits of the African Charter on the Rights and
Welfare of the Child' (2002) 10 *International Journal of Children's Rights* 157, 158; Art 1(3)
of the African Children's Charter.

[100] Viljoen, n 94 above.

[101] Lloyd, n 94 above, 184.

to ratify Additional Protocol I, it did deem many of its provisions as forming part of customary international law.[102] The provisions expressly mentioned included 'that all feasible measures be taken in order that children under fifteen do not take a direct part in hostilities'.[103] Furthermore, in 2004, the Appeals Chamber of the Special Court for Sierra Leone (SCSL) held that the international law crime of enlisting, conscripting or using child soldiers, as formulated under the Statute of the SCSL and the Rome Statute, had crystallised into a customary international law crime.[104] What is more, no party to the proceedings before the SCSL argued against the existence of such a customary rule at the time of the proceedings (although they would disagree on the scope and nature of the rule, and the existence of such a rule was disputed at the time of the commission of the offence).[105]

There is no denying that the prohibition of the use and recruitment of child soldiers has crystallised into a norm of customary international law. This section assesses the nature, scope and definition of this customary rule (or rules). The existence of a customary rule or rules relevant to child soldiering is important for two primary reasons: states not party to the relevant international instruments will also be bound, and customary law largely transcends the formal distinction between IAC and NIAC.[106] The fact that non-party states are bound is founded upon the separate existence of the customary norm, ie such states will only be bound by the customary norm and states parties will be bound by both the treaty and the customary norm.[107] Furthermore, states cannot withdraw from or denounce customary norms.[108]

Customary law is 'international custom, as evidence of a general practice accepted as law'.[109] To find the existence of a customary norm, both *usus* and *opinio juris sive necessitates*—that is, state practice and the belief that such custom applies as a matter of law—are required to be present.[110]

---

[102] MJ Matheson, 'The Sixth Annual American Red Cross-Washington College of Law Conference on International Humanitarian Law: A Workshop on Customary International Law and the 1977 Protocols Additional to the 1949 Geneva Conventions' (1987) 2 *Americal University Journal of International Law & Policy* 415, 421.

[103] Ibid.

[104] *Prosecutor v Sam Hinga Norman Decision on Preliminary Motion Based on Lack of Jurisdiction* SCSL-2004–14-AR72(E) (31 May 2004) (*Child Recruitment* decision). For an explanation and criticism of this judgment see generally Chapter 5.I.A below.

[105] Ibid.

[106] For example, 149 of the 161 customary international humanitarian law rules identified by the ICRC apply to both IAC and NIAC.

[107] *Military and Paramilitary Activities in and against Nicaragua (The Republic of Nicaragua v The United States of America)*, ICJ Reports 1986, 95 (*Nicaragua* case).

[108] Ibid, 113–14. Except for the case of persistent objectors.

[109] Art 38(b) of the Statute of the International Court of Justice, Annexed to the Charter of the United Nations (entered into force 24 October 1945) 1 UNTS XVI.

[110] *North Sea Continental Shelf (Libyan Arab Jamahiriya v Malta)*, ICJ Reports 1985, 29–30.

State practice has been defined as 'any act, articulation or other behaviour of a state, as long as the behaviour in question discloses the State's conscious attitude with respect to its recognition of a customary rule'.[111] This includes 'real' and 'verbal' acts, meaning that treaty ratification and negotiating positions (*travaux préparatoires*) are included.[112] Furthermore, such practices have to be attributable to states, and other states must be able to learn of such behaviour within reasonable time.[113] There is no *numerus clausus* as to the manners in which state practice can be expressed, but it includes diplomatic correspondence, declarations on foreign or legal policy and national legislation. State practice must also be 'general', thus meaning common, widespread and representative.[114] *Opinio juris* has been held to be conduct exercised by a state by reason of it being 'a duty incumbent on them and not merely for reasons of political expediency'.[115] This duty must be 'a belief that this practice is rendered obligatory by the existence of a rule of law requiring it'.[116] It is thus a subjective determination on the part of the relevant state.

The ICRC study on customary international humanitarian law found that there are two customary rules within the IHL branch of law that relate to the prevention of child soldiering. First, rule 136: 'children must not be recruited into armed forces or armed groups';[117] and secondly, rule 137: 'children must not be allowed to take part in hostilities'.[118]

The study found an abundance of state practice supporting both the rule against recruitment and the rule against use.[119] Finding state practice to the effect that states do not use and recruit children below a certain age is not a tall order in itself, as clearly no state recruits or uses children younger than four, as an arbitrary example. Thus, insofar as state practice is concerned, the real question becomes what the age threshold is. Although there is a significant movement towards a

---

[111] ME Villiger, *Customary International Law and Treaties*, 2nd edn (The Hague, Kluwer, 1997) 16.

[112] M Byers, *Custom, Power and the Power of Rules* (Cambridge, Cambridge University Press, 1999) 134; MH Mendelson, *The Formation of Customary International Law* (The Hague, Brill, 1998) 204–07; for the opposite view see AM Weisburd, 'Customary International Law: The Problem of Treaties' (1988) 21 *Vanderbilt Journal of Transnational Law* 1; A D'Amato, *The Concept of Custom in International Law* (Ithaca, NY, Cornell University Press, 1971) 88.

[113] Villiger, note 111 above, 16–17.

[114] *Fisheries (United Kingdom v Norway)*, ICJ Reports 1951, 131; *North Sea Continental Shelf (Federal Republic of Germany v Denmark; Federal Republic of Germany v Netherlands)*, ICJ Reports 1969, para 74.

[115] *Asylum (Colombia v Peru)*, ICJ Reports 1950, 277; also see *Lotus (France v Turkey)* PCIJ (1927) Series A No 10, 28.

[116] *North Sea Continental Shelf* case, above n 114, para 77.

[117] JM Henckaerts, L Doswald-Beck and C Alvermann, *Customary International Humanitarian Law: Rules* (Cambridge, Cambridge University Press, 2007) rule 136.

[118] Ibid, rule 137.

[119] JM Henckaerts and L Doswald-Beck, *International Committee of the Red Cross: Customary International Humanitarian Law Volume II: Practice (Part II)* (Cambridge, Cambridge University Press, 2005) 3109–42.

straight-eighteen threshold, in terms of the ICRC study current state practice still holds younger than fifteen as the threshold age. However, custom is fluid, thus further legal development may well see a raise in the age threshold to younger than eighteen. I am of the view, however, that studies that aim to codify customary international law, such as this ICRC study, may potentially impact negatively on future interpretations of substantive customary norms, specifically in relation to the development of such norms.

General state practice dictates that there can only be one customary rule on one issue.[120] This begs the question whether state practice can be discernibly divided between such practice giving rise to an IHRL rule and such practice giving rise to an IHL rule. Sassòli and Olson argue that, 'in relation to the same problem, there cannot be a customary "human right" and a different customary "humanitarian rule". The focus is always placed on the practice and the opinio juris manifested in relation to problems as similar as possible to the one to be resolved.'[121] The methodology of the ICRC study placed equal reliance on state practice founded on IHRL (both during times of armed conflict and peace) as it did on state practice founded on IHL. The *Child Recruitment* case followed the same reasoning.[122] Such an approach is warranted as the ICRC study states that IHRL was included in state practice as 'international human rights law continues to apply during armed conflicts'.[123] On this basis, it is accepted that state practice, as directed by IHRL obligations, can bolster the threshold state practice required for the existence of a customary norm that includes application in the context of IHL. The question then is whether this is equally true vice versa?

The overlap between IHL and IHRL in the context of child soldiering is of such a nature that both bodies of law are often applicable to the same situation. However, unlike IHRL's continued application during times of armed conflict, IHL does not continue to apply during times of peace. Therefore, strictly speaking, if the ICRC argument is followed, reliance should not be placed on state practice emanating from within IHL to find a customary rule in IHRL. Furthermore, the substantive content of state practice within the IHL and IHRL realms should also be considered. For example, the now established IHL customary rule that 'children must not be allowed to take part in hostilities' has corresponding IHRL state practice, and indeed is founded in part upon such state practice, to the same effect. It is impossible for this part of the substantive IHRL to apply during times of peace as it directly speaks to participation in hostilities. Therefore, the degree of overlap between the

---

[120] Villiger, n 111 above, 30.
[121] Sassòli and Olson, n 54 above, 605.
[122] *Prosecutor v Sam Hinga Norman*, n 104 above.
[123] Henckaerts et al, n 117 above, xxxi.

relevant state practice from within IHL and IHRL is directly proportional to each other. In contrast, recruitment (as opposed to 'use') is prohibited during times of peace. The degree of overlap between state practice within IHL and IHRL is thus reduced, and state practice from within IHL cannot contribute to the existence of a customary IHRL norm applicable during times of peace. However, it can so contribute in relation to that customary norm as it applies during armed conflict. Nevertheless, overwhelming state practice supports the existence of a customary rule to the effect that 'children must not be recruited into armed forces or armed groups' during times of peace and armed conflict.

State practice supports the existence of two customary rules: the rule that children must not be recruited into armed forces or armed groups; and the rule that children must not be allowed to take part in hostilities. Due to the fluid nature of customary international law, and the general rule that there cannot be two customary norms on one substantive issue of state practice, there is no distinction between IHL and IHRL within the framing of the rules, though there is in their application. The *opinio juris* requirement is notoriously difficult to comply with. There is an obvious link between *usus* and *opinio juris*, as the latter qualifies the first, although care must be taken that they are not equated and *opinio juris* cannot be presumed on the basis of state practice.[124] Nevertheless, in the context of child soldiering, the sources confirming state practice are stacked overwhelmingly in favour of a finding that states regard the prohibitions against the use and recruitment of child soldiers as 'accepted as law'.

Finally, as customary international law is composed of state practice and *opinio juris*, theoretically the substantive norms contained in treaties relate only to the content of customary law insofar as those treaties dictate state practice and *opinio juris*. In the context of, for example, the prohibition of the use of children younger than fifteen in armed conflict, state practice and *opinio juris* possibly support the existence of a customary norm of greater proscriptive content than any of the treaty norms discussed. However, in practice, the first port of call in defining a customary norm is often widely ratified treaty norms of similar content to that of the envisaged customary norm.

Therefore, in my view, treaties often play an undue or superfluous role in defining customary law. In some instances, state practice and/or *opinio juris* fall short of the treaty norms relied upon, resulting in the recognition of a customary law rule, the substantive content of which is not supported by state practice and/or *opinio juris*. In other instances, state practice and *opinio juris* exceed the substantive content of the treaty norms relied upon, resulting in the recognition of a customary law rule

---

[124] See the *Nicaragua* case and the *North Sea Continental Shelf* case (nn 107 and 110, respectively).

that is more restricted than the relevant state practice and *opinio juris*. Although there are many child soldiers internationally, a relatively small number of states account for all child soldiers. A great majority of states do not use children younger than eighteen in hostilities in any capacity. More states recruit, as opposed to use, children younger than eighteen, however, a majority of states also refrain from doing so. It is thus likely that state practice and *opinio juris* support a rule or rules of customary law prohibiting the use and recruitment of child soldiers with greater proscriptive content than any current treaty norm. I would go as far as saying that, taking into account the number of states who have ratified instruments that prohibit the use of children younger than eighteen for direct participation in hostilities and taking account of the number of states who do not practice such use of children, both de jure and de facto, that the customary law threshold for the prohibition of the use of child soldiers has now reached the straight-eighteen threshold. However, this is certainly not true in respect of the prohibition of the recruitment of child soldiers.

## A. Status of Ratification of Relevant Instruments[125]

| Instrument | Entry into force | Parties |
|---|---|---|
| Geneva Convention IV | 21 October 1950 | 196 |
| Additional Protocol I | 7 December 1978 | 174 |
| Additional Protocol II | 7 December 1978 | 167 |
| Convention on the Rights of the Child | 2 September 1990 | 194 |
| African Children's Charter | 29 November 1999 | 47[a] |
| ILO Convention 182 | 19 November 2000 | 179 |
| CIAC Protocol | 12 July 2002 | 156 |

[a] The number of ratifying countries is lower due to the nature of the instrument — it is a regional IHRL instrument. The total number of possible ratifications is 54.

### IV. SUMMARY

The relationship between IHL and IHRL is of great importance in relation to child soldier prevention, but has received very little attention from commentators. The differences between these regimes, and their relationship to one another, has been discussed. The effects hereof are numerous. Most importantly, IHL applies only during armed conflict

[125] Information correct as at 1 June 2014.

and creates obligations upon state and non-state actors alike, whereas IHRL applies at all times, but creates obligations only upon states. There are further practical distinctions that relate directly to application, which will be discussed in Chapters 5 and 6. In a concrete situation, for example, Additional Protocol II provides stronger protection to a thirteen-year-old who is used in hostilities than the African Children's Charter does. However, the African Court on Human and Peoples' Rights has subject-matter jurisdiction over the African Children's Charter and there are no comparable IHL enforcement mechanisms. Reliance may therefore be placed on the African Children's Charter provision instead of the corresponding Additional Protocol II provision. Such enforcement considerations will be dealt with in Chapters 5 and 6.

Great emphasis has been placed on the weaknesses of the substantive norms prohibiting child soldiering. However, these weaknesses mostly relate to the scope of protection offered, that is to say, the number of children protected by the relevant provision. The only limitation that relates directly to the legal enforceability of these norms is the qualification that all feasible measures must be taken that children do not participate in hostilities. However, in order to rely on this qualification, an armed force or group will have to show that all feasible measures were taken to prevent such participation in each and every military engagement where children were used. As of yet, no armed force or group has relied on this qualification to defend their use of child soldiers. Further refinement of these norms should be pursued with the aim of offering better protection to more children; however, the limitations of the legal provisions in force do not render them unenforceable.

Customary international law largely transcends the distinction between IHL and IHRL. As was discussed, this approach is more warranted in some cases than in others. The drafting and adoption of the CIAC Protocol was a massive undertaking that was first initiated during 1991 and only came into force during 2002. Unfortunately, the text that was finally adopted is rather disappointing for the reasons discussed above. Considering the magnitude of the process to get such a global instrument adopted, it is unlikely that the treaty provisions prohibiting child soldiering that are in force presently will be revised for many years to come. The development of customary international law presents an avenue through which child soldier prevention can be further refined. However, many enforcement mechanisms have subject-matter jurisdiction over specific treaty norms only. The progressive development of customary norms is still of great value, as some mechanisms do have subject-matter jurisdiction over such norms; customary norms are taken into account in the interpretation of treaty norms; and when the relevant treaty norms are eventually revised, the state of customary law will play a significant role in determining the proscriptive content of such treaty norms.

# 5

## International Criminal Responsibility and the Prosecution of Individuals for the Enlistment, Conscription and Use of Child Soldiers

E VER SINCE THE child soldier phenomenon started receiving critical attention by the international community, the establishment of the International Criminal Court (ICC)—and developments within the ICC—have been the most significant in entering an era of application. Indeed, Thomas Lubanga Diylo, the first person to be prosecuted by the ICC, was charged, and convicted, only with the enlistment, conscription and use of child soldiers.[1] This chapter deals with international criminal tribunals that operate within technical parameters of jurisdiction, and therefore takes a rather technical form. This is unavoidable because, in order for judicial mechanisms to reach their potential in addressing social problems such as child soldiering, the positive law must be correctly understood and applied. In the case of child soldiering, the judicial interpretation and enforcement of the positive law is in its infancy and therefore requires much analysis.

The Special Court for Sierra Leone (SCSL; the Court) will not issue any further indictments, and all matters in relation to which indictments were issued have been disposed of. The jurisprudence of the SCSL has contributed significantly to the development of international criminal law (ICL) regarding child soldiering. Indeed, every case that has been finalised before this court resulted in at least one conviction on the ground of the enlistment, conscription or use of child soldiers, including its most high-profile case, that of *Prosecutor v Charles Taylor*.[2]

At the time of writing, three of the six defendants in the four cases to have entered the trial phase before the ICC are charged with the enlist-

---

[1] *Prosecutor v Thomas Lubanga Dyilo*, Trial Chamber I, Judgment, ICC-01/04-01/06 (2012) (*Lubanga* judgment).
[2] *Prosecutor v Charles Ghankay Taylor*, Trial Chamber II, SCSL-03-1-T (2012).

ment, conscription or use of child soldiers.[3] This includes the *Lubanga* case, where the defendant has been convicted of the enlistment, conscription or use of child soldiers, with an appeal pending. Indeed, to date, final Trial Chamber judgments have been rendered in respect of three individuals, all of whom were charged with child soldier use, enlistment or conscription—resulting in one conviction and two acquittals.[4] Lubanga was sentenced to fourteen years' imprisonment.

Two aspects of international criminal justice are of specific relevance to child soldier prevention. First, the positive ICL, as it is likely to be applied by the ICC; and secondly, the role of international prosecutions in achieving social change. Both aspects are addressed in this chapter; however, more emphasis is placed on the application and enforcement of ICL.

## I. THE ENLISTMENT, CONSCRIPTION AND USE OF CHILD SOLDIERS AS A WAR CRIME: BACKGROUND AND DRAFTING HISTORY

The Statute of the SCSL criminalises 'other serious violations of international humanitarian law', which includes 'conscripting or enlisting children under the age of 15 years into armed forces or groups or using them to participate actively in hostilities'.[5] The Statute of the ICC criminalises 'war crimes', which include:

> (2)(b) Other serious violations of the laws and customs applicable in international armed conflict, within the established framework of international law, namely, any of the following acts:
> . . .
> (xxvi) Conscripting or enlisting children under the age of fifteen years into the national armed forces or using them to participate actively in hostilities.[6]
> . . .
> (2)(e) Other serious violations of the laws and customs applicable in armed conflicts not of an international character, within the established framework of international law, namely, any of the following acts:
> . . .

---

[3] Thomas Lubanga Diyo, Germain Katanga and Mathieu Ngudjolo Chui were all charged with the use, enlistment or conscription of children, and all were charged in relation to the situation in the Democratic Republic of the Congo (DRC). While Lubanga was convicted, Katanga was acquitted of the child soldiering charge, but convicted on other charges and Chui was acquitted of all charges. Appeals in respect of each of these matters are pending. *Lubanga* case, n 1 above; *Prosecutor v Germain Katanga*, Trial Chamber II, ICC-01/0-01/07 (2014) (*Katanga* case); and *Prosecutor v Mathieu Ngudjolo Chui*, Trial Chamber II, ICC-01/0-02/12 (2012) (*Chui* case).

[4] Ibid, *Lubanga* judgment.

[5] Art 4(c), Statute of the SCSL.

[6] Art 8(2)(b)(xxvi), Rome Statute.

(vii) Conscripting or enlisting children under the age of fifteen years into armed forces or groups or using them to participate actively in hostilities.[7]

For ease of reference, the formulation of this crime as contained in both the Statute of the SCSL and the Rome Statue of the International Criminal Court (Rome Statute)[8] will be referred to as the 'child soldier crime'.

In his report of 2000 on the establishment of the SCSL, the Secretary-General of the United Nations stated that it was clear that child recruitment and use was prohibited in terms of customary international law.[9] He went on to say that it is far less clear whether such use and recruitment had, at the times when the crimes relevant to the SCSL were committed, entailed individual criminal responsibility under customary international law.[10] Accordingly, the Article 4(c) crime proposed for the SCSL by the Secretary-General was formulated more restrictively: 'abduction and forced recruitment of children under the age of 15 years into armed forces or groups for the purpose of using them to participate actively in hostilities'.[11] This formulation, in the Secretary-General's opinion, represented customary international law at that time. The President of the Security Council, however, unilaterally and without providing reasons, amended the formulation of the crime to reflect the wording of the Rome Statute.

The temporal jurisdiction of the ICC is strictly prospective.[12] The SCSL is an ad hoc tribunal, with retrospective jurisdiction. The doctrine of strict legality (*nullum crimen sine lege/nulla poena sine lege*) holds that one can only be held criminally responsible for a deed if that deed was prohibited as a crime at the time of commission.[13] Although the stated

---

[7] Ibid, Art 8(2)(e)(vii).

[8] Rome Statute of the International Criminal Court (Rome Statute) (entered into force 1 July 2002) 2187 UNTS 90.

[9] 'Report of the Secretary-General on the Establishment of a Special Court for Sierra Leone', UN S/2000/915 (4 October 2000), para 17 (Secretary-General's Report).

[10] Ibid, paras 17–18: 'owing to the doubtful customary nature of the ICC Statutory crime which criminalizes the conscription or enlistment of children under the age of 15, whether forced or "voluntary", the crime which is included in art 4(c) of the Statute of the Special Court is not the equivalent of the ICC provision. While the definition of the crime as "conscripting" or "enlisting" connotes an administrative act of putting one's name on a list and formal entry into the armed forces, the elements of the crime under the proposed Statute of the Special Court are: (a) abduction, which in the case of the children of Sierra Leone was the original crime and is in itself a crime under Common Article 3 of the Geneva Conventions; (b) forced recruitment in the most general sense—administrative formalities, obviously, notwithstanding; and (c) transformation of the child into, and its use as, among other degrading uses, a "child-combatant".'

[11] Report of the Secretary-General, draft Statute of the Special Court for Sierra Leone, Art 4(c).

[12] Art 11 of the Rome Statute.

[13] International law has departed from the doctrine of substantive justice and accepted the doctrine of strict legality. This doctrine is entrenched in Art 22 of the Rome Statute, and is also accepted by the SCSL, ICTY and ICTR. With regard to the SCSL see *Prosecutor v Sam Hinga Norman, Decision on Preliminary Motion Based on Lack of Jurisdiction*, SCSL-2004-14-AR72E (31 May 2004), para 25 (*Child Recruitment* decision); Secretary-General's Report,

aims of the drafters of the Rome Statute were to codify existing law, they were not subject to any legal limitation on developing and creating new treaty crimes. Conversely, to comply with the principle of legality, the subject-matter jurisdiction of the SCSL had to be limited to deeds that were deemed criminal in customary or conventional international law binding on Sierra Leone at the time of its commission.

## A. The Child Recruitment Decision

Sam Hinga Norman, a defendant in the *CDF* case, brought a preliminary motion before the Appeals Chamber of the SCSL.[14] He challenged the Court's material jurisdiction over the crime of 'conscripting or enlisting children under the age of 15 years into armed forces or groups or using them to participate actively in hostilities' on four grounds: first, child recruitment was not a crime under customary international law at the times relevant to the indictment.[15] Secondly, this violates the principle of legality. Thirdly, while Additional Protocol II to the Geneva Conventions and the Convention on the Rights of the Child (CRC) created obligations on states not to recruit children, it did not criminalise such acts. Lastly, the Rome Statute is not a codification of customary international law.[16]

The first time an international tribunal dealt with such a challenge to legality in relation to the subject-matter jurisdiction of the tribunal was in the *Hostages* case before the Nuremberg Tribunal.[17] In that case, the defendants argued that Control Council Order Number 10 was *ex post facto* law as it did not exist at the time of the alleged crimes. The Nuremburg Tribunal found against the defendants and held that the alleged crimes were already crimes under international law, 'some by conventional law and some by customary law'.[18] Some may question whether this was indeed true at that time; nevertheless, the Tribunal clearly deemed itself bound by the principle of legality.

In *Prosecutor v Sam Hinga Norman, Decision on Preliminary Motion Based on Lack of Jurisdiction* (the *Child Recruitment* decision), the Court

---

n 9 above, para 22. Furthermore see *Prosecutor v Duško Tadić, Decision on the Defence Motion for Interlocutory Appeal on Jurisdiction* IT-94-1-AR-72 (2 October 1995), paras 90–95 (*Tadić Jurisdiction* judgment).

[14] *Child Recruitment* decision, ibid. The matters against Norman, Fofana and Kondewa were joined in what came to be known as the *CDF* case (*Prosecutor v Norman, Fofana and Kondewa*, Indictment, SCSL-2004-14-PT (11-21) (5 February 2004)). Norman died on 22 February 2007; the proceedings against him were thus terminated.

[15] The phrase 'times relevant to the indictment' lacks clarity. However, the indictment used the same phrase. Thus at the earliest it refers to 30 November 1996.

[16] *Child Recruitment* decision, n 13 above, para 1.

[17] *Trial of Wilhelm List and Others* Case No 47 United Nations War Crimes Commission, Law Reports of Trials of War Criminals, Volume VIII (1949) (*Hostages* case), paras 634–35.

[18] Ibid.

delivered a controversial three to one majority decision finding against the defendant.[19] The Court held that the crime as formulated in Article 4(c) had already entailed criminal responsibility as a customary norm by 30 November 1996, and that the principle of legality would therefore not be violated.[20] This judgment was based on an unconvincing exposé of international and municipal legal measures prohibiting the use and recruitment of child soldiers. There are particular aspects to the judgment that are unsatisfactory. First, in finding that the prohibition of the use and recruitment of child soldiers has crystallised into a norm of customary international law, the Court never compared the proscriptive content of Article 4(c) with the proscriptive content of the prohibition in customary law, as supported by state practice and *opinio juris*. Secondly, the Court erred in its approach to determine whether a customary norm entails individual criminal responsibility in international law. Thirdly, the Court largely confused the existence of a customary norm criminalising child soldier use and recruitment with the principles of legality and specificity. These points of critique are further discussed below. Given their relationship to one another, the second and third points are discussed together.

### i. The Proscriptive Content of the Relevant Customary Crime

In a strong and convincing dissent, Judge Robertson closely assessed the content of the various provisions that formed the basis of the customary norm. He concluded that the more limited crime as initially formulated by the Secretary-General had crystallised under customary international law by 30 November 1996, but not the more expansive crime as contained in Article 4(c).[21]

As previously stated, the formulation of the crime as found under the Rome Statute was imported into the Statute of the SCSL. The Rome Statute was the first legal instrument of any kind to have prohibited, not to mention criminalised, the enlistment of children instead of their recruitment. The text of the Rome Statute was adopted on 17 July 1998 and the Statute of the SCSL came into force on 1 July 2002. Even though it was drafted after the Rome Statute, since the Statute of the SCSL has

---

[19] For a commentary in support of the majority decision see generally A Smith, 'Child Recruitment and the Special Court for Sierra Leone' (2004) 2 *Journal International Criminal Justice* 1141, where this author argues: 'given this preponderance of evidence demonstrating the existence of state practice and *opinio juris*, there can be little doubt that the majority decision was correct in holding that the conscription, enlistment and use in hostilities of children under the age of 15 attracted individual criminal responsibility as at November 1996'. However, Smith fails to draw a distinction between establishing the existence of a norm of customary international law, and whether such a norm entails criminal responsibility.

[20] Art 1(1) of the Statute of the SCSL.

[21] *Child Recruitment* decision, Judge Robertson's dissent, para 4.

retrospective effect, it was the first instrument with legal force to pro-hibit and criminalise the enlistment of children instead of merely their recruitment. Throughout this chapter much attention is paid to the fact that enlistment as opposed to recruitment is criminalised in the Statute of the SCSL. The reason for this is that enlistment is a broader concept than recruitment.[22]

The temporal jurisdiction of the SCSL commenced on 30 November 1996, and although no express end date is provided, the civil war ended on 18 January 2002.[23] Even though the Rome Statute was intended to contain customary international law crimes only, during 2000 Bassiouni, the Chairman of the Drafting Committee for the Diplomatic Conference on the Establishment of an International Criminal Court, stated that Article 8(2)(e)(vii) of the Rome Statute was 'progressive'.[24] Scharf, the US Representative at the Rome Conference stated during the conference that 'the use of children under the age of 15 years in hostilities was not currently a crime under customary international law and was another area of legislative action outside the purview of the Conference'.[25] The commencement of the temporal jurisdiction of the SCSL thus predates the adoption of the Rome Statute by almost two years; the de facto end date of its temporal jurisdiction also predates the coming into force of the Rome Statute. The Special Court thus made an error of law in fail-ing to take account of the proscriptive content of the relevant customary norm at the times relevant to the indictment.

The question remains what the effect would have been, should the Court have found, as Judge Robertson did, that a customary norm had crystallised by 30 November 1996, but that its proscriptive content fell short of the formulation in Article 4(c). There are two feasible options. The Court may have found that Article 4(c) forms part of its subject-matter jurisdiction, but to an extent limited to the proscriptive content of the customary norm, as it existed on 30 November 1996.[26] Alter-natively, the Court may have found that it lacked the competence to prosecute individuals under Article 4(c) altogether. I am of the view that the second option would be correct in law, as the first would lead to judges exercising powers beyond their mandate. Such a finding would have effectively barred the Court from prosecuting individuals for the

[22] See Chapter 3.II. C above.

[23] This date is also supported by the UN Secretary-General. See Secretary-General's Report, n 9 above, para 27.

[24] MC Bassiouni, 'The Normative Framework of International Humanitarian Law: Over-laps, Gaps and Ambiguities' (2000) 75 *International Law Studies* 3, 20.

[25] United Nations Diplomatic Conference of Plenipotentiaries on the Establishment of an International Criminal Court, Committee of the Whole, 'Summary Record of the 4th Meeting', A/CONF.183/C.1/SR.4 (20 November 1998), para 54.

[26] The Court may also identify specific dates relevant to concrete cases of child enlist-ment, conscription or use, and determine what the proscriptive content of the norm was on that date.

child soldier crime, which would have had detrimental consequences for the Court, as well as the movement for the prevention of child soldiers. However, this could have been avoided by exercising better judgment at the time of the drafting and adoption of the Statute.

As I argued in Chapter 4, the content of customary international law bears no direct link to treaty law, but, rather, is dependent on state practice and *opinio juris*—which is often influenced by treaty norms. As such, conventional law plays an indirect role in formulating the content of customary international law.[27] Theoretically, state practice and *opinio juris* may have supported the existence of a customary norm materially the same as Article 4(c); however, this was never argued by the Court.

*ii. Differentiating between the Existence of a Criminal Norm and the Principles of Legality and Specificity*

All war crimes emanate from IHL; however, all violations of IHL norms do not imply criminal responsibility. Thus, the mere existence of a customary IHL norm prohibiting the enlistment, conscription or use of child soldiers does not mean that such conduct necessarily entails criminal responsibility. The questions whether the violation of an IHL norm entails criminal responsibility and whether the principle of legality is complied with are closely related, but are not the same. International law has developed rules that dictate the requisites for a norm that did not traditionally entail criminal responsibility to become one that does entail it. The principle of legality does not concern itself with such development of the law; instead, it is a more technical rule that safeguards the rule of law values inherent in criminal law.[28] To illustrate the difference between these inter-related rules, consider the following: it is possible for a tribunal to find that a particular rule did indeed entail criminal responsibility at a given time, but that there is no way in which a defendant could have reasonably been aware of this.[29] As such, the principle of legality would be violated should the person be prosecuted.

No international instruments in force during the temporal jurisdiction of the SCSL contained a prohibition of child soldiering that expressly criminalised the conduct contained in Article 4(c). After finding that the enlistment, conscription or use of child soldiers formed part of customary law, the SCSL nevertheless had to determine whether such conduct

---

[27] See Chapter 4.III above.

[28] Van B Schaack, 'The Principle of Legality in International Criminal Law: Legality & International Criminal Law' (2009) 103 *American Society of International Law Proceedings* 101.

[29] I am not arguing that legality is dependent on the subjective knowledge of a particular defendant. The example relates to any defendant within the territorial and temporal jurisdiction relevant to the case at hand.

could result in criminal responsibility. For this purpose, the Court relied on the following formulation provided in the *Tadić Jurisdiction* case:[30]

> The following requirements must be met for an offence to be subject to prosecution before the International Tribunal under Article 3 [of the International Criminal Tribunal for the former Yugoslavia (ICTY) Statute]:
> (i)   The violation must constitute and infringement of a rule of international humanitarian law;
> (ii)  the rule must be customary in nature or, if it belongs to treaty law, the required conditions must be met;
> (iii) the violation must be 'serious', that is to say, it must constitute a breach of a rule protecting important values, and the breach must involve grave consequences for the victim . . .;
> (iv)  the violation of the rule must entail, under customary or conventional law, the individual criminal responsibility of the person breaching the rule.[31]

This formulation was used in *Tadić* to lay down requirements that 'must be met for an offence to be subject to prosecution',[32] which is not the same as determining when individual criminal responsibility attaches to a breach of IHL—as was used in the *Child Recruitment* decision. Indeed, the fourth requirement specifically asks the question whether individual criminal responsibility attaches to a person who breaches the norm. It is a circular argument at best to state that one holds certain conduct to be criminal in terms of a test in which one of the questions is whether the conduct is criminal.

In *Tadić*, the court does in fact go on to specifically contemplate the fourth requirement.[33] In so doing, the court refers to various authorities supporting its ultimate finding that violations of Common Article 3 to the Geneva Conventions do entail individual criminal responsibility. This includes various pieces of national legislation; municipal prosecutions for such violations; agreements between parties to the conflict; and Security Council Resolutions.[34] Most tellingly, the court held:

> as it applies to offences committed in the former Yugoslavia, the notion that serious violations of international humanitarian law governing internal armed conflict entail individual criminal responsibility is also fully warranted from the point of view of substantive justice and equality . . . such violations were punishable under the Criminal Code of the Socialist Federal Republic of Yugoslavia and the law implementing the two Additional Protocols of 1977. The same violations have been made punishable in the Republic of Bosnia and Herzegovina by virtue of the decree-law of 11 April 1992. Nationals of the former Yugoslavia as well as, at present, those of Bosnia-Herzegovina

---

[30] *Child Recruitment* decision, n 13 above, para 26.
[31] *Tadić Jurisdiction* judgment, n 13 above, paras 90–95.
[32] Ibid, para 94.
[33] Ibid, para 128.
[34] Ibid, paras 128–36.

were therefore aware, or should have been aware, that they were amenable to the jurisdiction of their national criminal courts in cases of violations of international humanitarian law.[35]

It is important to keep in mind that the defendant did not raise legality as a bar to the exercise of subject-matter jurisdiction by the ICTY.[36] Given the importance of the principle of legality, the court did address this concept briefly, but only after it had concluded that the relevant IHL norms do entail criminal responsibility.[37]

The *Child Recruitment* decision is clearly and materially distinguishable from the *Tadić* decision in that the enlistment of children under fifteen was not criminalised in Sierra Leone at the relevant times.[38] Furthermore, where the *Tadić* Appeals Chamber had an abundance of materials in the nature of those referred to above to rely on, such material was lacking in the *Child Recruitment* decision.[39] The judgment for the majority did go to some lengths to highlight municipal legislation and Security Council Resolutions relevant to child soldiering. However, in most cases these sources either post-dated the temporality of the defendant's alleged criminal conduct or occurred in very close proximity to such conduct.

At the commencement of this section I highlighted three points of critique against the judgment in the *Child Recruitment* decision. I have since substantiated my arguments that the proscriptive content of Article 4(c) did not accord with that of the proscriptive content of the prohibition in customary law; and that the Court erred in its approach to determining whether a customary norm entails criminal responsibility. If these arguments are accepted, the principle of legality would be violated by implication, as the conduct relevant to Article 4(c) would not be deemed criminal.[40] However, for the sake of completeness, the Court's approach to the principle of legality is discussed below.

After it is established that the prohibited conduct entails individual criminal responsibility, the concrete case before the court must still pass scrutiny under the legality principle. If the principle of legality is

---

[35] Ibid, para 135. The conclusion reached in the *Tadić* case has been reaffirmed by the ICTY in *Prosecutor v Blaškić* IT-95-14-A (2004), para 176 (*Blaškić* judgment).

[36] Ibid, para 139.

[37] Ibid, paras 133–43.

[38] Ibid, para 133.

[39] A Cassese, *International Criminal Law*, 2nd edn (Oxford, Oxford University Press, 2008) 85 states that in assessing whether a breach of IHL is a war crime one is entitled to examine 'military manuals; national legislation of states belonging to the major legal systems of the world; or, if these elements are lacking, the general principles of criminal justice common to nations of the world, as set out in international instruments, acts, resolutions and the like, and the legislation and judicial practice of the state to which the accused belongs or on who's territory the crime has allegedly been committed'.

[40] This not to say that the questions whether a criminal norm exists and whether legality is complied with are the same. While it is true that if a criminal norm does not exist the principle of legality will be violated by implication, the reverse does not hold true.

absolute, it would imply that, in a case such as *Tadić*, where a norm was for the first time regarded as entailing criminal responsibility, the principle of legality will be violated. However, the law is a dynamic, living body of rules capable of development; this is particularly true in the case of common law and customary international law. Greenwood contends that the legality principle will not necessarily be violated, as

> that principle does not preclude all development of criminal law through the jurisprudence of courts and tribunals, so long as those developments do not criminalise conduct which, at the time it was committed, could reasonably have been regarded as legitimate.[41]

Greenwood goes on to argue that the principle of legality will not be violated where the relevant conduct is universally considered as wrongful and doubt only exists as to its wrongfulness under a particular system of law. He specifically refers to *Regina v R*, a House of Lords decision, where it was found that a husband can be convicted of raping his own wife.[42]

The Court further supported its finding that the principle of legality had not been breached, as a prohibition of child enlistment, conscription or use 'is found in the national legislation of the states which includes criminal sanctions as a measure of enforcement'.[43] It was never pertinently argued in the judgment that any state criminalised enlistment of children as opposed to recruitment, conscription or use,[44] not to mention such criminalisation in Sierra Leone specifically. Significantly, not a single legal provision in effect prior to 30 November 1996 prohibited the enlistment of children under fifteen. The Court went on to say that:

> Finally, one can determine the period during which the majority of states criminalised the prohibited behaviour, which in this case, as demonstrated, was the period between 1994 and 1996. It took a further six years for the recruitment of children between the ages of 15 and 18 to be included in treaty law as individually punishable behaviour. The development process concerning the recruitment of child soldiers, taking into account the definition of children as persons under the age of 18, culminated in the codification of the matter in the CRC Optional Protocol II.[45]

---

[41] C Greenwood, 'International Humanitarian Law and the *Tadić* Case' (1996) 7 *European Journal of International Law* 265, 281.

[42] Ibid, note 58; *Regina v R* (1992) 1 AC 599 (House of Lords).

[43] Ibid, para 42.

[44] As Judge Robertson stated in his dissent in the *Child Recruitment* decision, n 13 above, para 40, note 51, UNICEF was only able to list five states which had a specific criminal law against 'child recruitment' prior to July 1998. These states are Colombia, Argentina, Spain, Ireland and Norway. This does not necessarily mean that these states criminalised 'enlistment', as opposed to recruitment or conscription.

[45] *Child Recruitment* decision, n 13 above, para 50.

It is patently incorrect that 'the majority of states' criminalised the 'prohibited behaviour', which includes child enlistment, between 1994 and 1996.[46]

The Court dealt with the principle of specificity in a cursory manner. This principle is directly related to the principle of legality. Where the latter holds that a crime must exist at the time of commission before someone can be prosecuted for the deed, the former determines the degree to which this pre-existing crime must be clear and defined. The Court argued that the elements of crimes (EOC) formulated with regard to the Rome Statute together with the legislation of the world community specified the elements of the crime.[47] First, there was not a single state that formally criminalised the enlistment of children younger than fifteen years old as opposed to conscription, recruitment or use prior to 30 November 1996. Furthermore, the EOC of the Rome Statute was only adopted at the first session of the Assembly of States Parties to the Rome Statute during August 2002, after the temporal jurisdiction of the SCSL had ended.

The principle of legality is not absolute. Throughout the history of ICL, tribunals have interpreted this principle rather expansively;[48] perhaps too expansively. It is nevertheless important that the Court in the *Child Recruitment* decision deemed the doctrine of strict legality as binding upon it.[49] It is submitted that the enlistment of a child under the age of fifteen years for a non-combat-related activity could 'reasonably have been regarded as legitimate' at the time of commission of the deed. Thus, the Court's finding in this regard remains questionable.

The *Child Recruitment* decision cleared the way for all prosecutions before the SCSL where the defendant was charged under Article 4(c)—which, indeed, includes every defendant indicted by the SCSL. The criticism levelled at this judgment does not taint any future prosecutions before the ICC. First, the ICC has prospective jurisdiction only. Secondly, it is much more likely that the enlistment, conscription or use of children younger than fifteen had crystallised into a criminal norm of customary international law by 1 July 2002 rather than by 30 November 1996.

---

[46] See n 44 above.

[47] Elements of Crimes of the Rome Statute of the International Criminal Court (2002) ICC-ASP/1/3.

[48] Van Schaack, n 28 above, 101–04.

[49] *Child Recruitment* decision, n 13 above, para 25.

## B. The Drafting of the Rome Statute

The Rome Statute was drafted and finalised before the Statute of the SCSL. However, ICC jurisprudence only began developing after that of the SCSL.

The child soldier prohibitions were the subject of much debate at the Preparatory Committee. As regards the wording of Article 8(2)(b)(xxvi), the Preparatory Committee submitted four alternatives to the Rome Diplomatic Conference:

1. forcing children under the age of fifteen years to take direct part in hostilities;
2. recruiting children under the age of fifteen years into armed forces or using them to participate actively in hostilities;
3. (i) recruiting children under the age of fifteen years into armed forces or groups; or (ii) allowing them to take part in hostilities; and
4. [no such war crime].[50]

During the Rome Diplomatic Conference there was considerable debate regarding four issues: the degree of participation in hostilities required; the specific activities proscribed; whether or not the word 'national' should qualify the term 'armed forces'; and the age threshold.[51] Ultimately, option 2 above was adopted, with two amendments: the word 'recruit' was substituted with the words 'conscripting or enlisting' and the term 'armed forces' was qualified by the word 'national'. These amendments are rather interesting. The substitution of the word 'recruiting' was at the insistence of the United States, and was motivated by the fact that their military recruitment is aimed at relatively young children. This suggests that they foresaw the potential interpretation of the prohibition of child soldier recruitment, as it exists in IHL and IHRL (where the word 'recruiting' was already used at the time), being such that a recruitment drive, eg a television campaign aimed at young people as a group, may violate this provision. In other words, no child need actually join the armed force for the violation to occur. This interpretation is very doubtful and, moreover, it is curious that the words 'enlisting and conscripting' were preferred, as virtually all commentators not only consider this term to encapsulate the term 'recruiting' completely, but also deem 'enlisting and conscripting' to be broader than 'recruiting'.

It is also of interest to take note that the inclusion of 'national armed forces' as opposed to 'armed forces' was debated during the Diplomatic Conference, as this issue was somewhat controversial throughout the

---

[50] 'Draft Statute for the International Criminal Court and Draft Final Act', United Nations Diplomatic Conference of Plenipotentiaries on the Establishment of an International Criminal Court (1998) A/CONF.183/2/Add.1, 21.

[51] M Cottier, 'Article 8(2)(b)(xxvi)' in O Triffterer, *Commentary on the Rome Statute of the International Criminal Court* (Oxford, Hart Publishing, 2008) para 227.

*Lubanga* trial and pre-trial, and what is to come on this front in the appeal is not yet known. After a lengthy and prima facie convincing discussion, Pre-Trial Chamber I, in the *Lubanga* Confirmation of Charges Decision, determined that 'the term "the national armed forces" is not limited to the armed forces of a state'.[52] The rationale was first that the ICTY has construed the term 'national' to refer not only to nationality as such, but also as belonging to the opposing forces in armed conflict.[53] Secondly, to interpret 'national' to mean 'governmental' undermines the object and purpose of the Statute of the Court.[54] Finally, Additional Protocol I provides an interpretive basis upon which to interpret 'national armed forces' to include non-state groups with certain characteristics of a government.[55]

In contrast to the Confirmation of Charges Decision, in the Trial Chamber judgment the majority held that the armed conflict relevant to the charges was a non-international armed conflict, and as such further discussion of the 'national armed forces' requirement was not forthcoming.[56] However, in her dissenting opinion, Judge Odio Benito argued that this issue was a live issue in the case at hand, and that it was one that impacted heavily on arguments before the court and should thus be addressed in the judgment. She concluded that:

> It would be contrary to the 'object and purpose' of the Rome Statute and contrary to internationally recognised human rights (and thus contrary to Article 21(3) of the Rome Statute) to exclude from the prohibition of child recruitment, an armed group, solely for the nature of its organization (State or non-state armed group).[57]

While I agree with the shared sentiment of Pre-Trial Chamber I and Judge Odio Benito, neither took into account the fact that the qualifier 'national' was specifically debated and negotiated in Rome, and consciously included. It was a group of Arab states that lobbied for the qualifier 'national' to be included, so as to avoid a situation where young Palestinians joining the Intifada were proscribed by the Rome Statute. Taking this history into account, it appears that Judge Odio Benito's interpretation remains sound.

---

[52] *Prosecutor v Thomas Lubanga Dyilo*, Pre-Trial Chamber I, Decision on the Confirmation of Charges, ICC-01/04-01/06 (2007) (*Lubanga Confirmation of Charges* decision), paras 268–85.

[53] *Lubanga Confirmation of Charges* decision, ibid. *Prosecutor v Delalić et al* IT-96-21-A Appeal Judgment (2001), para 98. In *Delalić*, the ICTY's finding was made in the context of Art 4(1) of Geneva Convention IV.

[54] *Lubanga Confirmation of Charges* decision, ibid, para 281.

[55] Art 43 of Protocol I Additional to the Geneva Conventions of 12 August 1949, and relating to the Protection of Victims of International Armed Conflicts, adopted 8 June 1977 (entered into force 7 December 1978) 1125 UNTS 17512. See also ibid, paras 272–85; *Prosecutor v Katanga and Ngudjolo Confirmation of Charges* ICC-01/04-01/07 (2008), para 249 (*Katanga and Ngudjolo Confirmation of Charges* decision).

[56] *Lubanga* judgment, n 1 above, para 568.

[57] *Lubanga* judgment, ibid, Dissenting Opinion of Judge Odio Benito, para 13.

## II. 'USING, CONSCRIPTING OR ENLISTING'
## CHILDREN IN TERMS OF THE POSITIVE LAW

The jurisprudence of the SCSL was ground-breaking insofar as bringing to account those responsible for the enlistment, conscription and use of children is concerned. Nevertheless, its value for future prosecutions in the context of the ICC should not be overstated. Although the crime proscribed by the SCSL is a verbatim restatement of the Rome Statute, there are various and significant differences between the approaches of the SCSL Statute and the Rome Statute to general principles of ICL. What is more, by definition, the SCSL jurisprudence does not take direct account of the different features of child soldier prosecutions in the context of international and non-international armed conflict. This section is focused on contemporary ICL and its prospects in addressing child soldiering. The Rome Statute and ICC thus form the basis of discussion; the SCSL and its jurisprudence is drawn on only insofar as it contributes to an understanding of the contemporary crime proscribing child soldiering and its scope of prosecution.

The EOC of Article 8(2)(b)(xxvi) of the Rome Statute, proscribing the child soldier crime in international armed conflict, are:

1. The perpetrator conscripted or enlisted one or more persons into the national armed forces or used one or more persons to participate actively in hostilities.
2. Such person or persons were under the age of 15 years.
3. The perpetrator knew or should have known that such person or persons were under the age of 15 years.
4. The conduct took place in the context of and was associated with an international armed conflict.
5. The perpetrator was aware of factual circumstances that established the existence of an armed conflict.

Similarly, the EOC of Article 8(2)(e)(vii) of the Rome Statute, proscribing the child soldier crime in non-international armed conflict, are:

1. The perpetrator conscripted or enlisted one or more persons into an armed force or group or used one or more persons to participate actively in hostilities.
2. Such person or persons were under the age of 15 years.
3. The perpetrator knew or should have known that such person or persons were under the age of 15 years.
4. The conduct took place in the context of and was associated with an armed conflict not of an international character.
5. The perpetrator was aware of factual circumstances that established the existence of an armed conflict.

The only difference between the elements of the child soldier crime in international armed conflict (IAC) and non-international armed conflict

(NIAC) is found in the first and fourth elements. In the context of IAC, the first element provides 'into the national armed forces', whereas in the context of NIAC the first element provides 'into an armed force or group'. Similarly, the fourth element uses the language 'an armed conflict not of an international character' in the context of NIAC and 'an international armed conflict' in the context of IAC. These elements account for the *chapeau* requirements, objective requirements (*actus reus*) and subjective requirements (*mens rea*) of the child soldier crime. The remainder of this section is divided accordingly.

## A. *Chapeau* Requirements

*Chapeau* requirements are those requirements that must be met in order to charge a specific class of international law crimes. The concept of 'war crimes' as a distinct genus of international crimes is premised on the basis that the offence must be committed in the context of either an international or a non-international armed conflict.[58] The *chapeau* requirements of war crimes are formulated under various statutes, most relevantly the Rome Statute. The Statute of the SCSL provides very little in this regard. The *RUF* case of the SCSL has, however, provided some needed clarity on this issue. The Court held that there are two relevant *chapeau* requirements: the existence of an armed conflict at the time of the alleged offence and the existence of a nexus between the alleged offence and the armed conflict.[59]

The existence of such a nexus is a question of fact, and is to be determined on a case-by-case basis.[60] However, the Sierra Leone conflict occurred within the context of non-international armed conflict, and the Court's finding with regard to the relevant *chapeau* requirements is supported by the findings of the International Criminal Tribunal for Rwanda (ICTR), also in the context of non-international armed conflict.[61] In the *Tadić Appeals* decision the ICTY held that, in the context of international armed conflict, 'it is sufficient that the alleged crimes were closely related to the hostilities occurring in other parts of the territories controlled by the parties to the conflict'.[62] The EOC sheds some light on the position

---

[58] LC Green, *The Contemporary Law of Armed Conflict*, 2nd edn (Manchester, Manchester University Press, 2000) 18–19.

[59] *Prosecutor v Sesay, Kallon and Gbao*, Trial Chamber 1, SCSL-04015-T (2 March 2009) (*RUF* Trial judgment), para 107. See also *Prosecutor v Fofana and Kondewa* SCSL-04014-T (2 August 2007), para 138 (*CDF* Trial judgment).

[60] Ibid.

[61] *Prosecutor v Kayhishema and Ruzindana* ICTR-9501-T (1999), paras 186–88; *Prosecutor v Rutaganda* ICTR-96-3-T (1999), para 102.

[62] *Tadić Jurisdiction* judgment, n 13 above, para 70; see also *Prosecutor v Delalić, Mucić, Delić and Landžo* IT-96-21-T (1998), paras 69–70 (*Čelebići* Trial judgment).

before the ICC, without materially differentiating between international and non-international armed conflict:

4. The conduct took place in the context of and was associated with an international armed conflict [armed conflict not of an international character].
5. The perpetrator was aware of factual circumstances that established the existence of an armed conflict.[63]

No legal evaluation on the part of the perpetrator as to the existence of an armed conflict or its character (as international or non-international) is required.[64] A perpetrator is also not required to be aware of the facts that established the character of the conflict.[65] The ICC has held that the Rome Statute criminalises the same conduct regardless of the characterisation of the conflict as international or internal,[66] giving further credence to the movement to abolish this distinction.[67] With regard to the existence and nexus between the armed conflict and the alleged crime, it was stated in the *Lubanga Confirmation of Charges* decision that:

chamber follows the jurisprudence of the ICTY, which requires the conduct to have been closely related to the hostilities occurring in any part of the territories controlled by the parties to the conflict. The armed conflict need not be considered the ultimate reason for the conduct and the conduct need not have taken place in the midst of battle. Nonetheless, the armed conflict must play a substantial role in the perpetrator's decision, in his or her ability to commit the crime or in the manner in which the conduct was ultimately committed.[68]

Without disputing the progressive aspects of the Rome Statute, in certain respects the Rome Statute is more restrictive than customary international law.[69] The ICC has jurisdiction over war crimes '*in particular* when committed as part of a plan or policy or as part of a large-scale commission of such crimes'.[70] This provision was entered as a compromise, as some states were in favour of a high threshold that would have seen the words 'in particular' replaced with 'only when committed as part of'.[71] This provision does not provide elements or prerequisites to the exercise of jurisdiction by the Court, but instead

---

[63] EOC, Art 8(2)(b)(xxvi) and 8(2)(e)(vii).

[64] EOC, introduction to Art 8.

[65] Ibid.

[66] *Lubanga Confirmation of Charges* decision, n 52 above, para 204.

[67] Cassese, n 39 above; also see Bassiouni, n 24 above.

[68] *Lubanga Confirmation of Charges* decision, 52 above, para 287. See also *Katanga and Ngudjolo Confirmation of Charges* decision, para 247.

[69] Cassese, n 39 above, 94.

[70] Art 8(1), Rome Statute. Original emphasis.

[71] K Dormann, 'War Crimes under the Rome Statute of the International Criminal Court, with a Special Focus on the Negotiations on the Elements of Crimes' (2003) 7 *Max Planck Yearbook of United Nations Law* 343, 349.

provides guidance to the prosecutor in his enquiry whether to launch an investigation into an alleged war crime.[72]

Within the context of international armed conflict, child soldier enlistment, conscription and use is criminalised and categorised as 'other serious violations of the laws and customs applicable in international armed conflict, *within the established framework of international law*'.[73] The equivalent provision in NIAC is the same except 'international armed conflict' is replaced by 'armed conflicts not of an international character'.[74] This requirement is repeated in the EOC as well, where it is said that 'the elements for war crimes . . . shall be *interpreted* within the established framework of the international law of armed conflict'.[75] Article 8, as a whole, is categorised according to the nature of the conflict: international or non-international, and according to the applicable law, either conventional or customary.[76] Bassiouni is of the view that sub-articles 2(b) and 2(e) incorporate 'what the drafters believed to be customary law'.[77] However, he points out that these sections also reflect existing conventional law.[78] Elsewhere in the same work, Bassiouni contends that the child soldiering provisions under Article 8(2)(e)(vii) is 'progressive', indicating that this provision did not form part of customary international law.[79]

Cassese's view on the meaning of the term 'within the established framework of international law' is that the court has a mandatory duty to determine contemporary customary international law each time it hears a charge under Article 8(2)(b) or (e).[80] Such a charge can only be sustained if contemporary international law recognises it. Even though the crimes listed in these sub-articles were deemed to be of a customary nature by the drafters at the time of drafting,[81] Cassese's position is sustainable given that the EOC states that war crimes 'shall be interpreted within the established framework of international law'. The question ultimately becomes whether the contemporary status of customary inter-

---

[72] Ibid. K Kittichaisaree, *International Criminal Law* (Oxford, Oxford University Press, 2001), 133 agrees that this provision does not add a further element to war crimes, but states that it is a jurisdictional threshold. See also H Von Hebel and D Robinson 'Crimes within the Jurisdiction of the Court' in RSK Lee (ed), *The International Criminal Court: The Making of the Rome Statute—Issues, Negotiations, Results* (The Hague, Martinus Nijhoff, 1999) 79, 107–08.

[73] Art 8(2)(b) of the Rome Statute. Emphasis added.

[74] Ibid, Art 8(2)(e).

[75] EOC, introduction to Art 8. Emphasis added.

[76] Bassiouni, n 24 above, 21.

[77] Ibid; see also Von Hebel and Robinson, n 72 above, 104.

[78] Bassiouni, n 24 above, 21.

[79] Ibid, 20; United Nations Diplomatic Conference, n 25 above, para 54.

[80] For the continuous evolution of customary rules of IHL see T Meron, *War Crimes Law Comes of Age* (Oxford, Oxford University Press, 1998) 262–77.

[81] Bassiouni, n 24 above, 21.

national law limits or expands the court's subject-matter jurisdiction.[82] I share Cassese's view: a charge should only be sustained if that crime is recognised as such under customary international law. Should the Rome Statute be more conservative than customary law on a particular matter, the Rome Statute definition and elements should be applied. Effectively, this interpretation will be *in favorem libertatis*, although this is not necessarily the rationale for it.

## B. Objective Requirements

In IAC, the EOC provides 'the perpetrator conscripted or enlisted one or more persons into the national armed forces or used one or more persons to participate actively in hostilities'.[83] Similarly, in NIAC, the EOC provides 'the perpetrator conscripted or enlisted one or more persons into an armed force or group or used one or more persons to participate actively in hostilities'.[84] Regardless of the categorisation of the armed conflict, the EOC also provides 'such person or persons were under the age of 15 years'.

The *actus reus* element of the use, conscription or enlistment of children can be committed in three different ways.[85] First, enlistment is the least severe form of the crime; this entails the acceptance and enrolment of a person younger than fifteen when she/he volunteers. Secondly, conscription entails a degree of compulsion on the part of the recruiter. Finally, use is predicated on active participation in hostilities.[86] As all three incarnations of this crime are continuous crimes,[87] the commission of the crime occurs for as long as the child remains enlisted, conscripted or used for active participation in hostilities, or until the child is no

---

[82] Art 21 of the Rome Statute states the applicable law thus:

1. The Court shall apply:
(a) In the first place, this Statute, Elements of Crimes and its Rules of Procedure and Evidence;
(b) In the second place, where appropriate, applicable treaties and the principles and rules of international law, including the established principles of the international law of armed conflict.

[83] Element 1, EOC, Art 8(2)(b)(xxvi).

[84] Ibid, Art 8(2)(e)(vii).

[85] *Lubanga* judgment, n 1 above, para 609; *RUF* Trial judgment, n 59 above, para 249: 'Consistent with established jurisprudence, the Chamber adopts the definition of "committing" a crime as "physically perpetrating a crime or engendering a culpable omission in violation of criminal law". The *actus reus* for committing a crime consists of the proscribed act of participation, physical or otherwise directly, in a crime provided for in the Statute, through positive acts or culpable omissions, whether individually or jointly with others.'

[86] *Child Recruitment* decision, Judge Robertson's dissent, para 5.

[87] *Lubanga Confirmation of Charges* decision, n 52 above, para 248.

longer younger than fifteen. Furthermore, each of the three incarnations of the crime is a complete crime.

## *i. Enlistment and Conscription*

The *actus reus* of the crime of enlistment of children under fifteen has been a subject of confusion, perhaps because it is the most novel aspect to the formulation of the crime.[88] Schabas states that the replacement of the word 'recruiting' in an earlier draft of the Rome Statute with 'conscripting or enlisting' 'suggests something more passive, such as putting the name of a person on a list'.[89] The Secretary-General of the United Nations adopted the same approach in his report to the Security Council on the establishment of the SCSL.[90] The SCSL was the first court to pronounce on this matter. Trial Chamber 1 and Trial Chamber 2 heard the *CDF* and *AFRC* matters (respectively) concurrently.[91] Trial Chamber 1 found that enlistment encompasses both conscription and enlistment.[92] On the other hand, Trial Chamber 2 held that enlistment means 'accepting and enrolling individuals when they volunteer to join an armed force or group'.[93] Trial Chamber 1's interpretation was suspect from the beginning, as it renders the word 'conscription' superfluous. This issue formed one of the grounds of appeal in the *CDF* case. The Appeals Chamber correctly endorsed Trial Chamber 2's finding in the *AFRC* case.[94] More recently, the ICC rejected the defence argument in *Lubanga* that 'the act of enlistment consists in the integration of a person as a soldier, within the context of an armed conflict, *for the purposes of* participating actively in hostilities on behalf of the group'.[95]

On the question of the role of the accused in the enlistment of children, the Appeals Chamber in the *CDF* case held that

> for enlistment there must be a nexus between the act of the accused and the child joining the armed force or group . . . Whether such a nexus exists is a question of fact which must be determined on a case-by-case basis.[96]

Furthermore, in the context of a non-state armed group, enlistment cannot be narrowly construed as a formal process. It should rather be regarded

---

[88] See the discussion of the term 'recruitment' in Chapter 3.II.C above.

[89] W Schabas, *An Introduction to the International Criminal Court* (Cambridge, Cambridge University Press, 2001) 50.

[90] Secretary-General's Report, n 9 above, para 17–18.

[91] *Prosecutor v Brima, Kamara and Kanu* SCSL-04-16-T (20 June 2007), para 735 (*AFRC* Trial judgment).

[92] *CDF* Trial judgment, n 59 above, para 192.

[93] *AFRC* Trial judgment, n 91 above, para 733.

[94] *Prosecutor v Fofana and Kondewa* SCSL-04-14-A (28 May 2008), paras 140–44 (*CDF* Appeal judgment).

[95] *Lubanga* judgment, n 1 above, para 609. Original emphasis.

[96] Ibid, para 141.

in a broad sense so as to include any conduct that accepts a child as a part of the militia, which includes making him or her participate in military operations.[97] The ICC has also held that enlistment is a 'voluntary act' whereas conscription is 'forcible recruitment', which means that consent can never be a defence against a charge of enlistment.[98]

Giving meaning to the 'conscription' of children under fifteen is the least contentious in law of the three incarnations of the child soldier crime. This crime requires an element of force or compulsion to be applied by the recruiter to distinguish it from enlistment.[99] In some instances, such compulsion would be by the force of law.[100] Conscription is usually associated with citizenship duties, where governments require their citizens to serve in the governmental armed forces on a mandatory basis. This occurs within many western democracies, such as Switzerland, even when not at war. Conscription in the context of the child soldier crime is broader than that, as conscription can occur in the context of an armed group distinct from the state.[101] In the *AFRC* case it was stated that 'conscription' encompasses coercive acts such as abductions and forced recruitment.[102] In distinguishing between enlistment and conscription, which turns on the degree of participation of the child in becoming associated with an armed group or force, the SCSL has consistently argued that this distinction is 'contrived', as the ability of a child younger than fifteen to express free will and volition in a conflict setting is a questionable endeavour.[103] This accords with Coomaraswamy's view that children do not have a 'death concept'; however, she places the age threshold at younger than eighteen.[104] During the *Lubanga* proceedings, Coomaraswamy testified, and the Court accepted her testimony, that 'the line between voluntary and forced recruitment is therefore not only legally irrelevant but practically superficial in the context of children in armed conflict'.[105] The Court in *Lubanga* went further than previous tribunals in discussing the possibility of a defence of consent and finding that consent cannot be a proper defence against a charge of child soldier enlistment. Kurth argues convincingly that, had

[97] Ibid, para 144; *RUF* Trial judgment, n 59 above, para 185.
[98] *Lubanga Confirmation of Charges* decision, n 52 above, para 247. See also *Child Recruitment* decision, Judge Robertson's dissent, para 5.
[99] *Lubanga Confirmation of Charges* decision, ibid, para 246; *Child Recruitment* decision, Judge Robertson's dissent, para 5.
[100] *Child Recruitment* decision, ibid; *AFRC* Trial judgment, n 91 above, para 734.
[101] *AFRC* Trial judgment, ibid.
[102] Ibid; *RUF* Trial judgment, n 59 above, para 186.
[103] *RUF* Trial judgment, ibid, para 187; *CDF* Trial judgment, n 59 above, para 192.
[104] I interviewed Ms Coomaraswamy on 7 February 2011 in New York, USA. At the time she served as Special Representative to the Secretary-General on Children in Armed Conflict.
[105] *Lubanga* judgment, n 1 above, para 611.

the age threshold been younger than eighteen, the Court's finding in this regard would have been much more controversial.[106]

Finally, within the context of international armed conflict, the child soldier crime is formulated so as to criminalise the enlistment and conscription of children into 'the national armed forces'. This aspect to the prohibition was dealt with above in the context of the drafting history to the Rome Statute.

### ii. Use to Participate Actively in Hostilities

The phrase 'use of one or more persons to participate actively in hostilities' raises a number of issues that require analysis. First, can a child be so used in hostilities without having been either conscripted or enlisted? Added to this is the question whether a charge of enlistment or conscription can be sustained together with a charge of use of a child soldier, as this may violate the rule against duplicity.

As it has been held that enlistment should be broadly construed so as to include any conduct that accepts a child as a part of the militia, it is clear that either enlistment or conscription will always occur before the use of the child for participation in active hostilities.[107] In *Lubanga*, the court held: 'it follows that the status of a child under 15 who has been enlisted or conscripted is independent of any later period when he or she may have been "used" to participate actively in hostilities'.[108]

In the *Blockburger* case, the US Supreme Court set the test to determine whether a person can be charged with more than one crime where an act simultaneously breached various rules covering the same subject matter.[109] Such charges will be sustainable 'only if each statutory provision involved has a materially distinct element not contained in the other. An element is materially distinct from another if it requires proof of a fact not required by the other.'[110] Enlistment is a lesser crime than conscription, not an incomplete crime; the same is true of conscription vis-à-vis use. There is at least one distinct objective element that needs to be proven with regard to the use of child soldiers on the one hand and enlistment and conscription on the other: it has to be shown that the

---

[106] ME Kurth 'The *Lubanga* Case of the International Criminal Court: A Critical Analysis of the Trial Chamber's Findings on Issues of Active Use, Age, and Gravity' (2013) 5(2) *Goettingen Journal of International Law* 431, 437.

[107] It is nevertheless theoretically possible for a child to engage in hostilities without forming part of an armed group and without an adult being responsible for using the child, for example, a child spontaneously going to arms.

[108] *Lubanga* judgment, n 1 above, para 609.

[109] *Blockburger*, US, Supreme Court, 1932, 284 US, 299 US SCt 180, 304. This test was endorsed by the ICTY in *Prosecutor v Kupreškić and others* IT-95-16 TC (14 January 2000), para 681 et seq; see also D Mundis, 'Blockburger Test' in A Cassese, (ed) *The Oxford Companion to International Criminal Justice* (Oxford, Oxford University Press, 2009) 257–58.

[110] *Čelebići* Trial judgment, n 62 above, para 412.

child was used to participate actively in hostilities. It is thus submitted that a charge of both enlistment/conscription and use can be sustained against the same defendant with regard to the same victim.[111]

One of the most contentious questions within IHL has long been what constitutes direct/active participation in hostilities. In Chapter 3 I discussed direct participation in hostilities insofar as it relates to IHL. This section is focused on the parallel development of this concept within ICL.

I have already argued that 'direct' and 'active' participation in hostilities amount to the same standard.[112] While I maintain this point of view, on the same reasoning expressed in Chapter 3, there are developments within ICL that must be canvassed. The ICTR held, in the *Akayesu* case, that the wording is so similar that direct and active mean the same insofar as they qualify the degree of participation in hostilities.[113] The SCSL,[114] the *Targeted Killings Case* and the International Committee of the Red Cross guidance on direct participation in hostilities all support this view.[115] The Report of the Preparatory Committee on the Establishment of an International Criminal Court provided:

> The words 'using' and 'participate' have been adopted in order to cover both *direct participation in combat* and also *active participation in military activities linked to combat* such as scouting, spying, sabotage and use of children as decoys, couriers or at military checkpoints. It would not cover activities clearly unrelated to the hostilities such as food deliveries to an airbase or the use of domestic staff in an officer's accommodation. However, use of children in a direct support function such as acting as bearers to take supplies to the front line, or activities at the front line itself, would be included within the terminology.[116]

Many commentators, as well as the ICC itself, have interpreted this to indicate that 'direct' and 'active' participations in hostilities present different standards. However, this interpretation is not sound. The words 'direct' and 'active' in this context are not used to qualify participation

---

[111] These crimes should be charged in separate counts in the indictment. See *CDF* Appeals judgment, n 94 above, para 139, where it is stated that 'these modes of recruiting children [enlistment; conscription and use] are distinct from each other and liability for one form does not necessarily preclude liability for the other'. See also *Lubanga Warrant of Arrest*. See also *Prosecutor v Lubanga*, Warrant of Arrest, ICC-01/04–01/06 (2006).

[112] See generally Chapter 3.II.B.

[113] *Prosecutor v Akayesu* ICTR-96-4-T (1998), para 629. See also *Prosecutor v Semanza* ICTR-97-20-T (2003), para 365.

[114] *CDF* Trial judgment, n 59 above, para 131. See also *RUF* Trial judgment, n 59 above, para 102.

[115] *Public Committee against Torture in Israel v Government of Israel et al* HCJ 769/02 (11 December 2005), para 30; N Melzer, *Interpretive Guidance on the Notion of Direct Participation in Hostilities under International Humanitarian Law* (Geneva, ICRC, 2009), 43.

[116] Report of the Preparatory Committee on the Establishment of an International Criminal Court, A/CONF.183/2/Add.1 (14 April 1998) 21, note 12, cited in *CDF* Trial judgment, n 59 above, para 193. Emphasis added.

in hostilities, as is the case in the Rome Statute; rather, they qualify 'participation in combat' and 'participation in military activities linked to combat'. Moreover, the quoted passage was intended to define not 'direct' and 'active', but rather 'using' and 'participate'.

The ICC held in the *Lubanga Confirmation of Charges* decision that these standards are not the same:

> 'Active participation' in hostilities means not only direct participation in hostilities, combat in other words, but also covers active participation in combat-related activities such as scouting, spying, sabotage and the use of children as decoys, couriers or at military check-points.[117]

The incorporation of the language of the Preparatory Committee's report indicates that the court endorsed the argument based on the report. Having interpreted active participation more broadly than direct participation, the question remains exactly how widely the ICC will interpret this provision in concrete cases.

The ICC Pre-Trial Chamber has held, in obiter dictum, that delivering food to an airbase and working as domestic staff in the quarters of married officers do not meet the threshold of active participation.[118] On the other hand, it was held in ratio decidendi that the guarding of military objectives and the acting as a bodyguard meet the threshold.[119] The SCSL has held that the 'concept of hostilities encompasses not only combat operations but also military activities linked to combat such as the use of children at military checkpoints or as spies'.[120] Similar to the ICC, the SCSL has held that food-finding missions and working as a domestic servant in officers' quarters do not amount to active participation in hostilities,[121] whereas acting as a bodyguard, mounting ambushes, participating in armed patrols, committing crimes against civilians, guarding military objectives and children acting as spies may do.[122] However, it should be borne in mind that this is not a list that can blindly be followed: whether a specific case meets the threshold depends 'on the particularities of each armed conflict and the *modus operandi* of the warring factions'.[123] Similar to the ICC, the SCSL held in the *AFRC* case that:

> the use of children to participate actively in hostilities is not limited to participation in combat. An armed force requires logistical support to maintain

---

[117] *Lubanga Confirmation of Charges* decision, n 52 above, para 261.
[118] Ibid, para 262.
[119] Ibid, para 263.
[120] *RUF* Trial judgment, n 59 above, para 1720.
[121] Ibid, para 1743. However, in the *AFRC* Trial judgment, n 91 above, para 737, it was stated, in *ratio decidendi*, that 'finding and/or acquiring food' may amount to active participation.
[122] *RUF* Trial judgment, n 59 above, paras 1714–43.
[123] Ibid, para 1720.

its operations. Any labour or support that gives effect to, or helps maintain, operations in a conflict constitutes active participation. Hence carrying loads for the fighting faction, finding and/or acquiring food, ammunition or equipment, acting as decoys, carrying messages, making trails or finding routes, manning checkpoints or acting as human shields are some examples of active participation as much as actual fighting and combat.[124]

Thus, in contrast to the *Lubanga Confirmation of Charges* decisions and the *RUF* case, it was held, in obiter dictum, that finding or acquiring food may amount to active participation in hostilities. In the *RUF* case, the Court argued that children did not carry arms openly while on food finding missions, thus it did not amount to active participation.[125] This again shows that determining whether acting in a given capacity amounts to active participation needs to be made on a case-by-case basis, and indeed this has recently been confirmed in the *Lubanga* Trial Chamber judgment.[126]

An issue that has developed quite a lot of controversy following the *Lubanga* judgment is the question whether the sexual abuse of child soldiers, especially girl soldiers, amounts to use in the context of active participation in hostilities. Central to this issue was the use of girl soldiers as sex slaves. The majority found that such conduct was irrelevant in the context of Articles 8(2)(b)(xxvi) and 8(2)(e)(vii). This finding is correct in law. The failure of the *Lubanga* case to address these horrific violations is due to the failure of the Office of the Prosecutor to charge Lubanga for these violations, which the Rome Statute specifically proscribes. Judge Odio Benito disagreed, holding:

> Sexual violence committed against children in the armed groups causes irreparable harm and is a direct and inherent consequence to their involvement with the armed group. Sexual violence is an intrinsic element of the criminal conduct of 'use to participate actively in the hostilities'. Girls who are used as sex slaves or 'wives' of commanders or other members of the armed group provide essential support to the armed groups.[127]

Such a creative interpretation of the concept 'use' cannot be accepted. Indeed, it is greatly regrettable that Lubanga was not charged with gender crimes, but this cannot be remedied by making the crime that he was charged with into something that it is not.

---

[124] *AFRC* Trial judgment, n 91 above, para 737.
[125] *RUF* Trial judgment, n 59 above, paras 1714–43.
[126] *Lubanga* judgment, n 1 above, para 915.
[127] *Lubanga* judgment, Dissenting Opinion of Judge Odio Benito, n 1 above, para 20.

## C. Subjective Requirements

*Mens rea* denotes 'a state of mind, a psychological element required by the legal order for the conduct to be blameworthy and consequently punishable'.[128] The Rome Statute contains a provision devoted exclusively to *mens rea*, and regulates *mens rea* in relation to all crimes over which the ICC has jurisdiction:

> 1. Unless otherwise provided, a person shall be criminally responsible and liable for punishment for a crime within the jurisdiction of the Court only if the material elements are committed with intent and knowledge.

> 2. For the purposes of this article, a person has intent where:
> (a) In relation to conduct, that person means to engage in the conduct;
> (b) In relation to a consequence, that person means to cause that consequence or is aware that it will occur in the ordinary course of events.

> 3. For the purposes of this article, 'knowledge' means awareness that a circumstance exists or a consequence will occur in the ordinary course of events. 'Know' and 'knowingly' shall be construed accordingly.[129]

The main question is what degree of *mens rea* is required to sustain a conviction before the ICC. In essence, fault is composed of *dolus* (intent) and *culpa* (negligence). Intent is divided into *dolus directus*,[130] *dolus indirectus*[131] and *dolus eventualis*.[132] *Culpa* comprises negligence and gross negligence (*culpa lata*).

Cassese is of the view that international criminal law generally requires intent in the strict sense,[133] but recognises lesser forms of *mens rea* in limited cases; for example, *dolus eventualis* is inherent in command responsibility and common purpose/joint criminal enterprise.[134] Cassese draws a distinction between 'intent' and '*dolus eventualis*'. He has further criticised the fault requirement as included in the Rome Statute for requiring a stricter form of *dolus* than *dolus eventualis* (he would argue that 'intent' (*dolus directus*) is required and 'recklessness' (which he seems

---

[128] Cassese, n 39 above, 53.
[129] Art 30, Rome Statute.
[130] The perpetrator foresees and desires the consequences of her/his actions.
[131] The perpetrator foresees secondary consequences that will set in as a certainty in consequence to her/his actions. Although these consequences are not desired, she/he nevertheless committed the act and those consequences do set in.
[132] The perpetrator foresees the possibility of harmful consequences, and reconciles her/himself with the possibility of such consequences and nevertheless proceeds with the relevant activity. For an extensive discussion of these definitions see JD Van der Vyver, 'The International Criminal Court and the Concept of *Mens Rea* in International Criminal Law' (2004) 12 *University of Miami International & Comparative Law Review* 57, 62–63.
[133] Cassese, n 39 above, 60.
[134] *Blaškić* judgment, n 35 above, para 42.

to equate to *dolus eventualis*) is insufficient).[135] There is a tendency among ICL commentators to use the terms '*dolus eventualis*' and 'recklessness' synonymously, when there is in fact a technical difference between the terms.[136] Van der Vyver argues that the Rome Statute is sound in this regard as the ICC concerns itself with 'the most serious crimes of concern to the international community as a whole'.[137] Considering that the determination of the seriousness of a crime does not lie with *actus reus* alone but includes *mens rea*, Van der Vyver's position is to be preferred.

The ICTY held in the *Stakić* case that *dolus eventualis* is sufficient to meet the intent requirement for the *mens rea* element for the crime of murder as a crime against humanity.[138] The Trial Chamber specifically and correctly emphasised that *dolus eventualis* does not include a standard of negligence or gross negligence. With regard to the crime of extermination, the court in *Stakić* dismissed the prosecutor's contention that criminal liability can be founded when intention, recklessness or gross negligence is present, stating that only *dolus directus* and *dolus eventualis* will be sufficient.[139] This would also mean that *dolus indirectus* would be sufficient. The prosecutor's contention was based on the ICTR's finding in the *Kayishema* case.[140] However, little weight should be attached to ICTY jurisprudence, where the Anglo-American perception of the fault requirement played a more significant role.[141] The *Blaškić* case indicates the ICTY's adherence to the Anglo-American fault requirement well. This judgment speaks of *dolus eventualis* as 'recklessness which may be likened to serious criminal negligence', which is not the correct definition of *dolus eventualis*.[142] The fault requirement as included in the Rome Statute can trace its roots back to a civil law lineage where, unlike the case in America, *dolus* is never equated to any form of *culpa* (negligence).[143]

Unless the specific crime provides otherwise, the Rome Statute requires 'intent and knowledge' for a conviction. Cassese argues that, in terms of the standard of construction, the grammatical construction must yield to a logical interpretation when the principle of effectiveness

---

[135] A Cassese, 'The Statute of the International Criminal Court: Preliminary Reflections' (1999) 10 *European Journal of International Law* 144, 153–54.

[136] See generally Van der Vyver, n 132 above.

[137] Ibid, 64–65. It should, however, be noted that this provision is considered to be a provision to guide the discretion of the prosecutor, and is not a jurisdictional threshold.

[138] *Prosecutor v Stakić* IT-97-24-T (2003), para 587.

[139] Ibid, para 642.

[140] *Prosecutor v Kayishema* ICTR-95-1-T (1999), para 146. See also *Prosecutor v Musema* ICTR-96-13-T (2000), para 215.

[141] Van der Vyver, n 132 above, 59. Van der Vyver further points out that the Anglo-American conception of fault was not as readily adopted by the ICTR.

[142] *Blaškić* judgment, n 35 above, para 152.

[143] Ibid.

(*ut res magis valeat quam pereat*) so requires. The General Introduction to the EOC supports Cassese:

> Where no reference is made in the Elements of Crimes to a mental element for any particular conduct, consequence or circumstance listed, it is understood that the relevant mental element, ie intent, knowledge *or* both, set out in Article 30 applies. (emphasis added)

However, the relative 'weakness' of the EOC must be highlighted. Article 9 of the Rome Statute states that 'Elements of Crimes shall assist the Court in the interpretation and application' and goes on to state that 'the Elements of Crimes and amendments thereto shall be consistent with this Statute'. It may well be argued that the General Introduction is inconsistent with the Statute in this regard. What should be remembered is that, if the requirements of intent and knowledge are to be interpreted in an either/or fashion, it does not only mean that intent alone will suffice, but also vice versa. Therefore I am of the view that both 'intent and knowledge' should be present. Taking into account the Rome Statute definition of 'knowledge', the only effect of this provision is to limit the fault requirement to *dolus directus* and *dolus indirectus*.

There are various opinions as to which degrees of *dolus* this article encapsulates. There is general agreement that *dolus directus* and *dolus indirectus* are both sufficient. Piragoff and Cassese are of the view that *dolus eventualis* is also sufficient, whereas Van der Vyver opines that *dolus eventualis* is not.[144] The wording of the text, which states 'awareness that a . . . consequence will occur', suggests that Van der Vyver's position is correct. Thus, I am of the view that, in terms of Article 30 of the Rome Statute, both intent and knowledge are required to sustain a conviction and that *dolus directus* and *dolus indirectus* are the only forms of intent that will suffice, unless otherwise provided. This approach will surely be deemed conservative. However, when the formulation of the Rome Statute is invoked, and considering that the ICC is to hear 'the most serious crimes of international concern', this conclusion is warranted.[145]

The Statute of the SCSL provides no guidance on the requisite threshold of *mens rea*. However, it was held in the *RUF* case that the required *mens rea* threshold will be met if the prosecution proves that 'the accused acted with intent to commit the crime, or with the awareness of the substantial likelihood that the crime would occur as a consequence of his conduct'.[146] Thus, *dolus eventualis* is sufficient to meet the *mens rea* requirement before the SCSL. In the context of the child soldier crime,

---

[144] DK Piragoff, 'Mental Element' in A Cassese et al (eds), *Commentary on the Rome Statute of the International Criminal Court* (Oxford, Oxford University Press, 1999) 533; Cassese, n 39 above, 74; Van der Vyver, n 132 above, 66.

[145] Art 1, Rome Statute.

[146] *RUF* Trial judgment, n 59 above, para 250.

in order to meet the fault threshold, the SCSL has held that the person must be aware that the child is under the age of 15 and that the child may be trained for or used in combat.[147]

The EOC does indeed provide otherwise (than the general *mens rea* provision in Article 30 of the Rome Statute) in the context of the child soldier crime, in that the EOC provides: 'the perpetrator knew or should have known that such person or persons were under the age of fifteen'. A standard of negligence is thus imported into the child soldier crime.[148]

### III. THE POTENTIAL OF INTERNATIONAL CRIMINAL LAW TO COMBAT THE CHILD SOLDIER PHENOMENON

Given its direct link to IHRL and IHL, the existence of ICL is warranted on the basis that child soldier prohibitions entail criminal responsibility. Theories of punishment are thus central to the pursuits of ICL as a discipline. Such theories of punishment have long been debated in the context of municipal criminal law. Some commentators have transplanted these theories mutatis mutandis to ICL,[149] where others warn that the peculiarities of ICL must be borne in mind, and theories of punishment emanating from municipal criminal law must not be transplanted to ICL blindly and as a matter of course.[150] Theories of punishment are varied. However, in viewing the ICC as a mechanism to achieve social change, two specific aspects of punishment are of importance: deterrence and capacity-building in municipal legal systems.

#### A. The ICC as a Deterrent to the Enlistment, Conscription or Use of Child Soldiers

In an era of application, it is necessary that mechanisms such as the ICC play a role in deterring the commission of crimes such as the enlistment, conscription and use of child soldiers. As is the case with municipal criminal justice systems, the deterrence value of criminal prosecutions in

---

[147] *CDF* Appeal judgment, n 94 above, para 141; *RUF* Trial judgment, ibid, para 192.

[148] WA Schabas, *The International Criminal Court: A Commentary on the Rome Statute* (Oxford, Oxford University Press, 2010) 252. *Katanga and Ngudjolo Confirmation of Charges* decision, n 55 above, paras 251–52; M Bothe, 'War Crimes' in A Cassese et al, *The Rome Statute of the International Criminal Court: A Commentary Volume I* (Oxford, Oxford University Press, 2002) 416.

[149] For example, R Cryer et al, *An Introduction to International Criminal Law and Procedure*, 2nd edn (Cambridge, Cambridge University Press, 2010) 22 argue that the objectives of punishment do not differ that significantly between municipal criminal justice systems and ICL.

[150] See, eg M Drumbl, 'Collective Violence and Individual Punishment: The Criminality of Mass Atrocity' (2004–2005) 99 *North-Western Law Review* 539.

international criminal tribunals has been the subject of extensive debate.[151] The deterrence debate has been conducted around the parameters of various deterrence theories. The primary pragmatic critique of international criminal prosecutions as a form of deterrence is 'approaches that treat people as rational calculators'.[152] Justice Chaskalson, a former Judge President of the South African Constitutional Court, followed such an approach in his majority decision in *S v Makwanyane*.[153] Chaskalson argued that the death penalty is not a deterrent, as perpetrators do not weigh the punishment they may potentially receive upon conviction at the time of the commission of the crime. Instead, they justify their actions by a belief that they will not be caught.[154]

Yet, as Cryer et al argue, there can be little doubt that criminal justice systems implementing punishment disproportionately to the relevant crime and punishing innocent family members of perpetrators will have a more significant deterrent effect.[155] While there is no place for such unjust criminal justice systems in a rule-of-law-oriented society, the example illustrates that criminal prosecutions potentially play a role in deterrence.

Deterrence is one of the Rome Statute's central goals: 'determined to put an end to impunity for the perpetrators of these crimes and thus to contribute to the prevention of such crimes'.[156] The ICTY has indicated that deterrence is a proper aim of that Tribunal, but that it should not be overemphasised.[157] Unlike the ad hoc tribunals, the ICC has prospective jurisdiction only, and therefore is likely to play a more meaningful role in deterrence. Judge Kirsch, the first President of the ICC, has been joined by many commentators in his view that 'by putting potential perpetrators on notice that they may be tried before the Court, the ICC is intended to contribute to the deterrence of these crimes'.[158]

---

[151] See, eg W Punyasena, 'Conflict Prevention and the International Criminal Court: Deterrence in a Changing World' (2006) 14 *Michigan State Journal of International Law* 39; M Smidt, The International Criminal Court: An Effective Means of Deterrence? (2001) 167 *Military Law Review* 156.

[152] Cryer et al, n 149 above, 26. Also see the same source for a more philosophical critique.

[153] *S v Makwanyane and Others* 1995 (3) SA 391 (CC).

[154] Ibid. This approach is an oversimplification of a complex issue and is better suited, and perhaps more accurate, in the debate around appropriate punishment, as it was used in this case.

[155] Cryer et al, n 149 above, 26.

[156] Preamble, Rome Statute.

[157] *Tadić Jurisdiction* judgment, n 13 above, para 48; *Prosecutor v Nikolić*, ICTY IT-02-60/1 (12 December 2003), paras 89–90.

[158] Parliamentarians for Global Action 'A Deterrent International Criminal Court— The Ultimate Objective', available at http://www.pgaction.org/uploadedfiles/deterrent%20 paper%20rev%20Tokyo.pdf. See this source also for comments by Chief Prosecutor Ocampo, Bassiouni, High Commissioner Arbour (as she then was) and others. See also DJ Scheffer, 'The International Criminal Tribunal Foreword: Deterrence of War Crimes in the 21st Century' (1999) 23 *Maryland Journal of International Law & Trade* 1.

Cynics of the ICC, and international criminal justice more broadly, may be quick to cite the arrest warrant issued during March 2009 against Sudanese President Omar al-Bashir as an example of the shortcomings of the ICC. At the time of writing, President al-Bashir is still at large and still in power. This, it may be argued, negatively affects the deterrent value of the ICC. As a counter-balance, however, the successful prosecution of Charles Taylor by the SCSL indicates the reach of international criminal justice well. It should also be added that President al-Bashir has not been unaffected by the warrant for his arrest; for example, his international travel has been severely limited.[159] From a deterrence point of view, the value of prosecutions against defendants such as al-Bashir and Taylor are twofold. First, other heads of state are placed on notice that their actions are also subject to the jurisdiction of the ICC or other tribunals, even where the relevant state is not a state party to the Rome Statute.[160] Secondly, the fact that leaders and heads of state are subject to such prosecutions likely has an impact on lower-level commanders operating in the field. It seems that ICL has progressively more impact on deterrence.[161]

During fieldwork in the Democratic Republic of the Congo (DRC), I was routinely viewed with suspicion when I spoke about child soldiering to people who had been involved in the Ituri conflict as fighters (direct participants in hostilities). The complete opposite happened when I spoke to victims. Although this was expected to some extent, the level of engagement by the victims was overwhelming, in contrast to the complete lack of engagement by the fighters. This, I soon discovered, was primarily due to a fear on the part of the former fighters that I was an ICC investigator, and a corresponding hope on the part of the victims. I therefore adapted the way in which I engaged with both victims and fighters, strongly indicating that I was an independent researcher, and I immediately noticed more balanced and less polarised responses from both groups.[162] Fear of prosecution does not necessarily result in deterrence. However, knowledge of the possibility of prosecution is a precondition for deterrence. While in the Ituri district of the DRC, I was very surprised at the level of awareness of the existence of the ICC, and the ongoing prosecution of *Lubanga*.

---

[159] L Stone, 'Implementation of the Rome Statute in South Africa' in C Bhoke and J Biegon (eds), *Prosecuting International Crimes in Africa* (Pretoria, Pretoria University Law Press, 2011) 326.

[160] See generally EL Lutz and C Reiger (ed), *Prosecuting Heads of State* (Cambridge, Cambridge University Press, 2008).

[161] Cryer et al, n 149 above, 26, quoting F Harhoff, 'Sense and Sensibility in Sentencing — Taking Stock of International Criminal Punishment' in O Engdahl and P Wrange (eds), *Law at War: The Law As It Was and the Law As It Should Be* (The Hague, Brill, 2008) 128.

[162] In some cases it was hard to convince people that I was indeed an independent researcher. Over time, I built up a network with local people and relied upon them to vouch that I was an independent researcher.

## B. The Role of the ICC in Building Capacity in Municipal Legal Systems

Much has been written about the fact that the jurisdiction of the ICC operates complementarily to that of municipal criminal jurisdictions. Indeed, without this feature the Rome Statute would probably never have come into force. The most important feature of this complementary relationship insofar as criminal deterrence is concerned is the municipal incorporation by states of the Rome Statute.[163] Indeed, the Rome Statute's potential to prevent child soldiering lies more in its municipal incorporation, and the resulting municipal enforcement of international criminal norms, than on prosecutions before the ICC. Most importantly, such municipal incorporation results in an increase by many-fold of the capacity of courts to prosecute people for crimes proscribed in the Rome Statute. As is further discussed in Chapter 7, the first municipal prosecutions for the enlistment, conscription or use of child soldiers have already been concluded in the DRC.

Upon municipal incorporation, the jurisdictional scope of enforcement of crimes proscribed by the Rome Statute may be expanded in terms of the relevant municipal legal system. Two areas where this will be of primary relevance in relation to the prevention of child soldiering are the expansion of jurisdiction to include universal jurisdiction and the age of criminal responsibility.

### i. Universal Jurisdiction

Outside of the context of matters that appear before the ICC by way of Security Council referral, the jurisdiction of the ICC is limited to territorial and active personality jurisdiction. However, many states are empowered, in terms of their municipal law,[164] to exercise universal jurisdiction in relation to specific crimes,[165] including genocide, war

---

[163] Although I argue strongly in favour of the municipal incorporation of the Rome Statute, I acknowledge that there are significant challenges to the effectiveness of prosecuting ICL crimes in municipal jurisdictions. Nevertheless, although the scope of this chapter and study do not allow for further analysis of this issue, I am of the view that these challenges can largely be overcome and are not fatal to such prosecutions. See generally WN Ferdinandusse, *Direct Application of International Criminal Law in National Courts* (Amsterdam, Asser Press, 2005).

[164] In order to exercise universal jurisdiction, the municipal legal system of a state must provide for such jurisdiction, see *R v Bow Street Metropolitan Stipendiary Magistrate and others, Ex Parte Pinochet Ugarte (Amnesty International and Others Intervening) (No 3)* [1999] 2 All ER 97, 177 (HL). For the parameters of universal jurisdiction in terms of international law see also *Case Concerning the Arrest Warrant of 11 April 2000 (Democratic Republic of the Congo v Belgium)*, ICJ Reports 2002, 3 et seq.

[165] For examples of countries that exercise universal jurisdiction see LC Green, '"Grave Breaches" or Crimes Against Humanity' (1997–1998) 8 *USAFA Journal of Legal Studies* 19, 27–28.

crimes and crimes against humanity.[166] Some authorities suggest that the exercise of universal jurisdiction in relation to war crimes is more limited in NIAC, but is proper in IAC generally.[167] Universal jurisdiction has been defined as:

> the right of a state to institute legal proceedings and to try the presumed author of an offence, irrespective of the place where the said offence has been committed, the nationality or the place of residence of its presumed author or of the victim.[168]

In relation to states which have incorporated the Rome Statute municipally and which exercise universal jurisdiction in relation to war crimes, both the capacity and the reach of prosecution of ICL norms are vastly expanded. Both the United Nations Fact Finding Mission on the Gaza Conflict and the former United Nations Special Rapporteur on Torture have called upon states to expand their jurisdiction to include universal jurisdiction and to utilise such jurisdiction in order to bring an end to impunity.[169]

It is undoubtedly the case that the relative deterrent role ICL plays in relation to the commission of war crimes is related to the scope and number of prosecutions of war crimes. Therefore, if universal jurisdiction is utilised by more states progressively in relation to child soldiering, ICL will, over time, operate more effectively as a deterrent to the enlistment, conscription and use of child soldiers. Significant challenges remain, however. Most importantly, before prosecution can be initiated, a state will have to secure custody of the alleged perpetrator in a lawful manner. For universal jurisdiction to effectively contribute to the prevention of child soldiering, increased international cooperation in the suppression and prosecution of crime will also be required.

---

[166] See M Danilenko, 'ICC Jurisdiction and Third States' in Cassese et al, n 148 above, 1879.

[167] A Zimmermann, 'Die Schaffung eines standigen Internationalen Strafgerichtshofes: Perspectiven und Probleme vor der Sraatenkonferenz in Rom' (1998) 47 *Zeitschrift fur Auslandisches Offentliches Recht und Volkerrecht* 86.

[168] 'Brussels Principles against Immunity and for International Justice, Principle 13, Combating Impunity', Proceedings of the Symposium held in Brussels, 11–13 March 2002, 157.

[169] Report of the United Nations Fact Finding Mission on the Gaza Conflict UN Doc A/HRC/12/48 (25 September 2009), para 1975(a). M Nowak, 'Study on the Phenomena of Torture, Cruel, Inhuman or Degrading Treatment or Punishment in the World, Including an Assessment of Conditions of Detention', A/HRC/13/39/Add.5 (Human Rights Council, 5 February 2010).

## ii. The Age of Criminal Responsibility

The criminal responsibility of children, for crimes committed while being child soldiers is a very contentious issue.[170] Given the import of this issue, it is dealt with separately in the next section.

## IV. THE CRIMINAL RESPONSIBILITY OF CHILD SOLDIERS

Shortly after the establishment of the SCSL on 16 January 2002, the Chief Prosecutor of the Tribunal David Crane announced at an event, while addressing Sierra Leonean students, that 'the children of Sierra Leone have suffered enough both as victims and perpetrators. I am not interested in prosecuting children. I want to prosecute the people who forced thousands of children to commit unspeakable crimes.'[171] Crane made this decision notwithstanding the fact that the Statute of the SCSL makes special provision for prosecution of people aged between fifteen and eighteen at the time of the commission of the crime. In relation to such perpetrators, the Statute of the SCSL provides:

> he or she shall be treated with dignity and a sense of worth, taking into account his or her young age and the desirability of promoting his or her rehabilitation, reintegration into and assumption of a constructive role in society, and in accordance with international human rights standards, in particular the rights of the child.[172]

The purpose for such jurisdiction was aimed at the rehabilitation and reintegration of former child soldiers. The SCSL is empowered to make the following orders in relation to youth perpetrators:

> care guidance and supervision orders, community service orders, counselling, foster care, correctional, educational and vocational training programmes, approved schools and, as appropriate, any programmes of disarmament, demobilization and reintegration or programmes of child protection agencies.[173]

Crane made this decision on the basis that the Tribunal's mandate is 'to prosecute persons who bear the greatest responsibility for serious

---

[170] See, eg M Happold, 'Child Soldiers: Victims or Perpetrators' (2008) 29 *University of La Verne Law Review* 56; P Konge, 'International Crimes & Child Soldiers' (2010) 16 *Southwestern Journal of International Law* 41; L Seneviratne, 'Accountability of Child Soldiers: Blame Misplaced' (2008) 20 *Sri Lanka Journal of International Law* 29; DM Rosen, 'Who Is a Child—The Legal Conundrum of Child Soldiers' (2009–10) 25 *Connecticutt Journal of International Law* 81.

[171] Special Court for Sierra Leone Public Affairs Office press release, 'Special Court Prosecutor Says He Will Not Prosecute Children' (2 November 2002).

[172] Ibid, Art 7(1).

[173] Ibid, Art 7(2).

violations of international humanitarian law and Sierra Leonean law'.[174] He argued that this certainly does not include children.

The ICC only has jurisdiction in relation to people who were eighteen years of age or older at the time of the commission of the crime.[175] However, the age of criminal responsibility in terms of the Statute of the SCSL is more complicated, as it provides for three categories of perpetrators.[176] First, the SCSL has no jurisdiction over people younger than fifteen at the time of the commission of the crime. Secondly, the SCSL has ordinary jurisdiction over persons aged eighteen years or older at the time of the commission of the crime. Finally, the SCSL has specific limited jurisdiction in relation to offenders aged fifteen to eighteen, as discussed above.

The position regarding youth offenders before international tribunals is less complicated. The trend is certainly to limit the personal jurisdiction of such tribunals to persons aged eighteen and older at the time of the commission of the offence. At the same time, there are many commentators and rights organisations that insist that children should not be prosecuted for crimes committed as child soldiers by municipal criminal justice systems either. This is a much more contentious issue.

Drumbl is correct in arguing that there are a number of 'pull factors' dissuading the prosecution of child soldiers that exist separately from the arguments above, and that these are steeped in the passive victim persona afforded by the international community to the child soldier.[177] Drumbl argues further that there is a paradox in the fact that children are routinely prosecuted for serious offences within municipal legal systems while, at the same time, there seems to be a general hands-off approach to the prosecution of children for crimes committed while being child soldiers.[178] He accounts for this paradox, at least in part, with the fact that child soldiers are often the subject of brutality themselves.[179]

There are rights considerations attached to states that have too high a minimum age of criminal responsibility, such as eighteen. In such states, particularly if there are high incidences of crimes perpetrated by youth offenders, vigilante justice becomes more prominent. The criminal justice system offers no recourse against such offenders, leaving victims to their own devices. In the context of child soldiering, a very real problem is the integration of former child soldiers into their communities. The concern is thus that, if there is a blanket amnesty instead of a remedial

---

[174] Statute of the SCSL, Art 1.
[175] Rome Statute, Art 26.
[176] Statute of the SCSL, Art 7(1).
[177] MA Drumbl, *Reimagining Child Soldiers in International Law and Policy* (Oxford, Oxford University Press, 2012), 102–03 and 128–33.
[178] Ibid.
[179] Ibid, 128–29.

criminal justice system, communities might also seek vigilante justice. Indeed, this has happened many times.

In the context of the administration of international criminal justice, I am of the view that children younger than eighteen should not be prosecuted, primarily for the same reasons that Crane argued, and, additionally, international tribunals are not well equipped to handle the prosecution of youth offenders in a manner consonant with their rights. Therefore, the debate regarding the criminal responsibility of children for crimes committed while being child soldiers is more relevant in the context of municipal prosecutions. There is no inherent reason why states should not prosecute children. However, such prosecutions must be conducted in strict compliance with the relevant municipal legal system, as well as IHRL provisions regarding the administration of juvenile justice and the rights of the child.[180] Children will likely not be criminally responsible for their actions due to factors other than unlawfulness or wrongfulness, eg extreme mental distress and intoxication. This, however, is to be determined on a case-by-case basis.

The prosecution of children is unlikely to have a deterrent effect on recruits voluntarily joining armed groups, as these children more often than not see no other course of action than to join such groups. Such prosecutions will have no effect on deterring the conscription or use of children in armed conflict.

## V. SUMMARY

Notwithstanding my criticism of the *Child Recruitment* judgment, the child soldier jurisprudence that has since developed in the SCSL indicates well that the Rome Statute formulation of the crime (as was also adopted by the SCSL Statute) is indeed capable of enforcement. The symbolic value of the ICC's first prosecution relating to child soldiering to the exclusion of all other international crimes is significant, as it is an indication that the Prosecutor of the ICC deems the ICC a mechanism capable of contributing to the prevention of child soldiering.

Questions remain as to the inherent ability of the Rome Statute, the ICC and ICL in general to act as a deterrent. Commentators are presenting positive research on this front. Should it be feasible, and after the ICC has built up a more significant jurisprudence of its own, it may be possible to address deterrence from a quantitative point of view. For the time being, the limited qualitative work on this front may be varied, but it is premature to draw overtly negative findings in this regard. Basing

---

[180] See generally the obligations of states in terms of the Convention on the Rights of the Child (entered into force 2 September 1990) 1577 UNTS 3. Arts 37 and 40 are of relevance in juvenile justice.

the level of potential deterrence of the ICC on the experiences of its predecessor ad hoc tribunals is of limited value, as the ICC is the first permanent international criminal tribunal with prospective jurisdiction. More importantly, unlike the statutes of such predecessor ad hoc tribunals, the Rome Statute is to be implemented by states parties into their municipal law.

In relation to the ultimate research question of this study, being 'what is needed for "an era of application"?', the capacity of the ICC may be expanded in future, but the demand for justice will likely always outweigh the ICC's ability to prosecute and dispense justice. International criminal tribunals are, by definition, in the business of dispensing 'selective justice'.[181] McCormack and Cryer argue, in their respective works, that such selectivity is two-dimensional.[182] The closed list of crimes that comprise the ICL regime is the first layer of selectivity; the second layer relates to the decision as to who will be prosecuted for violations. In the context of child soldiering, the first layer has been overcome—the prohibition of the enlistment, conscription and use of child soldiers is now a war crime in terms of ICL. Indeed, it is now recognised as a customary crime. This in itself is significant, specifically considering that the drafters of the Rome Statute set out to codify existing customary international law crimes, of which the child soldier crime was not one at the time. The more expansive definition of the crime, which includes 'enlistment' and 'conscription' instead of 'recruitment', is also very welcome. Many are of the view that the child soldier crime should have employed an age limit of younger than eighteen.[183]

Cryer refers to the second level of selectivity as 'selectivity *ratione personae*'.[184] Here, too, developments thus far have been extremely positive. As stated, the first defendant to be tried by the ICC was charged and convicted solely with the enlistment, conscription and use of child soldiers.[185] This level of selectivity is, however, endemic to international criminal tribunals. In order to enter 'an era of application', states should incorporate the Rome Statute into their municipal law and should show the necessary political will to enforce the child soldier crime in their municipal courts. The level of effectiveness of such prosecutions can

---

[181] See generally R Cryer, *Prosecuting International Crimes: Selectivity and the International Criminal Law Regime* (Cambridge, Cambridge University Press, 2005).

[182] Cryer, ibid, 191, Cryer also cites TLH McCormack, 'Selective Reaction to Atrocity' (1996–97) 60 *Albany Law Review* 681, 683.

[183] Several delegations supported the call from non-governmental organisations to lift the age threshold of the child soldier crime to younger than eighteen during the negotiation and drafting of the Rome Statute. This was, however, never strongly pursued, as it was clear that customary international law did not support such a standard. Cottier, n 51 above, 468–69.

[184] Cryer, n 149 above, 191.

[185] *Lubanga* case, n 1 above.

and should be further advanced by prosecuting offenders through the instrumentality of universal jurisdiction.

This chapter has not addressed modes of liability directly, as such modes in ICL are generic. Individuals can be prosecuted for the child soldier crime as direct perpetrators on the basis of joint criminal enterprise, and also on the basis of command responsibility, either as military or civilian commanders.[186] Finally, child soldiers are often subject to various forms of treatment by their own forces that constitute separate complete crimes in ICL, including war crimes and crimes against humanity, eg torture and sexual crimes. Although both boys and girls are subject to such sexual crimes, girls suffer such abuse disproportionately to boys. In a narrow sense, gender does not play a direct role in relation to the child soldier crime; however, it plays a very direct role in the plight of child soldiers. The analysis in this chapter must be viewed against the backdrop of the multiple further crimes that are committed against child soldiers, and offenders must be prosecuted for these crimes in addition to the child soldier crime.

---

[186] Arts 25 and 28, Rome Statute.

# 6

# *International Institutional Law and the Prevention of Child Soldiering*

E VER SINCE THE International Court of Justice (ICJ) recognised the international legal personality of international governmental organisations (IGOs) in 1949, the scope of application and regulation of such organisations has expanded exponentially. Unbeknown to your average consumer, most products, from food to technology, are regulated in some way by an IGO, such as the World Trade Organization.[1] Such organisations also play a key role in human rights enforcement. Indeed, such international institutions lie at the heart of an era of application. Herch Lauterpacht recognised as early as 1950 that the project of progressing from human rights norm creation to norm enforcement was intrinsically linked to the rise to prominence of international organisations such as the United Nations (UN).[2]

There is an impressive and ever-growing list of international organisations, both governmental and non-governmental, that engage with the issue of child soldier prevention. It is thus not feasible to discuss each of these. Instead, focus is placed on those institutions that possess the potential to directly enforce child soldier prohibitions. Outside of the International Criminal Court (ICC) and the Special Court for Sierra Leone (SCSL), these institutions are limited to mechanisms forming part of either the UN or the African Union (AU). The UN is an international organisation, whereas the AU is a regional organisation. Functionaries within both have a mandate to ensure that states protect, promote, respect and fulfil their international human rights law (IHRL) obligations.

The ICC and the jurisprudence of the SCSL was the subject of analysis in the previous chapter. Neither of these mechanisms forms part of

---

[1] See generally J Klabbers, *An Introduction to International Institutional Law*, 2nd edn (Cambridge, Cambridge University Press, 2009).

[2] See generally E Lauterpacht, *International Law and Human Rights* (London, Stevens & Sons, 1950) 79.

the UN.[3] The UN has, however, founded a number of ad hoc criminal tribunals. These tribunals form part of the UN proper; the most notable examples are the International Criminal Tribunal for the former Yugoslavia and the International Criminal Tribunal for Rwanda. Neither of these tribunals have subject-matter jurisdiction over crimes directly related to child soldiering. Nevertheless, the UN deserves mention in this regard, as these tribunals showcased to the international community the need for a permanent international criminal tribunal, and directly led to significant further developments within substantive international criminal law.

A variety of mechanisms forming part of the UN directly engage with child soldier prevention. These mechanisms span the divide from political to quasi-judicial, and, indeed, the ICJ, the principal judicial organ of the UN, can also potentially adjudicate matters related to child soldier prevention.[4] On the regional level, it is only the African Court on Human and Peoples' Rights (African Court) and the African Committee of Experts on the Rights and Welfare of the Child (African Children's Committee) that have the potential to directly engage with child soldier prevention. Both of these mechanisms have subject-matter jurisdiction over the African Charter on the Rights and Welfare of the Child (African Children's Charter),[5] and both form part of the African Union.

This chapter is divided into three sections. First, the proper role of the UN in addressing child soldier prevention is analysed. Hereafter, those functionaries within the UN most relevant to child soldier prevention are critically assessed. The aims of this section are to critique these functionaries and, more importantly, to attempt to identify ways in which to render them more effective. Finally, the African Court and African Children's Committee are assessed within the African Regional Human Rights System.

In writing this chapter I drew substantially on interviews I had conducted with the Special Representative to the Secretary-General on Children in Armed Conflict (SRSG) (as she then was), Radhika

---

[3] Although the ICC has a formal relationship with the UN, in terms of Article 2 of the Rome Statute of the International Criminal Court (Rome Statute) (entered into force 1 July 2002) 2187 UNTS 90, it is nevertheless an autonomous institution. The SCSL was founded in terms of an agreement between the UN and the Government of Sierra Leone; however, this tribunal also has the status of an independent international organisation.

[4] For a dispute relating to child soldiering to be adjudicated by the ICJ a state party to the Charter of the United Nations (entered into force 24 October 1945) (UN Charter) 1 UNTS XVI (who is *ipso facto* a party to the ICJ Statute) will have to submit such a dispute to the Court against another state. Both states will have to agree to the jurisdiction of the Court, and one state will have to allege that another state infringed its rights in using or recruiting child soldiers, and in so doing committed an internationally wrongful act against the state itself. Accordingly, the ICJ cannot be seen as a direct mechanism through which to prevent child soldiering.

[5] The African Charter on the Rights and Welfare of the Child (entered into force 29 November 1999) OAU Doc CAB/LEG/24.9/49(1990).

Coomaraswamy;[6] the Chairperson of the UN Committee on the Rights of the Child (CRC Committee), Jean Zermatten (then Deputy-Chairperson of the Committee);[7] and a CRC Committee Member and former child soldier, Awich Pollar.[8] I am indebted to them for affording me time in their busy schedules.

## I. THE PROPER LEVELS OF ENGAGEMENT WITH CHILD SOLDIER PREVENTION WITHIN THE UNITED NATIONS

The effective enforcement of even the most basic of laws and the existence of a law-abiding culture are often two of the first casualties of armed conflict. Correspondingly, during armed conflict, the prospects of child soldier prevention deteriorate significantly. The Security Council has acknowledged that child soldiering may potentially threaten the 'maintenance of international peace and security'.[9] This gives credence to the argument that conflict de-escalation and resolution is the proper method with which to combat the use and recruitment of child soldiers.[10] Moreover, conflict avoidance can potentially be achieved by creating early warning mechanisms that monitor signs of impending armed conflict, allowing the international community (including the UN) to take action to avoid conflict. Prior to the Rwandan genocide, for example, then UN Special Rapporteur on extrajudicial, summary or arbitrary executions, Bacre Ndiaye, reported the early warning signs of an impending genocide in Rwanda.[11] Yet his pleas for action went unanswered. It is very difficult, both legally and politically, to directly intervene in other sovereign states before armed conflict has commenced.[12] Nevertheless, identifying early warning signs can place the international community on ready alert to respond appropriately to impending conflict situations. The fact that Ndiaye, a UN mandate holder, warned of the potential for genocide renders the international community's failure to intervene in that situation even more inexcusable.

The question remains, which strategy holds the most potential for child soldier prevention: a broad-based approach aimed at the prevention,

---

[6] I interviewed Ms Coomaraswamy on 7 February 2011 in New York, USA.

[7] I interviewed Mr Zermatten on 2 February 2011 in Geneva, Switzerland.

[8] I Interviewed Mr Pollar on 1 February 2011 in Geneva, Switzerland.

[9] Art 24(1), UN Charter.

[10] J Kuper, 'Implementing the Rights of Children in Armed Conflict: Progress and Dilemmas', Public Lecture (School of Oriental and African Studies, 5 March 2010); P Ironside, Protection Specialist, UNICEF Child Protection Section, Stationed in Goma, DRC. I interviewed Ms Ironside in Goma, DRC on 8 November 2008.

[11] 'Report by BW Ndiaye, Special Rapporteur, on his mission to Rwanda from 8 to 17 April 1993', E/CN.4/1994/7/Add.1 (11 August 1993).

[12] S Chesterman, TM Franck and D M Malone, *Law and Practice of the United Nations: Documents and Commentary* (Oxford, Oxford University Press, 2008) 449.

resolution and avoidance of armed conflict (broad-based approach) or a narrower approach directly aimed at preventing child soldiering notwithstanding ongoing armed conflict (direct approach)? Although many commentators and other role players insist that there are, and have been since the mid-1990s, 300,000 child soldiers globally, I am of the view that this figure was likely never accurate.[13] That notwithstanding, there has been at the very least a marginal reduction in child soldier numbers since the mid-1990s.[14]

There are clear examples where the direct approach has yielded positive results.[15] Furthermore, when I discussed the pros and cons of the broad-based and direct approaches with SRSG Coomaraswamy, she argued strongly that the direct approach is more successful and holds more potential for further success. Nevertheless, I attribute the decline in child soldier numbers globally during the last two decades primarily to a reduction in armed conflicts where children made up significant proportions of fighters and combatants, including Sierra Leone, Liberia and Sri Lanka—three conflicts that have become synonymous with child soldiering.[16] This does not mean that the broad-based approach is better suited. One first has to determine what caused the resolution of these conflicts, and what the potential is for the re-escalation of child soldiering elsewhere. In the case of Sri Lanka, the protracted civil war ended with the defeat of the Liberation Tigers of Tamil Eelam by the Sri Lankan Armed Forces—not through any form of external peace initiative.[17] In Sierra Leone and Liberia peacekeeping forces from the UN and the Economic Community of West African States Monitoring Group (ECOMOG) played a more direct role in suppressing those conflicts.[18] It is debatable what contribution these forces made to resolving these

---

[13] See Chapter 2 above.

[14] Ibid.

[15] Numerous such successes have been achieved in the DRC. See Chapters 6 and 7 in this regard. More recently, on 16 June 2011, the Chadian government, after engagement with the SRSG, signed an agreement with the UN, to phase out child soldiering. In particularm 'the Chadian Government has committed to: step-up efforts to ensure that the Chadian National Forces (ANT) and recently integrated armed groups are child-free; enable verification of military installations by the United Nations to monitor compliance with the action plan; align national legislation with its international obligations for children; take punitive measures against those who continue to violate the agreement; and to put in place other preventive measures'. See 'Press Release of the Special Representative of the Secretary-General for Children and Armed Conflict—Chad Signs an Action Plan to End Recruitment and Use of Children in its National Army and Security Forces', OSRSG/061611-12.

[16] See Chapter 2 above.

[17] See 'Report of the Secretary-General's Panel of Experts on Accountability in Sri Lanka' (31 March 2011).

[18] JOC Jonah, 'The United Nations' in A Adebajo and I Rashid, *West Africa's Security Challenges: Building Peace in a Troubled Region* (Boulder, CO, Lynne Rienner Publishers, 2004) 319–41, where this author discusses the peace operations by ECOMOG and the UN both in Sierra Leone and Liberia.

conflicts. Moreover, in the context of both Sierra Leone and Liberia, the very forces that suppressed the conflict were responsible for serious human rights violations. In fairness, these forces may have contributed to preventing these states from falling into a state of virtual perpetual armed conflict, as is the case in Eastern DRC.

In Chapter 2 I differentiated between the supply and demand of child soldiers.[19] I argued that the supply of child soldiers will likely remain strong due to deeper systemic problems, such as extreme poverty; thus, to be effective in preventing child soldiering, international law should operate to stem the demand for child soldiers, as it does. The broad-based approach will, however, impact equally on the supply and demand of child soldiers. The Security Council, a principal organ of (and the most powerful mechanism within) the UN, has assumed primary responsibility for the maintenance of international peace and security.[20] Indeed, the principle of non-aggression is one of the most central ideals of the UN.[21] The broad-based approach is essential in the context of child soldier prevention and may well yield more future positive results. However, this approach is already implemented across all spheres of the UN on a daily basis. Moreover, it forms the principle business of the UN. This is not to say that there is not still massive scope for improvement in efforts aimed at conflict de-escalation and resolution.

As parallel processes, the broad-based and direct approaches are equally needed to suppress child soldiering. However, the direct approach has received much less attention and, more importantly, taking a vantage point from a child soldier prevention point of view, adds no substantial value to initiatives aimed at conflict de-escalation and resolution. Therefore, this chapter presents an analysis of the direct approach.

## II. A CRITICAL APPRAISAL OF UNITED NATIONS INITIATIVES ENGAGED WITH CHILD SOLDIER PREVENTION

The UN is a vast and enormously complex organisation. The status of any given functionary within the UN is best determined in relation to the principal organ that has oversight over the given functionary, as these organs are the apex functionaries within the UN. The first important observation in this regard is that those functionaries that yield the most power have an advantage insofar as potential effectiveness is concerned. Although the Office of the SRSG on Children and Armed Conflict is not a particularly powerful functionary, it is the

---

[19] Chapter 2 above.
[20] Art 24(1) of the UN Charter.
[21] Ibid.

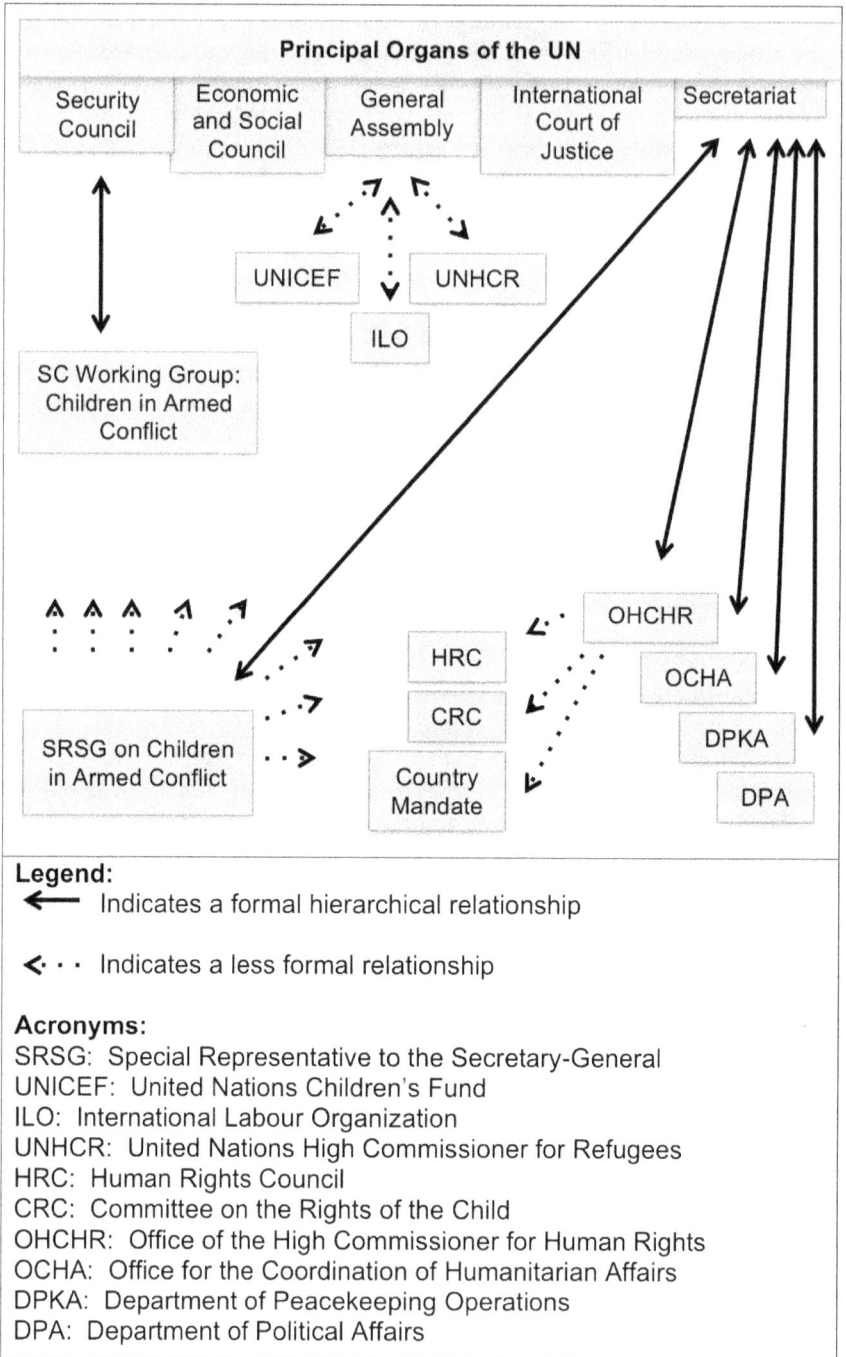

**Principal Organs of the UN**

Security Council | Economic and Social Council | General Assembly | International Court of Justice | Secretariat

UNICEF   UNHCR

ILO

SC Working Group: Children in Armed Conflict

OHCHR

HRC   OCHA

CRC   DPKA

SRSG on Children in Armed Conflict   Country Mandate   DPA

**Legend:**

← Indicates a formal hierarchical relationship

<··· Indicates a less formal relationship

**Acronyms:**
SRSG:  Special Representative to the Secretary-General
UNICEF:  United Nations Children's Fund
ILO:  International Labour Organization
UNHCR:  United Nations High Commissioner for Refugees
HRC:  Human Rights Council
CRC:  Committee on the Rights of the Child
OHCHR:  Office of the High Commissioner for Human Rights
OCHA:  Office for the Coordination of Humanitarian Affairs
DPKA:  Department of Peacekeeping Operations
DPA:  Department of Political Affairs

Figure 1

most important in relation to child soldier prevention, as it is the focal point within the UN of such engagement. Figure 1 represents a limited organogram of UN functionaries directly or indirectly engaged with child soldier prevention.

There are more functionaries within the UN that relate to child soldier prevention. However, those represented in the diagram are the most active in this regard. The scope of this chapter calls for a selective approach as to which functionaries are included in the analysis. In determining the most appropriate functionaries, I balanced the relative power of each functionary with its potential for direct engagement with child soldier prevention. On this basis, the CRC Committee, the SRSG on Children and Armed Conflict and the Security Council are all included in this analysis.

The only UN institutions that can render decisions binding upon member states are the Security Council and the ICJ, both of which are principal organs of the UN.[22] A number of the functionaries included in the diagram relate to child soldier prevention in narrow, specific circumstances. The work of the Office for the Coordination of Humanitarian Affairs, for example, is relevant specifically to the protection of displaced children from military use and recruitment. Child protection has been prioritised across UN functionaries, including in peace missions.[23] The mandate of each peace mission is unique, and an abstract analysis of child soldier prevention within the context of peace missions will be of limited value. Instead, the United Nations Organization Stabilization Mission in the Democratic Republic of the Congo (MONUSCO) forms part of the analysis in Chapter 7.

The UN has an exceptionally far reach, as it is a truly global organisation—it currently has 193 members, including each state that is fully recognised internationally and two observer non-member states, The Holy See and the State of Palestine. The newest member state, South Sudan. became a member of the UN on 14 July 2011.

## A. Historical Background

The quintessential human rights instrument of the twentieth century, the Universal Declaration of Human Rights (UDHR) of 1948, only references the rights of children once, and that rather vaguely.[24] Yet the founding

[22] Art 7 of the UN Charter.
[23] See section 6.II.C below.
[24] Art 25(2) of the Universal Declaration of Human Rights, General Assembly Resolution 217A (III), UN Doc A/810 (1948). The Declaration was adopted by the United Nations General Assembly on 10 December 1948. Indeed, it is not only the rights of children, but human rights in the broad sense, that were not seriously prioritised during the drafting of the UN Charter. The UN Commission on Human Rights was not founded by the Charter,

of the United Nations Children's Fund (UNICEF) predates even the UDHR—UNICEF was founded in 1946 to provide emergency food and healthcare to children in countries devastated in the aftermath of World War Two.[25] The first UN child rights instrument and the forebearer to the Convention on the Rights of the Child (CRC) was the Declaration of the Rights of the Child of 1959.[26] However, the plight of children during armed conflict was only recognised for the first time by a UN organ in 1974, with the adoption of the Declaration on the Protection of Women and Children in Emergency and Armed Conflict by the General Assembly.[27] This was soon followed by the International Year of the Child (1979), as proclaimed by the United Nations Educational, Scientific and Cultural Organization.[28] None of these early developments addressed the use and recruitment of child soldiers.[29] Indeed, the 1974 Declaration expressly excludes children who participate in hostilities from special protection.[30] Child rights only infiltrated UN structures on a significant level in 1989 with the adoption of the CRC.[31]

The first UN institution to recognise the need to act in response to the involvement of children in armed conflict was the CRC Committee, established shortly after the adoption of the Convention. In 1992 the Committee held a 'general discussion day' on the question of 'children in armed conflict'.[32] The following year it was decided to submit a request to the Secretary-General to appoint an expert to launch an in-depth investigation into the protection of children during armed conflict and to report thereon.[33] This recommendation was endorsed by the delegates to the World Conference on Human Rights, held in Vienna in 1993, and was included in the Vienna Declaration and Programme of Action.[34]

but was instead founded in 1946 by the Economic and Social Council under Article 68 of the UN Charter. See also Chesterman et al, n 12 above, 448.

[25] General Assembly Resolution 57 (I) of 11 December 1946.

[26] Declaration of the Rights of the Child, General Assembly Resolution 1386 (XIV), 14 UN GAOR Supp (No 16), 19, UN Doc A/4354 (1959).

[27] Declaration on the Protection of Women and Children in Emergency and Armed Conflict, General Assembly Resolution 29/3318 of 14 December 1974. The plight of children during armed conflict had long been recognised prior to this declaration even in certain ancient societies. The modern humanitarian law recognition of the plight of children during armed conflict is embodied in the Geneva Conventions (see Chapter 3 above for details).

[28] General Assembly Resolution 3l/169 of 1 January 1979.

[29] See Chapter 3 above for a detailed analysis of applicable international human rights law and international humanitarian law.

[30] Preamble, 1974 Declaration.

[31] The UN Convention on the Rights of the Child, General Assembly Resolution 44/25 (12 December 1989).

[32] Committee on the Rights of the Child, 'Report on the Second Session', CRC/C/10 (19 October 1992), para 64.

[33] Committee on the Rights of the Child, 'Report on the Third Session', CRC/C/16 (5 March 1993), para 176 and Annex VI in terms of Art 45(c) of the CRC.

[34] 'Vienna Declaration and Programme of Action', A/CONF.157/23 (12 July 1993), para 50.

The Secretary-General submitted the request to the General Assembly, which then passed Resolution 48/157 in 1993—the first General Assembly Resolution on children in armed conflict—mandating the appointment of an expert to conduct a study and to report on the situation of children in armed conflict.[35] Ms Graça Machel was duly appointed.[36] It is widely recognised that the UN's direct involvement in child soldier prevention came as a result of the ground-breaking 1996 Machel Report. Between 1992 and 1993, the Committee also first conceived of, and took the initiative to draft a first text of, a Protocol to the CRC on the Involvement of Children in Armed Conflict.[37]

## B. The Committee on the Rights of the Child

The CRC Committee is a UN treaty body, established in terms of the CRC to assess states parties' progress in meeting their obligations under the Convention.[38] The Committee's mandate also extends to both Optional Protocols to the CRC, with the Protocol on Children in Armed Conflict (CIAC Protocol) being relevant for present purposes.[39] This has the implication that the Committee has jurisdiction in relation to every state internationally, except Somalia. In order to achieve its mandate, the Committee is tasked with receiving reports from states parties which set out the measures adopted by the relevant state to give effect to the rights contained in the CRC and the Protocols, and the progress made on the enjoyment of these rights.[40] While acknowledging the shortcomings of rigid categorisation, the UN's human rights activities are divided between charter-based organs and treaty based organs.[41] Charter-based organs exercise their powers rather widely, and it is sometimes difficult to trace their actions to specific legal bases.[42] In contrast, treaty based organs, such as the Committee, are confined in scope to the mandate bestowed upon them expressly by the relevant international instrument.[43]

---

[35] General Assembly Resolution 48/157 of 20 December 1993.

[36] Ibid.

[37] 'Report on the Second Session', n 32 above, para 75. 'Report on the Third Session', n 33 above, para 176 and Annex VII.

[38] The Committee was established under Art 43(1) of the CRC.

[39] 'Optional Protocol to the Convention on the Rights of the Child on the Sale of Children, Child Prostitution and Child Pornography' (entered into force 18 January 2002) 1577 UNTS 3.

[40] Art 44(1), CRC.

[41] P Alston, 'Critical Appraisal of the UN Human Rights Regime' in P Alston (ed), *The United Nations and Human Rights: A Critical Appraisal* (Oxford, Oxford University Press, 1992) 4.

[42] Ibid.

[43] Ibid.

On 14 April 2014, the Optional Protocol to the Convention on the Rights of the Child on a communications procedure (Communications Protocol) came into force.[44] Until this point, the Committee's functions were technically limited to monitoring state compliance.[45] In practice, however, its work has always extended beyond this. The Committee has shown a tendency to interpret its role much less restrictively than a textual interpretation of its mandate would suggest.[46] Besides monitoring state party reports, being the Committee's main function, the Committee issues general interpretative comments on substantive provisions of the Convention. It also holds general thematic discussion days, and plays an active role in interpreting the Convention and making recommendations to states parties on how to achieve the goals and ideals of the CRC and the Protocols by issuing 'concluding observations' in response to reports filed and presented by states parties.

As stated, the CRC Committee's mandate is defined in terms of an international law instrument: the CRC. By implication, the shortcomings of the Committee relate either to the mandate of the Committee or the way in which the Committee exercises its mandate, or both. The Committee's limited mandate severely curtails its potential to be proactive in securing compliance with the Convention and the Protocols. Regarding the way in which the Committee exercises its mandate, the inability of the Committee to engage with actors other than states parties impacts on the success of the Committee. Furthermore, the Committee has a tendency to exceed its mandate, and I am of the view that this may lead to the dismissal of the Committee's recommendations by states parties.

*i. The Limitations of the Mandate of the Committee*

Until very recently, the CRC Committee was the only UN human rights treaty body the mandate of which did not incorporate an individual complaints procedure.[47] This was traditionally, and unconvincingly,

---

[44] Optional Protocol to the Convention on the Rights of the Child on a Communications Procedure (Communications Protocol) (entered into force 14 April 2014). For more information on the procedure see G de Beco, 'The Optional Protocol to the Convention on the Rights of the Child on a Communications Procedure: Good News' (2013) 13 *Human Rights Law Review* 367.

[45] In terms of Art 44(1) of the CRC, states parties are obliged to enter a report within two years of the entry into force of the CRC for the relevant state, and thereafter every five years. With regard to the CIAC Protocol, states parties are to submit a report to the Committee within two years of the entry into force of the Protocol detailing the measures it has taken to implement the provisions of the Protocol. Thereafter states are to include in their five-year reports filed in terms of the CRC further information with respect to the implementation of the Protocol.

[46] J Karp, 'Reporting and the Committee on the Rights of the Child' in AF Bayefsky, *The Human Rights Treaty System in the 21st Century* (The Hague, Martinus Nijhoff, 2000) 35–37.

[47] D Drahoslav Štefánek (Chairperson-Rapporteur) 'Report of the Open-Ended Working Group to Explore the Possibility of Elaborating an Optional Protocol to the Convention

explained with reference to the fact that initially the philosophy was to create a non-antagonistic committee that would work 'with' states to meet their obligations, instead of 'against' states.[48] However, it is likely that this reasoning was used to justify the failure of creating such a complaints mechanism during the drafting of the CRC. Zermatten explained to me that the inclusion of such a complaints procedure was hotly debated during the drafting of the CRC, but over time it became clear that states would not ratify the Convention if such a mechanism were to be included.[49] This gives further credence to Happold's argument that those who participated in the drafting of the CRC were preoccupied with codifying existing state practice instead of creating the stronger norms needed to safeguard the interests of children.[50]

Recognising the weakness of not having a direct complaints procedure, the Committee began to encourage children and their representatives to use the complaints procedures of other treaty bodies where feasible and possible.[51] Whether a treaty body other than the CRC will provide an avenue for redress to a victim is dependent on considerations such as whether the relevant state has ratified the instrument, whether the substantive rights in the instrument cover the nature of the harm the victim had sustained, and whether the admissibility and jurisdictional threshold requirements relevant to the specific complaints procedure have been met. The complaints procedure of the Committee Against Torture, for example, may be a viable avenue for redress in some cases of violent recruitment and use of child soldiers,[52] but will certainly not be so in all such cases.

on the Rights of the Child to Provide a Communications Procedure', A/HRC/13/43 (21 January 2010) 19.

[48] M Verheyde, *A Commentary on the United Nations Convention on the Rights of the Child: Art 43–45: the UN Committee on the Rights of the Child* (The Hague, Brill, 2006) 7–8; the *Travaux Préparatoires* of the Convention also supports this contention, see S Detrick (ed), *The United Nations Convention on the Rights of the Child: A Guide to the 'Travaux Préparatoires'* (The Hague, Martinus Nijhoff, 1992) 539. The Committee on Economic, Social and Cultural Rights is the only other UN human rights treaty body that did not incorporate an individual complaints procedure in terms of its original mandate. However, as of 2008, this Committee can also consider individual complaints (Optional Protocol (General Assembly Resolution A/RES/63/117)).

[49] Zermatten, n 7 above.

[50] M Happold, *Child Soldier in International Law* (Manchester, Manchester University Press, 2005).

[51] Committee on the Rights of the Child—Working Methods, XI, Individual Communications, www2.ohchr.org. 'The Convention on the Rights of the Child has no mandate to accept and review individual complaints. However, the Committee recommends children or their representatives to refer to other treaty bodies . . . Much the same can be said for the special procedures of the Commission on Human Rights, including the mechanisms for urgent action and appeals, including the Special Rapporteurs on the Sale of Children, Child Prostitution and Child Pornography; on Torture; on Extrajudicial, Summary or Arbitrary Executions, or the Working Group on Arbitrary Detention.'

[52] Art 17 of the Convention against Torture and Other Cruel, Inhuman or Degrading Treatment or Punishment (entered into force on 26 June 1987) (CAT) 1465 UNTS 85. Art

In June 2009, an 'open-ended working group to explore the possibility of elaborating an optional protocol to the CRC to provide a communications procedure' (CRC Working Group) was established by the Human Rights Council.[53] The CRC Working Group first met from 16 to 18 December 2009. The effectiveness of complaints procedures in quasi-judicial international human rights mechanisms is a point of contention. However, the complaints procedures of some treaty bodies are more effective than others.[54] Therefore, the effectiveness of such a procedure is dependent, in part, on the way it is formulated and the powers it is afforded. It was thus a massive failure not to have included such a procedure in the mandate of the CRC at the time that the convention was negotiated. This has the further implication that, until recently, the Committee never engaged with victims directly, which has far-reaching effects, even on the work of the Committee within its existing mandate (that is to say, the mandate before the Communications Protocol came into effect). Specifically, in making recommendations to states parties, the Committee is privy only to the state party's report, and the information and context presented therein. Furthermore, instead of having a mandate to actively enforce the CRC, it has a more passive mandate to monitor state compliance with the CRC.[55] This potentially diminishes the status of the Committee in the eyes of states.

The Chairperson-Rapporteur of the drafting committee, Drahoslav Štefánek, noted that the accessibility of the procedure to children and their representatives is key to its success.[56] After the release of a revised draft of the Protocol in January 2011, it seemed that the procedure was going to be flawed in many respects.[57] The draft provided for individual communications, by individuals or groups of individuals;[58] collective communications;[59] interim measures;[60] inter-state communications;[61] and

22 of the CAT further provides that a state party must enter a declaration to the effect that that state accepts the Committee's jurisdiction relating to individual complaints. Furthermore, the Committee will not investigate a matter that has already been brought before another committee by the same petitioner, based on the same facts.

[53] Human Rights Council Resolution A/HRC/RES/11/1 (17 June 2009).

[54] The Human Rights Committee, established in terms of Art 29 of the International Covenant on Civil and Political Rights (entered into force on 23 March 1976) (ICCPR) 999 UNTS 171, is an example of a relatively effective treaty body with a complaints procedure.

[55] Art 44 of the CRC.

[56] Štefánek, n 47 above.

[57] Revised proposal for a draft optional protocol prepared by the Chairperson-Rapporteur of the Open-ended Working Group on an optional protocol to the Convention on the Rights of the Child to provide a communications procedure, A/HRC/WG.7/2/4 (13 January 2011) (Revised Draft Protocol).

[58] Art 6 of the Revised Draft Protocol.

[59] Ibid, Art 7.

[60] Ibid, Art 8.

[61] Ibid, Art 15.

an enquiry procedure for grave or systematic violations.[62] While the draft excluded the possibility for states to make reservations to the Protocol,[63] states could, by declaration, exclude the competence of the Committee to hear individual communications that related to either of the Protocols to the CRC.[64] Furthermore, an 'opt-in' clause limited the Committee's competence to hear collective and inter-state communications to instances where the relevant state accepts such competence expressly, by way of declaration.[65] This selective ratification regime would effectively have allowed states to enter de facto reservations to each of the complaints procedures, except individual complaints in relation to the CRC only (as states would have been able to exclude the Protocols by declaration) and the enquiry procedure for grave or systematic violations. The draft made no provision for states which were party to either of the current Protocols to the CRC but not to the CRC itself, such as the US, which is a party to the CIAC Protocol but not to the CRC. The selective ratification regime would thus have effectively allowed such a state to ratify the Protocol without being subject to any complaints procedure, except for the enquiry procedure for grave or systematic violations.

Fortunately, there were a number of improvements made to the draft Protocol and these were ultimately adopted. However, some of the shortcomings remain. The Protocol calls for the recognition of the agency of the child, with due weight being given to the age and maturity of the child.[66] The individual communications procedure was retained, but states party to one of the CRC Protocols but not the CRC itself are not allowed to exclude the operation of the individual communications procedure to the Protocols.[67] The Protocol allows for interim measures,[68] and has a strong focus on friendly settlement of disputes,[69] which is perhaps somewhat naïve but, at the same time, well suited to the nature of a treaty body, that is to say, a quasi-judicial body with no direct enforcement capabilities. The final Protocol no longer provides for a collective complaints procedure, as the draft did. However, the inter-state communications procedure was retained,[70] and remains subject to a state filing a declaration opting-in to the procedure.[71] Finally, the enquiry procedure for grave or systematic procedures is significant.[72] It affords the Committee considerable *proprio moto* powers to initiate an investigation after

---

[62] Ibid, Art 16.
[63] Ibid, Art 24.
[64] Ibid, Art 6(2).
[65] Ibid, Arts 7(1) and 15(1).
[66] Art 2 of the Communications Protocol.
[67] Ibid, Art 5(1).
[68] Ibid, Art 6.
[69] Ibid, Art 9.
[70] Ibid, Art 12.
[71] Ibid, Art 12(1).
[72] Ibid, Art 13.

receiving information of grave or systematic violations of the CRC or either of its substantive Protocols. Unfortunately, while an opt-in declaration is not required, states are specifically empowered to declare that it does not recognise the Committee's powers in this regard.[73]

Before its coming into force, Zermatten expressed the view that the proposed collective complaints procedure had great potential to be effectively used to prevent child soldiering.[74] However, he also stated that many states were opposed to this procedure—including developed states.[75] Accordingly, it is unfortunately probable that many states will not accept the Committee's competence in relation to such complaints and, where they do, it might be so that they will exclude the inquiry procedure for grave or systematic violations. It is very unfortunate that the collective communications procedure was done away with. In the earlier draft it was formulated in the following terms: 'national human rights institutions and ombudsman institutions as well as non-governmental organizations . . . may submit collective communications alleging recurring violations affecting multiple individuals of any of the rights [in the CRC and its Protocols]'.[76] This procedure could well have been used effectively to redress child soldier violations, as it allowed NGOs to take the initiative. The inquiry procedure for grave or systematic violations also has potential for addressing child soldier prevention:

> If the Committee receives reliable information indicating grave or systematic violations by a State party of rights set forth in the Convention [or its Protocols] the Committee shall invite the State party to cooperate in the examination of the information and, to this end, to submit observations without delay with regard to the information concerned.[77]

Looking to the future, civil society has an immensely important role to play in lobbying states to ratify the Protocol without excluding any part of its operation. Admissibility presents a final stumbling block to many victims in accessing the Committee. The Committee should interpret the exhaustion of local remedies and the unavailability of such domestic remedies expansively, so as to guarantee greater protection to more children.[78] This argument is consonant with the recognition that the possibility of child victims of abuses such as military use and recruitment gaining access to municipal courts is a virtual impossibility in many parts of the world.[79]

---

[73] Ibid, Art 13(7).
[74] Zermatten, n 7 above.
[75] Ibid.
[76] Art 7(2) of the Revised Draft Protocol.
[77] Art 13(1) of the Communications Protocol.
[78] Ibid, Art 9.
[79] This is one of the key problems I observed in the DRC. Even where there are mechanisms that can effectively address violations committed against children, the children most in need of these mechanisms do not have access to them for a variety of reasons.

*ii. The Committee's Approach to Exercising its Mandate*

During my interview with Awich Pollar, he argued that, in relation to child soldiering, a major compliance gap exists in relation to non-state actors.[80] In this regard, he said that a lacuna exists in the mandate of the CRC as the Committee engages with states parties whereas non-state actors do not really feature in the mandate of the Committee. This, however, is a limitation inherent to IHRL, and mechanisms that exist to promote and enforce instruments such as the CRC. In Chapters 3 and 4 I presented an in-depth analysis of the relationship between IHRL and IHL that specifically emphasises the distinguishing features of these legal regimes. One such distinguishing feature is the fact that IHRL creates obligations upon states only whereas, in the context of armed conflict, IHL creates obligations on state and non-state actors alike.[81] The mandate of the CRC is to monitor state compliance with the CRC and its Protocols, and, with the coming into force of the complaints procedure, to play a more proactive role in enforcing state compliance. This includes the obligation upon states to 'undertake all appropriate legislative, administrative, and other measures for the implementation of the rights recognized in the [CRC]'.[82] The work of the Committee thus relates to non-state entities indirectly. The Committee aims to ensure that states parties prohibit non-state actors from using and recruiting child soldiers. In many instances this is extremely difficult, as the state party is likely engaged in armed conflict with the very entity in relation to which the state must prevent the use and recruitment of child soldiers. However, there are many states that are allied to non-state entities known for their use and recruitment of child soldiers. In such instances the Committee can pressurise states to ensure compliance. However, within the contemporary framework of IHRL, it is not possible to extend the mandate of the Committee to include direct engagement with non-state actors. This is so primarily because such actors do not incur international law obligations in terms of the CRC or its Protocols and the CRC Committee's subject-matter jurisdiction extends only to the CRC and its Protocols.

As stated above, the Committee actively interprets the Convention in its 'concluding observations', which it makes in response to state party reports. Often, however, the Committee's concluding observations extend beyond the Committee's mandate. At the Committee's 48th session, for example, it considered the initial report on the implementation of the

---

[80] Pollar, n 8 above.
[81] See Chapter 3 above.
[82] Art 4 of the CRC.

CIAC Protocol by the United States.[83] Among many recommendations, the Committee recommended:

> the State party to review and raise the minimum age for recruitment into the armed forces to 18 years in order to promote and strengthen the protection of children through an overall higher legal standard.[84]
> . . .
> that the United States of America proceed to become a State party to the Convention on the Rights of the Child in order to further improve the protection of children's rights.[85]
> . . .
> that the State Party consider ratifying the following international instruments, already widely supported in the international community: . . . The Convention on the Prohibition of the Use, Stockpiling, Production and Transfer of Anti-Personnel Mines and on their Destruction 1997.[86]

The first two recommendations relate directly to the subject-matter of the Committee's mandate. Although the US's policy of recruiting children of seventeen on a voluntary basis is within the confines of the Protocol,[87] the Committee nevertheless encouraged the increase of the minimum age for voluntary recruitment to eighteen. The Committee is justified in making such recommendations, as these comments were made in relation to the CIAC Protocol, the preamble of which provides:

> Noting that Article 1 of the Convention on the Rights of the Child specifies that, for the purposes of that Convention, a child means every human being below the age of 18 years unless, under the law applicable to the child, majority is attained earlier . . . Convinced that an optional protocol to the Convention that raises the age of possible recruitment of persons into armed forces and their participation in hostilities will contribute effectively to the implementation of the principle that the best interests of the child are to be a primary consideration in all actions concerning children.

This Protocol is expressly included in the mandate of the Committee. As such, there is no reason why the Committee cannot advocate for states parties to comply not only with the letter of the law, but also with the ultimate goals and aspirations of the instrument.

Conversely, no provision of the Convention on the Prohibition of the Use, Stockpiling, Production and Transfer of Anti-Personnel Mines and on their Destruction has direct bearing on any obligations owed by

---

[83] Committee on the Rights of the Child, 'Report on the Forty-eighth Session', CRC/C/48/3 (16 November 2009), para 25.
[84] Ibid, para 25(16).
[85] Ibid, para 25(23).
[86] Ibid, para 25(24)(c).
[87] 10 USC § 505.

the US in terms of the Protocol.[88] The enforcement of this convention has a bearing on the protection of children during armed conflict. Nevertheless, the Committee's recommendation goes beyond its mandate: 'examining the progress made by States Parties in achieving the realization of the obligations undertaken'.[89]

This, of course, raises some concerns related to *pacta sunt servanda*. The US ratified the Protocol knowing that it incurs specific obligations and agreeing to the jurisdiction of a quasi-judicial treaty body with a specific mandate determined by a legal instrument, nothing more. Recommendations such as the last one made by the Committee regarding the US report are not very useful, and are beyond the Committee's powers. This treaty body is already relatively weak, due to not having a direct enforcement mechanism. By making such recommendations, the Committee is likely making it easier for states to dismiss their recommendations, as these recommendations may come to be seen as the work of activists and not interpretations of legal obligations by a quasi-judicial mechanism.

It is very likely that the excessively wide interpretation the Committee employs in discharging its mandate is symptomatic of the very narrow and passive mandate it has been afforded. With the coming into force of the new Protocol, the Committee should recreate itself around this more proactive mandate—by staying strictly within the mandate but at the same time relentlessly pursuing compliance by states parties in terms of its mandate.

## C. The Security Council

The General Assembly was the first political organ of the UN to adopt a resolution on children in armed conflict, which it did in 1993.[90] Three years later, the Security Council began adopting resolutions in relation to specific countries in which it, inter alia, addressed child soldiering in the relevant country.[91] However, the issue of children in armed conflict was placed formally on the agenda of the Security Council in 1998. Since then:

- the Council has adopted a series of ten resolutions on children in armed conflict[92] (the resolutions that have thus

---

[88] Convention on the Prohibition of the Use, Stockpiling, Production and Transfer of Anti-Personnel Mines and on their Destruction (entered into force on 18 September 1997) 2056 UNTS 211.

[89] Art 43(1), CRC.

[90] General Assembly Resolution 48/157 20 of December 1993.

[91] The first such resolution was Security Council Resolution 1071 of 30 August 1996 in relation to the conflict in Liberia.

[92] Security Council Resolution 1261 of 25 August 1999; Security Council Resolution 1314 of 11 August 2000; Security Council Resolution 1379 of 20 November 2001; Secu-

far been adopted call various parties to action, including UN institutions and entities distinct from the UN. UN institutions must act in accordance with these resolutions, whereas they are of recommendatory persuasion to external entities);

- the Council devotes a day of debate to children in armed conflict each year;
- the Secretary-General reports annually to the Security Council itself on the situation of children in armed conflict, and directly names parties who act in violation of their obligations in using and recruiting child soldiers;[93]
- child protection has been integrated into the mandates of peacekeeping missions—and personnel are trained accordingly;[94]
- the 'well-being and empowerment of children affected by armed conflict' has been integrated into all peace processes. Furthermore, post-conflict recovery and reconstruction planning, programmes and strategies now prioritise issues concerning children affected by armed conflict;[95]
- child protection has been 'mainstreamed' in all relevant facets of the work of UN institutions;[96]
- a Monitoring and Reporting Mechanism (MRM) has been created in relation to children in armed conflict;[97] and
- a Security Council Working Group on children and armed conflict (SCWG) has been established.[98]

Nevertheless, like the rest of this chapter, the purpose of this section is not to create a narrative account of Security Council engagement with child soldiering.[99] Instead, it is to extrapolate those areas of engagement best suited to child soldier prevention and critically analyse the effectiveness of their work in this regard.

In terms of its Chapter VII powers, the Security Council can adopt resolutions binding upon UN member states.[100] It is thus the most pow-

---

rity Council Resolution 1460 of 30 January 2003; Security Council Resolution 1539 of 22 April 2004; Security Council Resolution 1612 of 26 July 2005; Security Council Resolution 1882 of 4 August 2009; Security Council Resolution 1998 of 12 July 2011; Security Council Resolution 2068 of 19 September 2012; Security Council Resolution 2143 of 7 March 2014.

[93] Security Council Resolution 1379, para 16.

[94] Security Council Resolution 1379, paras 2 and 10(a); Security Council Resolution 1460, para 9; Security Council Resolution 1539, para 7; Security Council Resolution 1612, para 12.

[95] Security Council Resolution 1882, para 15.

[96] Security Council Resolution 1539, para 8; Security Council Resolution 1612, para 18.

[97] Security Council Resolution 1612, paras 2–3.

[98] Ibid, para 8.

[99] For such an account see Happold, n 50 above, 34–53

[100] Art 24 of the UN Charter. For a detailed account of the Chapter VII Powers of the UN, see E De Wet, *The Chapter VII Powers of the United Nations Security Council* (Oxford, Hart Publishing, 2004).

erful entity that directly engages with child soldiering. Unfortunately, the Council is yet to adopt such a binding resolution in which it takes targeted action in relation to child soldiering. It does, however, have the potential to do so, as it held in 2000 that:

> the committing of systematic, flagrant and widespread violations of international humanitarian and human rights law, including that relating to children, in situations of armed conflict may constitute a threat to international peace and security, and in this regard reaffirms its readiness to consider such situations and, where necessary to adopt appropriate steps.[101]

This is a very significant step. First, as has been stated, for the Security Council to take targeted, binding action against parties who use or recruit child soldiers, it must issue a Chapter VII resolution—the situation therefore has to 'constitute a threat to international peace and security'.[102] Furthermore, for the Council to refer a matter to the ICC, it must adopt a resolution under Chapter VII of the UN Charter.[103] The implication of Resolution 1314 is that the Security Council will be able to refer a matter to the ICC where the alleged crimes are limited to the use or recruitment of child soldiers, as such deeds may threaten international peace and security (in a concrete case, however, the Council must be of the view that it does threaten such peace and security). Popovski points out that Resolution 1314's reference to international peace and security is not an empty threat.[104] The Security Council has adopted resolutions under Chapter VII related to children in armed conflict since Resolution 1314. For example, the Security Council adopted Resolution 1332 under its Chapter VII powers dealing with the situation in the DRC.[105] Among other things, the resolution demanded 'an effective end to the recruitment, training and use of children'.[106] It did not, however, impose any targeted measures against violating parties that failed to end the use and recruitment of child soldiers. While these resolutions do not pertain to child soldiering directly, the Security Council has thus far referred two situations to the Prosecutor of the ICC by way of Security Council Chapter VII Resolutions.[107] Child soldiering is proscribed by the Rome Statute of the ICC, and as such the international crime of child

---

[101] Security Council Resolution 1314 of 2000, para 9.

[102] Art 24(1) of the UN Charter.

[103] Art 13 of the Rome Statute.

[104] V Popovski, 'Children in Armed Conflict: Law and Practice of the United Nations' in K Arts and V Popovski (eds), *International Criminal Accountability and the Rights of Children* (Cambridge, Cambridge University Press, 2006) 44–45.

[105] Security Council Resolution 1332 of 14 December 2000.

[106] Ibid, para 10. Arts and Popovski, n 104 above, 44, states that 165 children were returned to UNICEF as a result of this resolution.

[107] Security Council Resolution 1593 of 31 March 2005 referred the situation in Darfur to the Office of the Prosecutor; and Security Council Resolution 1970 of 26 February 2011 referred the situation in Libya to the Office of the Prosecutor.

soldier enlistment, conscription or use can be charged in the context of such a Security Council referral.

Regular and continuous engagement with child soldier prevention from within the Security Council occurs only in the context of the MRM and the SCWG.

*i. Monitoring and Reporting Mechanism and the Security Council Working Group*

The MRM serves to 'collect and provide timely, objective, accurate and reliable information' on six situations affecting children that have been identified by the SRSG as most urgently deserving attention,[108] including 'recruiting or using child soldiers'.[109] The implementation of the MRM is focused on the parties to conflict named in the Secretary-General's report pursuant to Resolutions 1379 and 1882.[110] A country-level task force is set up in each of these countries and must submit a bimonthly report on 'grave violations against children'. The country-level task forces are composed of a variety of actors from within UN functionaries and NGOs. These task force reports are transmitted to the SRSG, who then reviews, consolidates and compiles the reports into monitoring and compliance reports. She then submits these reports to the SCWG. As of 3 August 2011, the MRM has been implemented in fifteen countries.[111] The work of the DRC country task force is discussed Chapter 7.[112]

The SCWG consists of all members of the Security Council and meets in closed session. The principal function of the SCWG is to review reports of the MRM.[113] In this context, the SCWG is tasked with making recommendations to the Security Council on possible measures to be taken against entities that, in terms of the MRM, violate any of the six grave breaches specifically identified, including recruiting or using child soldiers.[114] The Council has threatened persistent violators with targeted sanctions on numerous occasions.[115] In a recent resolution relevant to child soldiering, the Council requested 'enhanced communication between the Working Group and relevant Security Council Sanctions

---

[108] Ibid, para 5(c).

[109] Annual Report of the Secretary-General on Children in Armed Conflict (9 February 2005), para 68.

[110] For the operation of the MRM see ibid, 58–64.

[111] Report of the Special Representative of the Secretary-General for Children and Armed Conflict A/66/256 (3 August 2011), para 14.

[112] See Chapter 7 below.

[113] Ibid.

[114] To date, the working group has considered reports from 32 different countries and made recommendations relevant to each one.

[115] Security Council Resolution 1539, para 5(c); Security Council Resolution 1612, para 9; Security Council Resolution 1882, para 7(c); and Security Council Resolution 1998, para 9(c–d).

Committees, including through the exchange of pertinent information on violations and abuses committed against children in armed conflict'.[116] Furthermore, the Council has directed the SCWG, with the support of the SRSG, to 'consider, within one year, a broad range of options for increasing pressure on persistent perpetrators of violations and abuses committed against children in situations of armed conflict'.[117] This period expired on 12 July 2012. In complying with this request, the SRSG has already briefed the Security Council Committee concerning Somalia and Eritrea, proposing that grave violations against children be designated criteria for sanctions.[118] The Security Council has acted in this regard, adding such violations as designated criteria for sanctions in relation to Somalia and Eritrea.[119] The SRSG has, however, said that 'targeted and graduated sanctions should be applied against persistent perpetrators as a measure of last resort, when all other means have failed to end impunity for crimes committed against children'.[120]

While effect has been given to the first part of Otunnu's vision of creating a MRM, the second part, that reports produced by the MRM 'should, in turn, serve as "triggers for action"', is only just becoming a reality.[121] I am still sceptically aware that designating grave violations against children as criteria for sanctions does not necessarily mean that such sanctions will be imposed. The potential success of monitoring and reporting is based wholly on targeted action being taken once patterns of child soldier use and recruitment have been identified. To be effective in preventing child soldiering, I am of the view that the Security Council must follow up what can still be construed as political rhetoric—threats of sanction, with targeted action—with actually implementing such sanctions. Within the framework of the Council's Chapter VII powers, it should, where needed and only against persistent violators, adopt targeted action. Such action is similar to Resolution 1332, which was adopted in relation to the DRC and is discussed above— but, unlike Resolution 1332, targeted action, including sanctions, must be implemented against such persistent violators. Indeed, the first time the Council threatened violating parties with sanctions was in 2004.[122] Armed groups within nine specific countries have been consistently included in each of the Secretary-General's lists of violating parties that

[116] Security Council Resolution 1998, para 9(c).
[117] Ibid, para 21.
[118] Report of the Special Representative, n 101 above, para 60.
[119] Security Council Resolution 2002 of 29 July 2011.
[120] Report of the Special Representative, n 101 above, para, 59.
[121] O Otunnu, 'Protection of Children Affected by Armed Conflict Report of the Special Representative of the Secretary-General for Children and Armed Conflict', A/58/328 (29 August 2003), para 82.
[122] Security Council Resolution 1539, para 5(c).

have been published since 2004.[123] This indicates clearly that monitoring and reporting, an important component in the process of child soldier prevention, must be followed up with targeted sanctions to be effective in preventing child soldiering. What stands in the way of such sanctions is political will,[124] both by members of the Security Council in adopting such sanctions and by members of the UN in complying fully with Security Council resolutions.

## D. The Office of the Special Representative to the Secretary-General on Children and Armed Conflict

The Machel report recommended that a Special Representative to the Secretary-General on Children and Armed Conflict (SRSG) be appointed.[125] The first SRSG, Olara Otunnu was appointed in 1998, and served in that capacity until 2005. His successor, Radhika Coomaraswamy, took office during April 2006 and served until July 2012.[126] The current SRSG, Leila Zerrougui, was appointed during September 2012. The SRSG is mandated to:

(a) Assess progress achieved, steps taken and difficulties encountered in strengthening the protection of children in situations of armed conflict;
(b) Raise awareness and promote the collection of information about the plight of children affected by armed conflict and encourage the development of networking;
(c) Work closely with the Committee on the Rights of the Child, relevant United Nations bodies, the specialized agencies and other competent bodies, as well as non-governmental organizations;
(d) Foster international cooperation to ensure respect for children's rights in these situations and contribute to the coordination of efforts by Governments, relevant United Nations bodies, . . . regional and sub-regional organizations, other competent bodies and non-governmental organizations.[127]

In order to fulfil this mandate, the SRSG identified the following 'core activities':

---

[123] See Chapter 2 above.

[124] K Vandergrift, 'International Law Barring Child Soldiers in Combat: Problems in Enforcement and Accountability, Question and Answer Session' (2004) 37 *Cornell International Law Journal* 555, 556.

[125] G Machel, 'Promotion and Protection of the Rights of Children: Impact of Armed Conflict on Children' UN Doc A/51/306 (26 August 1996) (Machel Report), paras 266–69. The mandate was created in terms of General Assembly Resolution 51/77 of 12 December 1996.

[126] Ms Karin Sham Poo acted as SRSG on an interim basis from August to October 2005.

[127] General Assembly Resolution 57/77 of 12 December 1996, para 36.

(a) Public advocacy to build greater awareness and to mobilize the international community for action;
(b) Promoting the application of international norms and traditional value systems that provide for the protection of children in times of conflict;
(c) Undertaking political and humanitarian diplomacy and proposing concrete initiatives to protect children in the midst of war;
(d) Making the protection and welfare of children a central concern in peace processes and in post-conflict programmes for healing and rebuilding.[128]

The SRSG highlighted 'participation of children in armed conflict' as a key focus area early on.[129] Upon assuming office, Zerrougui initiated the 'Children, Not Soldiers' campaign, aimed at eradicating the use and recruitment of child soldiers by governmental forces by 2016. To the credit of all who have served as SRSG on children and armed conflict, they have engaged much more directly in efforts aimed at preventing child soldiering than their mandate may be interpreted.[130] Indeed, as was stated earlier, Ms Coomaraswamy expressed to me that her role as SRSG was best fulfilled by addressing grave violations committed against children during armed conflict directly, as opposed to more broad engagement. Unlike the situation with the CRC, this does not create any problems, as the SRSG is not a treaty body the mandate of which is determined in narrow terms by international law.

Two areas in which the SRSG has been particularly successful in direct action against the use and recruitment of child soldiers are undertaking field missions and obtaining concrete commitments from armed forces and groups to cease the recruitment and use of child soldiers.[131] Of course, such concrete commitments are only complied with in limited cases.[132] On the indirect level, the SRSG remains active in raising global awareness, engaging with civil society and enhancing legal and norma-

---

[128] O Otunnu, 'Protection of Children Affected by Armed Conflict Report of the Special Representative of the Secretary-General for Children and Armed Conflict', A/54/430 (1 October 1999), para 2.

[129] O Otunnu, 'Protection of Children Affected by Armed Conflict Report of the Special Representative of the Secretary-General for Children and Armed Conflict', A/53/482 (12 October 1998).

[130] The mandate of the Office of the SRSG for Children and Armed Conflict speaks generally to the Office's indirect role, as it utilises language such as 'assesses', 'raise awareness and promote' and 'foster international cooperation'.

[131] See Chapter 7 below. During her visit to the Central African Republic during May 2008, the SRSG obtained commitments from the Armée populaire pour la restauration de la République et de la démocratie (APRD) that they will release all children associated with their forces. On 7 July 2009 the APRD lived up to their commitment and released all 182 children associated with their forces to UNICEF. See R Coomaraswamy, 'Report of the Special Representative of the Secretary-General for Children and Armed Conflict', A/64/254 (6 August 2009), para 61.

[132] M Wessells, *Child Soldiers: From Violence to Protection* (Boston, MA, Harvard University Press, 2006) 236–37; PW Singer, *Children at War* (Oakland, CA, University of California Press, 2006) 143–44; Happold, n 50 above, 40–42.

tive frameworks.[133] NGO groups already champion most, if not all, of these areas of indirect engagement. Nevertheless, the office of the SRSG brings with it the authority of the Secretary-General of the UN. It may also be argued that this brings with it a degree of circumspection, as the UN is often perceived to be pro-government by non-state armed groups in countries where the UN has an established peace mission.[134]

Since 2001, the Secretary-General has been mandated to attach to his annual reports on children in armed conflict a list of parties to armed conflict that use or recruit child soldiers.[135] In practice, it is the SRSG that compiles these lists. Popovski is of the view that 'this was the end of tactful diplomacy'.[136] In other words, he asserts that directly engaging with armed groups and forces, and in so doing negotiating the end of the use and recruitment of child soldiers, is mutually exclusive with naming and shaming the violating parties. This argument is, however, premised on an assumption that violating states and armed groups will be less inclined to engage in 'tactful diplomacy' when their names may be put on a published list of offenders, which is questionable. Indeed, violating parties might be more willing to engage with the SRSG and provide concrete commitments in order to be excluded from the Secretary-General's list.

Although the SRSG has achieved much by way of engaging with governments and arguing for the disarmament, demobilisation and reintegration (DDR) of children, this is still a very critical, time-sensitive phase of ensuring compliance with child soldier prohibitions. The inherent value of legal norms to demand compliance may be lost if the relevant norms, or class of norms, have come to be seen as formal prohibitions, the violation of which has no adverse consequences. The successes of yesterday must not blind us from the suffering of today. As former UNICEF Executive Director, James Grant, said, 'as our capacity to do good has increased, it is gradually becoming unacceptable ethically not to use that capacity, or to exclude nations, communities or individuals from the benefits of progress. Morality marches with changing capacity.'[137] Isolated and anecdotal success does not amount to having entered 'an era of application'. The SRSG has functioned very effectively

---

[133] 'Report of the Special Representative of the Secretary-General for Children and Armed Conflict', A/66/256 93 (August 2011), para 20.

[134] See Chapter 7, where the United Nations Mission in the Democratic Republic of the Congo (MONUC) serves as a good example not only of the UN being perceived as biased, but of where the UN forces play an active role engaging enemy forces.

[135] Security Council Resolution 1379, para 16. This mandate has been slightly altered since; see Chapter 2 above.

[136] Popovski, n 104 above, 46.

[137] JP Grant, 'Child Health and Human Rights', address to the Committee on Health and Human Rights Lecture Programme (Institute of Medicine, 1994).

to date. This is probably largely due to the commitment and competencies of those who have held this position.

The one area in which the SRSG should focus more attention is her function as a focal point among all UN functionaries engaged in child soldiering.[138] Given the extent of the UN as an organisation, the scope for duplication of work is tremendous. Both Zermatten and Pollar indicated that the CRC Committee has no relationship with the SCWG.[139] The SRSG, on the other hand, remains actively involved with both the CRC Committee and the SCWG. However, she should also facilitate a relationship between these entities, and other key entities engaged with child soldier prevention, in light of the fact that these two bodies often engage with the same states on exactly the same subject matter; form part of the same organisation; and share the same goals.

### III. AFRICAN UNION ENGAGEMENT WITH CHILD SOLDIER PREVENTION

This section analyses the potential of the African Court to engage with child soldier prevention. The African Children's Committee is included in the analysis as it is an African intergovernmental organisation with the authority to transmit cases directly to the African Court. Neither of these bodies has generated any significant jurisprudence, and none specifically on child soldiering.

#### A. The African Committee of Experts on the Rights and Welfare of the Child

As was stated earlier, the African Children's Committee was created in terms of the African Charter on the Rights and Welfare of the Child, which provides that 'States Parties to the present Charter shall take all necessary measures to ensure that no child shall take a direct part in hostilities and refrain in particular, from recruiting any child'.[140]

The African Children's Committee has been in existence since 2001, but was rather inactive until November 2008, when the Committee exam-

---

[138] As she is mandated to 'foster international cooperation to ensure respect for children's rights in these situations and contribute to the coordination of efforts by Governments, relevant United Nations bodies, . . . regional and sub-regional organizations, other competent bodies and non-governmental organizations' (General Assembly Resolution 57/77, para 36(d)).

[139] Zermatten, n 7 above; Pollar, n 8 above.

[140] Art 22(2), African Children's Charter.

ined state reports for the first time.[141] The Committee's mandate is much broader than that of the CRC Committee, and includes examining state reports,[142] undertaking fact-finding missions,[143] promoting the African Children's Charter and the rights of the child in general.[144] It also has a mandate to hear individual and inter-state communications.[145]

A 'Communication on violations of the Rights of the Child in the North of Uganda' has been heard by the Committee which, among other things, relates to the use and recruitment of child soldiers in Northern Uganda. Unfortunately, the findings of the Committee on this communication, which has been finalised, has not yet been published.[146]

The Committee's findings have the force of recommendations, and the ineffectiveness of the Committee is one indicator of the level of political will among states parties to engage further with child rights. The Committee has recently been rejuvenated, and there has been a marked increase in the number of state reports received. It is hoped that more extensive use will be made of the Committee, such as the individual communication in relation to Northern Uganda. However, the strongest role of the Committee in relation to the prevention of child soldiering relates to the status of the Committee as an 'African intergovernmental organisations', meaning it is one of the gatekeeper entities that hold the key for access to the African Court.[147] It is this feature of the Committee that warrants its inclusion in this analysis.

## B. African Court on Human and Peoples' Rights

Outside of the war crimes tribunals, the only international judicial mechanism that potentially has subject-matter jurisdiction over child soldier prohibitive norms is the African Court, established pursuant to a Protocol to the African Charter on Human and Peoples' Rights (Court Protocol).[148] The Court commenced its functions during November 2006.

---

[141] J Sloth-Nielsen and BD Mezmur, 'Out of the Starting Blocks: The 12th and 13th Sessions of the African Committee of Experts on the Rights and Welfare of the Child' (2009) 9 *African Human Rights Law Journal* 336, 342–5.

[142] Art 43–44, African Children's Charter.

[143] Ibid, Art 45(1).

[144] Ibid, Art 42.

[145] Ibid, Art 44.

[146] '21st Session of the African Committee of Experts on the Rights & Welfare of the Child' (15–19 April 2013) ACERWC//RPT (XXI), para 96. In this report the Committee indicated that it had taken a decision on this communication, and that the 'decision will be published in the coming days'. A year has passed since, and the decision seems not to have been published yet.

[147] Art 5(1)(e) of the Protocol to the African Charter on Human and People's Rights on the Establishment of an African Court on Human and Peoples' Rights (entered into force 25 January 2004) OAU Doc OAU/LEG/EXP/AFCHPR/PROT (III) (Court Protocol).

[148] Ibid.

The child soldier prohibitive norm in question is Article 22 of the African Children's Charter. The African Court's counterparts in Europe and the Americas have a much more established jurisprudence. Nevertheless, neither the European Convention on Human Rights[149] nor the American Convention on Human Rights contains substantive provisions prohibiting child soldiering.[150] Furthermore, neither of these regional systems has a regional human rights instrument comparable to the African Children's Charter.

*i. Subject-Matter Jurisdiction*

The Court has jurisdiction over 'all cases and disputes submitted to it concerning the interpretation and application of the [African] Charter, this Protocol and any other relevant human rights instrument ratified by the States concerned'.[151] The Court thus has jurisdiction to interpret and apply the African Children's Charter in cases where it is relevant. However, the question remains open whether the Court's subject-matter jurisdiction extends far enough to include the CRC. Even if the Court is not competent to apply and enforce UN human rights treaties, its subject-matter jurisdiction remains the broadest of the three regional human rights courts.[152]

When the final version of the Court Protocol was adopted, it contained the words 'relevant human rights instrument', unlike the second draft, which had been tabled during the negotiation process towards adopting a Court Protocol and contained the words 'relevant African human rights instrument'.[153] This tends to indicate that the subject-matter jurisdiction of the Court was purposefully extended to include UN human rights treaties. However, according to Viljoen, the application of UN human rights treaties, such as the CRC, is problematic, so the court should interpret its subject-matter jurisdiction more narrowly and limit itself to African Human Rights Treaties. He makes this argument on the basis of three main reasons:

- should the relevant UN treaty provide its own enforcement mechanism, the party bringing the case will be in a position to 'forum shop'. In turn, this could mean a separate

---

[149] Convention for the Protection of Human Rights and Fundamental Freedoms (entered into force of 3 September 1953) ETS 5, 213 UNTS 222.

[150] American Convention on Human Rights (entered into force of 18 July 1978) OAS Treaty Series No 36, 1144 UNTS 123.

[151] Art 3(1), Court Protocol. See also Art 7 dealing with applicable law.

[152] F Viljoen, *International Human Rights Law in Africa* (Oxford, Oxford University Press, 2007) 444.

[153] Nouakchott Draft of the Protocol to the African Charter on Human and Peoples' Rights on the Establishment of an African Court on Human and Peoples' Rights (1997) OAU Doc OAU/LEGAL/EXP/AFCHPR/PRO (2).

jurisprudential development of the same treaty norm by two separate bodies;[154]

- where the relevant state party to the UN treaty did not accept an individual complaints procedure under that treaty, it may find itself answering to individual complaints through the workings of the Court Protocol;[155] and

- persons in states party to the Protocol may submit alleged violations of a UN treaty to a court with the power to render binding judgments, whereas persons in states party to the relevant UN treaty but not to the Court Protocol may not even submit individual communications to the applicable UN body, being the Committee on the Rights of the Child in the case of the CRC.[156]

The first two points raised do not arise in the context of the CRC, as the Committee on the Rights of the Child established in terms of the CRC does not have direct enforcement capabilities, nor has it until recently had an individual complaints mechanism (this has now changed).[157] However, the third reason has direct bearing on the CRC. Viljoen suggests two interpretations of the provision to prevent the 'absurd' implications it may have.[158] First, that the words 'states concerned' should be interpreted to mean 'all states parties to the [Court] Protocol'. In the context of the CRC, even such an interpretation would not prevent the Court from exercising jurisdiction over the CRC, as the only state that can potentially ratify the Protocol without having ratified the CRC is Somalia. It is the only African state that has not (yet) ratified the CRC and it is foreseeable that, should Somalia be in a position to ratify international instruments, it will ratify the CRC before the Court Protocol.[159] In fact, an equal number of African states are party to the CRC as are members of the African Union.[160] Viljoen's second suggestion is that the word 'relevant' should be so interpreted that UN treaties are not relevant or appropriate in the regional African human rights sense of the word.[161]

---

[154] Viljoen, n 152 above, 446.

[155] Ibid.

[156] Ibid.

[157] See Chapter 5 above.

[158] Viljoen, n 152 above, 446–47.

[159] The Transitional Federal Government (TFG) of Somalia announced on 20 November 2009 their plans to ratify the CRC. The previous TFG signed the CRC on 9 May 2002: see News Note, 'UNICEF Welcomes Decision by the Somali Transitional Federal Government to Ratify the Convention on the Rights of the Child' (UNICEF, 20 November 2009), available at www.unicef.org.

[160] In Africa only Somalia is not a party to the CRC and only Morocco is not a member of the African Union.

[161] Viljoen, n 152 above, 446–47.

On the other hand, many commentators argue that UN human rights treaties are included in the Court's subject-matter jurisdiction.[162] Both the text of the Court Protocol and its drafting history suggest that the Court does in fact enjoy such wide jurisdiction. Furthermore, a Protocol has been opened for ratification aimed at merging the African Court on Human and Peoples' Rights and the African Court of Justice (Merger Protocol).[163] Although this protocol is unlikely to enter into force, it is instructive to note that, in terms of the Merger Protocol, the Court will definitely have jurisdiction in relation to UN human rights treaties such as the CRC.[164] For the time being, primacy should be afforded to African regional instruments. UN treaties should only be interpreted and applied secondarily, if at all. The Court will surely, as a matter of course, deal with this issue early on. The discussion that follows is not dependent on which substantive child soldier prohibitive norm is applicable (African Children's Charter or CRC), as these treaty norms have been discussed independently in Chapter 4. Rather, the practicalities involved in the Court's exercise of jurisdiction over matters related to child soldiering are assessed.

*ii.* Locus Standi

The African Court has both contentious and advisory jurisdiction.[165] The following entities have access to the Court: the African Commission on Human and Peoples' Rights (the Commission); the State Party which has lodged a complaint to the Commission; the State Party against which the complaint has been lodged at the Commission; the State Party the citizen of which is a victim of human rights violation; and African IGOs.[166] States parties which have an interest in a matter may also request the

---

[162] Duy Phan argues that all Human Rights treaties are included, but that this is undesirable (H Duy Phan, 'A Blueprint for a Southeast Asian Court of Human Rights' (2008–09) 10 *Asian–Pacific Law & Policy Journal* 384, 398–99). Others argue that there is merit in such broad subject-matter jurisdiction (M Samb, 'Fundamental Issues and Practical Challenges of Human Rights in the Context of the African Union' (2009) 15 *Annual Survey of International & Comparative Law* 61, 69–69; G Mukundi Wachira, 'African Court on Human and Peoples' Rights: Ten Years On and Still No Justice' (Minority Rights Group International, 2008) 19); NJ Ubombana, 'Towards the African Court on Human and Peoples' Rights: Better Late than Never' (2000) 3 *Yale Human Rights and Development Law Journal* 45; RW Eno, 'The Jurisdiction of the African Court on Human and Peoples' Rights' (2002) 2 *African Human Rights Law Journal* 223, 226–27.

[163] The Protocol on the Statute of the African Court of Justice and Human Rights was adopted by the Eleventh Ordinary Session of the Assembly, held in Sharm El-Sheikh, Egypt on 1 July 2008 (Merger Protocol). For more on the history of the Merger Protocol see I Kane and AC Motala, 'The Creation of a New African Court of Justice and Human Rights' in MD Evans and R Murray (eds), *The African Charter on Human and Peoples' Rights: the System in Practice, 1986–2006* (Cambridge, Cambridge University Press, 2008) 406–40.

[164] Art 34(1) of the Merger Protocol.

[165] Art 4 of the Court Protocol.

[166] Ibid, Art 5(1)(e).

Court to be joined to the proceedings.[167] Lastly, relevant NGOs, with observer status before the Court, and individuals may be allowed to submit cases directly to the Court, provided that the relevant state party has made a declaration in terms of Article 34(6) of the Court Protocol accepting direct access by such parties to the Court.[168]

The likelihood of certain specific entities with standing to submit a matter to the Court is less than others. For example, it is unlikely that a state party against whom a complaint has been lodged at the Commission will submit the matter to the Court,[169] as the Court's judgment will be binding and enforceable, while the Commission's is not. Nevertheless, matters regarding child soldier prevention can be brought before the Court by any party with standing. Importantly, the African Children's Committee can also bring matters before the Court, as it is an African Intergovernmental Organisations.[170] The African Children's Committee should exercise this competency in serious matters regarding the use and recruitment of child soldiers. It is important to note that individuals have access to the complaints procedures of this Committee, thus the Committee can forward an individual complaint to the Court even where the relevant state had not made a declaration granting direct access to individuals.

In terms of child protection, direct access by NGOs and individuals surely offers the best potential avenue for protection. To date, twenty-seven out of a total of fifty-four countries have ratified the Court Protocol. Of these countries, only seven—Burkina Faso, Malawi, Mali, Tanzania, Ghana, Rwanda and Côte d'Ivoire—have entered a declaration allowing direct access to individuals and relevant NGOs with observer status before the Court.[171] Where the relevant state had not made a declaration, the communication will first have to be submitted to the Commission. However, for a matter to be admissible before the Commission, it has to be based on a violation of the African Charter on Human and Peoples' Rights (African Charter),[172] in addition to the other admissibility requirements as stipulated in Article 56 of the African Charter. The African Children's Charter is not a protocol to the African Charter; accordingly, a violation of the African Children's Charter does not amount to a violation of the African Charter.[173]

---

[167] Ibid, Art 5(1).

[168] Ibid, Art 5(3).

[169] The Commission was established in terms of Art 30 of the African Charter on Human and Peoples' Rights (entered into force on 21 October 1986) 1520 UNTS 217.

[170] The African Committee of Experts on the Rights and Welfare of the Child was established in terms of Art 32 of the African Children's Charter.

[171] As at August 2013.

[172] Art 56(2), African Charter; *Frederick Korvah v Liberia* Communication 1/88; *Frederick Korvah v Liberia*, Seventh Activity Report 1993–94, Annex IX.

[173] The Protocol to the African Charter on Human and Peoples' Rights on the Rights of Women in Africa (entered into force on 25 November 2005) CAB/LEG/66.6 does extend

The African Charter contains no explicit provisions on child soldiering. The question, then, is whether the matter has to be admissible before the Commission for the Commission to submit the matter to the Court. If it has to be, then the Commission will not be able to submit a communication to the Court that alleges the use and recruitment of child soldiers. The Commission's entitlement to submit such matters to the Court is exercised *ex mero motu*. As such, the likelihood is that this determination (ie whether the Commission must first determine admissibility before submitting the matter to the Court) will be subject to the interpretation of the Commission and not of the Court. There are three possibilities: the Commission will forward the matter to the Court without having dealt with it at all; the Commission will deal with the matter in part and then submit the matter to the Court; or the Commission will finalise the matter and then submit it.[174] The last option is widely supported by commentators.[175] In order for the Commission to make a decision on whether to submit the matter to the Court, the Commission should apply its mind to the matter at hand. Thus, my position is that, at the very least, the Commission will have to dispose of the matter partially. This will include a finding on admissibility. It is thus likely that the Court's subject-matter jurisdiction will be severely limited in instances where the matter is referred from the Commission—which will likely account for a great majority of cases that reach the court in relation to countries that did not make the Article 34(6) declaration.

The African Court has immense potential in the context of child soldier prevention. The realisation of this potential, however, is subject to numerous factors, the first being the number of states that enter declarations allowing direct access to individuals and NGOs with observer status.

The Court's remedial powers are very broad. It is entitled to make 'appropriate orders to remedy the violation', and this includes payment of fair compensation or reparations.[176] The Court is also entitled to adopt provisional measures.[177] In the context of child soldiering, the most obvious orders would be for states to cease the use and recruitment of child soldiers; enforce such legal measures on non-state groups; order the DDR of specific children; and pay reparations. The pessimistic reality

the substantive content of the African Charter as regards states parties to this Protocol, by reason that it is a Protocol (F Viljoen, 'Communications under the African Charter: Procedure and Admissibility' in Evans and Murray, n 163 above, 96).

[174] For a full discussion of the three possibilities see F Viljoen (ed), 'Judiciary Watch Report: The African Human Rights System: Towards the Coexistence of the African Commission on Human and Peoples' Rights and African Court on Human and Peoples' Rights' (Nairobi, Kenyan Section of the International Commission of Jurists, 2006).

[175] See, eg J Harrington, 'The African Court on Human and Peoples' Rights' in Evans and Murray, n 163 above, 305.

[176] Art 27(1) of the Court Protocol.

[177] Ibid, Art 27(2).

remains that, even though the Court delivers binding judgments, it is still subject to observance by the executive of the relevant state. Where the executive fails to adhere to the Court's findings, the judiciary of the relevant state should safeguard the sanctity of the Court's ruling. However, in many states in Africa the separation of the executive from the judiciary is theoretical at best.[178]

## IV. SUMMARY

When Otunnu spoke of entering 'an era of application' in relation to child soldier prevention, he did so *ex officio,* as a functionary forming part of the UN. As the international organisation charged with the maintenance of peace and security, and the safeguarding of the fundamental human rights of those who cannot safeguard their rights themselves, such as child soldiers, the UN forms the core of the international community's response. This was true in the context of norm creation—both the CRC and the CIAC Protocol were the products of initiatives internal to the UN. It must also be true in the context of norm application. In no way does this suggest that functionaries outside of the UN, such as the ICC and the African Court, play a second-tier role in preventing child soldiering. However, unlike these institutions, the reach of the UN is universal.

Each of the institutions discussed in this chapter operates on various levels of efficiency in preventing child soldiering. In some cases, such as the CRC Committee, its lack of success is due, in large part, to a weak mandate (this has recently been redressed, at least to some extent). In others, such as the African Court and the African Children's Committee, political will stands in the way of stronger engagement. Yet other functionaries, such as the SRSG, already operate at a very significant level of efficiency. Therefore, all these institutions and functionaries should constantly reassess their engagement with child soldier prevention and refine their approaches.

Some of the areas in which these institutions and functionaries can increase their level of engagement with child soldiering are significant, eg adopting the Protocol to the CRC creating an individual communications procedure in the CRC Committee; other areas where the level of engagement with child soldiering can be increased are more mundane. For example, the SRSG should pay more attention to her role as a focal point for UN engagement with child soldier prevention by facilitating a more streamlined relationship, or at least the exchange of

---

[178] CM Fombad, 'The Separation of Powers and Constitutionalism In Africa: The Case of Botswana' (2005) 25 *British Columbia Third World Law Journal* 301, 302.

reports and knowledge, between the CRC Committee and the SCWG. It should be borne in mind, however, that strengthening any one of the mechanisms analysed in this or any other chapter is unlikely to result in a significant decline in child soldiering. There are no 'silver bullet' solutions to issues such as child soldier prevention. However, each mechanism that is strengthened and rendered more effective, even to a limited extent, strengthens a strand in Cassel's rope that pulls human rights forward—and in this case, protects children from military use and recruitment—effecting social change incrementally.[179] Entering 'an era of application' does not require big changes to a few functionaries, but less significant changes to more functionaries, so that many strands of the rope are strengthened.

---

[179] D Cassel, 'Does International Human Rights Law Make a Difference?' (2001) 2 *Chicago Journal of International Law* 121, 126–134.

# 7

# Case Study: The Democratic Republic of the Congo

THE DEMOCRATIC REPUBLIC of the Congo (DRC) has become synonymous with atrocity and suffering. The DRC Mapping Report by the Office of the High Commissioner for Human Rights concluded that 'children did not escape the successive waves of violence that swept over the DRC, quite to the contrary: they were often its first victims'.[1] Indeed, children did not escape violence then, and they are still not escaping violence now. The DRC serves uniquely well as a case study regarding child soldier prevention, as virtually every incarnation of the child soldier phenomenon has occurred there during the last decade, and all the mechanisms and functionaries aimed at preventing child soldiering is or has recently been active in the DRC. This includes:

1. The existence of both international and non-international armed conflicts.
2. The use and recruitment of child soldiers by state armed forces, non-state actors and proxy forces.
3. National prosecutions for the crime of the use and recruitment of child soldiers.
4. The UN has a peace mission in DRC, the United Nations Organization Stabilization Mission in the Democratic Republic of the Congo (MONUSCO), that specifically incorporates child protection officers.[2] The new and unprecedented Force Intervention Brigade falls under the auspices of MONUSCO.

---

[1] 'Report of the Mapping Exercise Documenting the Most Serious Violations of Human Rights and International Humanitarian Law Committed within the Territory of the Democratic Republic of the Congo between March 1993 and June 2003' (Office of the High Commissioner for Human Rights, 2010), paras 37–39.

[2] MONUSCO was known as the United Nations Mission in the Democratic Republic of Congo (MONUC) until 2010. However, organisationally, MONUC transitioned to MONUSCO seamlessly. As such, the term MONUSCO will often be used to refer to the organisation both before and after 2010.

5. The ICCs first case, the *Lubanga* case, was referred to the ICC by the government of the DRC and the sole charge was the use and recruitment of child soldiers.[3]
6. Children have been used and recruited very extensively in armed conflict in the DRC for decades.

The case study serves to offer insight into the current international law response to child soldiering, and it makes three primary contributions: (i) it offers insights into whether international law has a role to play in preventing the use and recruitment of child soldiers; (ii) it presents a factual scenario against which to determine whether any headway has been made as of yet in the era of application; and (iii) it provides space where the practicalities of conclusions previously reached can be tested. The fieldwork I conducted in the DRC played a central role in informing my overall understanding of the practicalities of the child soldier phenomenon, and played an important role in directing the formulation and the structure of this book.

To this day, the use and recruitment of child soldiers occurs daily in the DRC, and in very recent history there have been escalations in child soldier use and recruitment. The Mouvement du 23-Mars (M23) comes to mind in this regard.

This chapter serves a different purpose to that of the other chapters that make up this book. Instead of investigating the legal environment in which child soldiering is to be prevented, or aiming at rendering the mechanisms that serve to prevent child soldiering more efficient, this chapter considers the engagement of these mechanisms with a contemporary country situation. Most of the mechanisms included in this chapter were previously discussed in Chapters 5 and 6. Accordingly, the conclusions drawn with regard to each of the mechanisms in those chapters, which are aimed at rendering the relevant mechanism more effective in preventing child soldiering, can be assessed in relation to a practical situation. The purpose of this chapter is thus not to draw new conclusions, but to test conclusions previously drawn.

I. METHODOLOGY

I had worked in areas plagued by child soldiering before I commenced this study and was always very impressed by the level of commitment of most people working to prevent the use and recruitment of child soldiers in the field. As there is no lack of commitment at this level of the enforcement process, I decided to do fieldwork, with one aim

---

[3] *Prosecutor v Thomas Lubanga Dyilo*, Trial Chamber I, Judgment, ICC-01/04-01/06 (2012) (*Lubanga* judgment).

being to establish what the real-world requisites are for the effective enforcement of child soldier prohibitive norms. As argued above, the DRC serves as the ideal case study in this regard. As such, this chapter is based on both field research and desk-based research. Within legal analysis, it is often difficult to bring into play data obtained through fieldwork. However, given the issues-based approach I advocate for, and the idea that the law must address social problems as they manifest rather than the perceptions of such problems that are often formed in strictly academic environments, I have opted to incorporate such data into the case study. Adopting an instrumentalist approach to law, and a 'law and sociology' theoretical basis, enhances the value of field research. Abstract legal reasoning will not necessarily contribute to social change if there are obstacles to change of which the abstract theorist is unaware.

I started planning the logistics for my field visit during early 2008. Although the conflict landscape in the DRC is always volatile and never predictable, it appeared at the time that the de-escalation in hostilities would have lasted until after my field visit. Indeed, my visit took place after the January 2008 peace agreement. Nevertheless, by the time I had got ready to depart for the DRC in October 2008, the conflict had escalated very significantly on two fronts. The 2008 Nord Kivu Conflict commenced on 26 October 2008 and lasted until 23 March 2009, which included my entire stay in the Nord Kivu province. It was also during this time that the Lord's Resistance Army (LRA) intensified their operations within the DRC. The 2008 Christmas massacre is the most notable example in this context. During the Christmas period of 2008, the LRA orchestrated attacks on several small villages in north-eastern DRC, hacking to death an estimated 500 people and abducting 160 children. The LRA's abduction of children had increased greatly from the second half of 2008.[4] For the period September 2008 to the end of March 2009, the LRA were responsible for the murder of 990 Congolese nationals and the abduction of 747 people, mostly children.[5]

In order to do a case study within the factual context of events, I conducted a four-month field visit to the DRC from October 2008 to January 2009. I decided to split my time between the Nord/Sud Kivu region, where the Nord Kivu War was ongoing, and the Ituri region, using the regional capitals Goma and Bunia as my base. I further decided not to conduct any fieldwork in relation to the LRA for two primary reasons: there was no way to do it safely, and conclusions drawn in relation to a fringe group with no clear political agenda can only be helpful in rela-

[4] M Fawke, 'UNHCR Visits Congolese Towns Attacked by Lord's Resistance Army' (UNHCR, 2008), available at www.unhcr.org.
[5] Comments made by R Redmond (UNHCR spokesperson) at the press briefing at the Palais des Nations in Geneva on 24 March 2009.

tion to the prevention of the use and recruitment of child soldiers in other areas to a very limited extent.

In determining the appropriate research methods and interview styles, the most important factors were what the study aimed to do and what it did not aim to do. It was not an anthropological study into the experiences of children in armed conflict. I therefore decided from the outset that I would not interview children (former or current child soldiers), as they would not be able to inform me on how child soldiering should be prevented. Furthermore, I had experience interviewing former child soldiers in Liberia and Sudan, in contexts unrelated to the current study, and had found their responses to be unreliable and of little academic value. This also prevented many potential ethical problems from arising in relation to interviewing children, specifically in a context where the interview relates to a child's memories of extremely disturbing events and where the information could indicate the criminal liability of the child for deeds she/he committed. As such, the respondent pool was made up of people working for the UN, in various capacities, and NGOs focused on preventing the use and recruitment of child soldiers. The overriding ethical consideration that no participant must be harmed or be subjected to scrutiny as a result of participation in this study was observed at all times.[6] The east and northeast of the DRC are very dangerous regions. This was particularly so in the Nord Kivu region in 2008. From an ethical point of view, researchers should not conduct research in circumstances where there is a grave threat to their life or well-being. However, I have extensive experience working in areas affected by armed conflict, specifically in Africa, and as a result I also have an extensive network of contacts in the region. These factors meant that I could conduct the fieldwork within acceptable parameters of safety and in an ethically sound manner.

Before departing for the DRC, I was aware that my methodology would have to be flexible. However, I did not anticipate the level of difficulty I encountered in getting respondents to speak on the record. The end of 2008 was a particularly volatile period in the DRC, and the UN, its agencies and the NGO community had their hands full. These organisations were not keen on sharing information in relation to their deployment at the time, as it could have had safety implications for their personnel. Therefore, while I was provided with very good intelligence on the use and recruitment of children on the ground, this was all done 'off the record'. Nevertheless, I managed to conduct a few very good interviews. Moreover, spending four months in war-affected regions of the DRC provided me with an insight into child soldier use and recruit-

    [6] J Boyden, 'Anthropology under Fire: Ethics, Researchers and Children in War' in J Boyden and J De Berry (eds), *Children and Armed Conflict* (Oxford, Berghahn, 2004) 238–41.

ment, and specifically the practicalities involved in preventing such use and recruitment, that I could never have obtained from desk research.

While the escalation of armed conflict is never desired, it may appear that doing fieldwork during a period of such escalation in armed conflict is well suited to achieving the research goals. The timing of my field-work did hold some advantages: for example, as discussed below, the re-escalation in hostilities presents an opportunity to gauge whether the successes achieved in the disarmament, demobilisation and reintegration (DDR) of child soldiers are attributable to the de-escalation in hostilities. However, such advantages are in fact few and far between. In address-ing the protection, or lack thereof, of children in armed conflict, and improvements in such protection, Kuper has stated:

> Clearly it is not feasible to conduct reliable empirical research, to stand in the midst of conflict and count child soldiers and/or child casualties, or to observe the treatment of children generally. Nor could such observation be sufficiently objective and comprehensive to be useful. So, how is it possible to ascertain if the relevant international law has any effect? Perhaps the most that can be done besides the painstaking analysis of individual conflicts, is to assess what seems likely to have any impact, and to take note of instances in which progress is made, for example when an army agrees to stop using soldiers under 18 years, or a rebel group agrees to release children it has captured.[7]

In a similar vein, the escalation of armed conflict does not present better opportunities for data collection; in fact, it seriously hampers such data collection. My research design was such that I aimed to interview a broad range of actors working for international organisations, most notably the UN and civil society, who operate in the field. I managed to arrange interviews with various people within the United Nations Mission in the Democratic Republic of the Congo (MONUC), the UN Peace Mission in the DRC. In only one of these meetings did the interviewee agree to me recording the interview and use the information publicly. This interview was with Estelle Nandy Ouattara, the child protection officer in MONUC's Bunia office.[8] Each of the other interviews conducted with MONUC staff was done on the basis that I was not to record the interview, or attribute the information to the individual interviewee. This was explained to me on the basis that, because of the escalation in armed conflict and the corresponding use and recruitment of child soldiers, the information is of strategic relevance and may not be published. However, MONUC had been criticised extensively during that same period within

---

[7] J Kuper, 'Children and Armed Conflict: Some Issues of Law and Policy' in D Fot-trell, *Revisiting Children's Rights: 10 Years of the UN Convention on the Rights of the Child* (Leiden, Brill, 2000).
[8] Interview conducted with Ms Ouattara on 13 November 2008, Bunia, DRC.

the media, and this likely contributed to the trouble I had in interviewing MONUC personal 'on the record'.

I did, however, manage to interview various people working within UN entities distinct from MONUC. In particular, I interviewed Ms Pernille Ironside, who was, at the time, a Child Protection Specialist for the United Nations Children's Fund (UNICEF) in Eastern DRC.[9] At present, Ironside is the UNICEF Child Protection Specialist in Emergencies, based in New York City. She is a great example that one person can make a huge contribution even in an organisation as vast as the UN.

Access to NGOs was equally difficult during this period, though for other reasons. With limited human and financial resources during periods of escalation in conflict, specifically if it occurs on an unpredictable level, NGOs have to utilise all their resources to their full capacity. As was communicated to me frequently, while NGOs fully support research such as this study, they simply do not have the time to commit to an interview. Of the NGOs, representative of whom I did manage to interview, the best data was obtained from Save the Children, Cooperazione Internazionale (COOPI) and the Salesian-run Don Bosco Ngangi centre for war orphans and at-risk children.

## II. THE CONTEMPORARY CONFLICT LANDSCAPE
## IN THE DRC: FROM THE DEMISE OF MOBUTO
## TO THE FORCE INTERVENTION BRIGADE

Joseph-Desiré Mobutu, who renamed himself Mobutu Sésé Seko Nkuku Ngbendu Wa Za Banga in 1971, meaning 'the all-powerful warrior who, because of his endurance and inflexible will to win, goes from conquest to conquest, leaving fire in his wake',[10] ruled the DRC (known as the Republic of Zaire for much of his rule) with an iron fist for more than three decades. By 1996, the DRC had spiralled into a virtual state of anarchy, with ethnic hatred very much at its core. The First Congo War began in November 1996 through the escalation of skirmishes on the mountainous borderlands of the DRC and Rwanda.[11] It ended barely seven months later, 2,000 kilometres away, with Laurent-Désiré Kabila's march on Kinshasa and the eventual overthrow of President Mobutu Sésé Seko.

The roots of the ongoing trepidations in the DRC are, however, found in its colonial history. The DRC has experienced continuous combat ever

---

[9] Interview conducted with Ms Ironside on 22 November 2008, Goma, DRC.

[10] M Wrong, *In The Footsteps of Mr Kurtz: Living on the Brink of Disaster in Mobutu's Congo* (New York, Harper Perennial, 2002) 4.

[11] For a full account of contemporary armed conflict in the DRC see JF Clark (ed), *The African Stakes of the Congo War* (New York, Palgrave Macmillan, 2002).

since it became independent on 30 June 1960. This is specifically true in the east and northeast of the country, and children have been used and recruited in every war fought in the DRC since independence. The Second Congo War, as well as numerous other conflicts that have subsequently occurred and are ongoing in the DRC, have at various times had an international and non-international character.[12]

Ethnicity has been the key factor in conflicts throughout the DRC for many years. At the core of the most recent conflicts lie the distinctions between Hutu and Tutsi[13] and between Hema and Lendu.[14] There are further ethnic groups who align themselves with one of the above-mentioned groups or with wholly separate identities, but who play less significant roles in armed conflict. Natural resources and politics create an even more volatile conflict landscape.[15] The recent conflicts have primarily been categorised as the First Congo War; the Second Congo War; the Kivu Conflict; the Ituri Conflict; and, more recently, the M23 rebellion. These conflicts overlap with one another and converge to the extent that a single perpetual conflict emerges.

Children are still recruited and used in active participation in hostilities in the DRC on a daily basis. Such use and recruitment occurs primarily in the context of the ongoing, low-intensity hostilities between the Hutu and Tutsi ethnic groups in the Kivu Provinces of the DRC, and the abduction of children by the (Ugandan) LRA in the northeast of the country. However, the Mai Mai groups (civil defence groups) that exist throughout the east of the DRC are often responsible for the escalation of violence in their areas.

Many so-called *génocidaires*, the perpetrators of the 1994 Rwandan genocide, crossed the border into the DRC soon after the genocide.[16] The strongest armed group consisting of former *génocidaires* is the Forces démocratiques de libération du Rwanda (FDLR), which is responsible for committing atrocities against people of Tutsi ethnicity on a continuous basis and who aim to ethnically cleans the Banyamulenge (ethnic Congolese Tutsis).[17] The Interahamwe, the principal architects of the Rwandan

---

[12] See, eg *Armed Activities on the Territory of the Congo (Democratic Republic of the Congo v Uganda)*, ICJ Reports 2005, 168.

[13] The Hutus and Tutsis are two rival ethnic groups in the Great Lakes region of Africa. Hutus far outnumber the Tutsis, but the Tutsis have taken up more elite positions in society. There are arguments that there is no longer any discernible difference between these two groups. This rivalry formed the basis of the 1994 Rwandan genocide.

[14] The Hema and Lendu are two ethnic groups located in the Ituri region of the DRC. The Hema are pastoralists and have a population of approximately 160,000 people. The Lendu number approximately 750,000 and are agriculturalists.

[15] ML Ross, 'How Do Natural Resources Influence Civil War? Evidence from Thirteen Cases' (2004) 58(1) *International Organization* 35.

[16] KC Dunn, 'A Survival Guide to Kinshasa: Lessons of the Father, Passed Down to the Son' in Clark, n 11 above, 56.

[17] K Vlassenroot, 'Citizenship, Identity Formation & Conflict in South Kivu: The Case of the Banyamulenge' (2002) 29(93/94) *Review of African Political Economy* 499.

genocide, are also allied with the FDLR. Opposed to the FDLR was the National Congress for the Defence of the People (CNDP). The CNDP operated under the leadership of General Laurent Nkunda until Nkunda's capture by the Rwandan Armed Forces on 22 January 2009. It is believed that Bosco Ntaganda took over from Nkunda as leader of the CNDP. However, the CNDP has since largely been integrated into the National Armed Forces of the DRC, the Forces Armées de la République Démocratique du Congo (FARDC).

I have mentioned before that sometimes there are individuals within the context of massive organisations, such as the UN, who make a tremendous singular contribution to the prevention of the use and recruitment of child soldiers. So, too, are there people on the opposite end of the spectrum, people who are responsible for the massive and continuous use and recruitment of child soldiers. Bosco 'The Terminator' Ntaganda is one such person. Ntaganda is of Tutsi ethnicity and was born in Rwanda. He commenced his career as a fighter/soldier during the early 1990s, when he joined the Rwandan Patriotic Army, fighting against the Hutu-led Rwandan government. After this, Ntaganda joined Thomas Lubanga's Union des Patriotes Congolais (UPC) and became chief of staff of the UPC's military faction, Forces Patriotiques pour la libération du Congo (FPLC). Significantly, the conflict in Ituri, in which the FPLC was involved. was an ethnic conflict between the Hema and Lendu. As a Tutsi, Ntaganda had no direct stake in that conflict. After the FPLC, Ntaganda joined Nkunda at the CNDP.

More recently, Ntaganda was a key figure in the M23 Rebellion, which lasted from 4 April 2012 until 7 November 2013. M23 was formed from the ranks of former CNDP forces who had been integrated into the national armed forces of the DRC following a peace agreement signed on 23 March 2009. The rebellion was focused against the government, as these forces believed the government to have violated the terms of the 23 March peace agreement. The highlight of the rebellion came with M23 taking control of Goma, the regional capital, on 20 November 2012.

Ntaganda unexpectedly surrendered himself to the United States Embassy in Kigali, Rwanda on 18 March 2013, and requested to be transferred to the ICC pursuant to a warrant that had been issued for his arrest. Many smaller factions, as well as the FARDC itself, have been and are involved in these hostilities. Most of them use and recruit child soldiers. This includes Mai Mai groups, who are civilian defence forces operating across the eastern parts of the DRC. Evidence strongly suggests that Bosco Ntaganda was responsible for the unlawful use and recruitment of child soldiers in virtually every armed group he operated in. Ntaganda stands charged before the ICC with the use, enlistment and conscription of children younger than fifteen. Each of the forms of child soldier crime (enlistment, conscription and use) are listed separately in the warrant of arrest.[18]

Since 2007, the LRA has been based primarily in the remote jungles of the Garamba National Park in north-eastern DRC.[19] This group continues to thrive purely on the basis of the vicious abduction of children.

III. MUNICIPAL AND INTERNATIONAL CRIMINAL
PROSECUTIONS FOR THE USE AND RECRUITMENT
OF CHILD SOLDIERS IN THE DRC

The DRC is the first state from which a national has been prosecuted, and successfully so, by the ICC. It is also the first state to have prosecuted an individual for the use and recruitment of child soldiers in a municipal court. Chapter 5 dealt with the legal-technical aspects of international criminal prosecutions. The purpose of this section is to investigate the role such prosecutions may play in preventing child soldiering in the DRC.

## A. The International Criminal Court

As was discussed in Chapter 5, the first finalised case before the ICC, *Prosecutor v Lubanga*, emanates from the DRC.[20] More specifically, Lubanga was the leader of the UPC, as well as the FPLC, the military wing of the UPC and one of the principal armed groups involved in the Ituri conflict. As already stated, the conflict in Ituri was largely between the Hema and Lendu ethnic groups. The UPC/FPLC was a Hema organisation. It is alleged that Lubanga was the President of the UPC and the Commander-in-Chief of the FPLC from September 2002 and at least until the end of 2003. He was convicted exclusively of the use and recruitment of child soldiers, and significantly his conviction included each of the three separate substantive child soldier offences, being the enlistment, conscription and use of child soldiers.[21] The Court held:

> The accused and his co-perpetrators agreed to, and participated in, a common plan to build an army for the purpose of establishing and maintaining political and military control over Ituri. This resulted, in the ordinary course of events,

---

[18] *The Prosecutor v Bosco Ntanganda*, Pre-Trial Chamber I, Warrant of Arrest, ICC01/04-02/06 (2006).

[19] 'Report of the Secretary-General on Children and Armed Conflict', A/64/742, S/2010/181 (13 April 2010), paras 157–59.

[20] *Lubanga* judgment, n 3 above.

[21] Ibid, para 1351.

in the conscription and enlistment of boys and girls under the age of 15, and their use to participate actively in hostilities.[22]

In the context of the DRC, the ICC has issued arrest warrants against five more individuals; of the six people indicted, Lubanga, Ntaganda, Ngudjolo Chui and Germain Katanga were/are charged with the use or recruitment of child soldiers. Whereas Lubanga was convicted on this charge, Katanga was convicted on other charges, but not the use, enlistment or conscription of child soldiers;[23] Chui was acquitted of all charges;[24] and the Ntaganda matter is still in the pre-trial phase.

On 24 February 2003, two armed groups predominantly belonging to the Lendu ethnic group, the Front des nationalistes et intégrationnistes (FNI) and the Force de résistance patriotique en Ituri (FRPI), launched an indiscriminate attack against the inhabitants of Bogoro, a small village in Ituri, the residents of which are mostly of Hema ethnicity. Chui was the highest-ranking FNI commander, and it is alleged that the mass atrocities committed during this attack were committed on his orders. Katanga was the ranking commander of the FRPI forces who participated in the attack. Had it not been for the attack on Bogoro, it is unlikely that arrest warrants for Katanga and Chui would have been issued.

It may well be premature to gauge the effect the ICC may have on deterring crimes in the DRC but, even with the Court's very limited jurisprudence, there are a number of valuable observations that can already be made. The situation in the DRC was referred to the Court as a state referral.[25] This at least shows a level of commitment by the Government of the DRC to ensure that justice prevails. It is very likely that political considerations influenced the decision of the DRC to refer the situation to the ICC, and, indeed, these political considerations may have been decisive. However, it is only the country situation that is referred by the state, not the individuals against whom arrest warrants will be issued. This largely mitigates the degree to which the ICC can be used by states to combat elements opposing the state.

The emphasis the ICC, and in particular the Office of the Prosecutor, has placed on the use and recruitment of child soldiers as a war crime is of great significance. Of the six people who have been charged in the DRC situation, it was alleged that four enlisted, conscripted or used children in armed conflict. In a country situation where killings and rape occur daily, along with the constant fear of renewed genocide, the

---

[22] Ibid.

[23] *The Prosecutor v Germain Katanga*, Trial Chamber II, Judgment, ICC-01/04-01/07-3436 (2014).

[24] *The Prosecutor v Mathieu Ngudjolo Chui*, Trial Chamber II, Judgment, ICC-01/04-02/12-3 (2012).

[25] ICC press release, 'Prosecutor Receives Referral of the Situation in the Democratic Republic of Congo', ICC-OTP-20040419-50 (2004).

fact that the prevention of child soldiering has emerged as the crime around which the fight against impunity has been rallied indicates that this crime is not a lesser crime when compared to other war crimes and crimes against humanity.

The arrest warrant for Ntaganda was originally issued under seal, as the Court feared that 'public knowledge of the proceedings in this case might result in Bosco Ntaganda hiding, fleeing, and/or obstructing or endangering the investigations or the proceedings of the Court'.[26] The warrant has been unsealed since April 2008.[27] Unfortunately, the combined effects of a lack of political will, weak enforcement structures and national protection resulted in a situation where, until his surrender, Ntaganda, who was then a general in the Congolese Army, made frequent public appearances without being arrested by either the DRC authorities or MONUSCO. There is evidence to suggest that, again until his surrender, Ntaganda operated as a senior commander in joint UN/ FARDC operations.[28]

While I was in the DRC, and in particular in Ituri, I was surprised at just how aware of the ICC the local people I spoke to were. Indeed, this was true to the extent that I soon learned that the reluctance on the part of many local people to speak to me at all was due to a fear that I was an ICC investigator, and that speaking to me could lead ultimately to being prosecuted by the ICC. Yet this awareness of the ICC and fear of prosecution among those who participated in atrocities may be lost if those against whom arrest warrants have been issued are free to maintain their public personas without fear of arrest. The eventual effect the ICC may have on deterring crime, and entering 'an era of application' in preventing child soldiering, is largely dependent on these initial years of operation of the Court, and the reputation the Court creates for itself.

## B. Municipal Courts in the DRC

In March 2006, the DRC became the first nation—and remains the only one to date—to prosecute an individual for the use and recruitment of child soldiers.[29] The defendant, Major Jean Pierre Biyoyo, an FARDC commander, was initially sentenced to death. However, the sentence was subsequently commuted to five years' imprisonment, and Biyoyo

---

[26] ICC press release, 'Warrant of Arrest against Bosco Ntaganda Unsealed', ICC-CPI-20080429-PR310 (2008).

[27] Ibid.

[28] Human Rights Watch press release, 'DR Congo: ICC-Indicted War Criminal Implicated in Assassinations of Opponents' (13 October 2010).

[29] 'Report of the Secretary-General on Children and Armed Conflict in the Democratic Republic of the Congo', S/2007/391 (28 June 2007) (2007 Secretary-General DRC Report), para 72.

escaped from prison three months later. In December 2008 Ironside told me that UNICEF, and the UN in general, were aware of Biyoyo's whereabouts and that he had rejoined his FARDC integrated unit, in which he held the rank of major. Yet the authorities have not attempted to rearrest this convicted escapee. The absurdity of this situation was further exacerbated by the promotion of Biyoyo, in 2010, to colonel in the FARDC.[30]

The former UN Special Representative to the Secretary-General on Children and Armed Conflict (SRSG), Ms Radhika Coomaraswamy, specifically raised the issue of Colonel Biyoyo with the government during her country visits to the DRC during March 2007 and April 2009.[31] The authorities nevertheless still failed to take action. It thus appears that the Government of the DRC is motivated more by the positive appearance created by the ratification and promulgation of conventions and laws prohibiting the use and recruitment of child soldiers than by any genuine political will to end impunity and eradicate child soldiering.

As the party most responsible for protecting children in the DRC, the national government is the primary entry point. The cornerstone of any national government's response to child rights is the enactment of targeted legislation. A more positive development was the coming into force of the DRC Child Protection Code (2009).[32] The Secretary-General's annual reports, filed pursuant to Security Council Resolution 1612, have specifically encouraged this development.[33] The 2008 report cited three municipal prosecutions related to the use and recruitment of children.[34] The defendants include Mai Mai Colonel Engangela (aka Colonel 106);[35] FARDC Major Bwasolo Misaba;[36] and the notorious Mai Mai commander Kyungu Mutanga (aka Gedeon). Gedeon is inter alia charged with the

[30] Interview conducted with Ms Ironside on 22 November 2008, Goma, DRC.

[31] R Coomaraswamy, 'Press Conference by Special Representative for Children and Armed Conflict' (UN Department of Public Information, News and Media Division, New York, 16 March 2007); Mission Report, 'Visit of the Special Representative for Children and Armed Conflict to The Democratic Republic of the Congo' (14–21 April 2009) 7.

[32] 'Concluding Observations of the Committee on the Rights of the Child: Democratic Republic of the Congo', Fiftieth Session of the Committee on the Rights of the Child, CRC/C/COD/CO/2 (January 2009), para 3.

[33] 'Report of the Secretary-General on Children and Armed Conflict in the DRC', S/2006/389 (13 June 2006) (2006 Secretary-General DRC Report), paras 7 and 45; 2007 Secretary-General DRC Report, n 29 above, para 60.

[34] 'Report of the Secretary-General on Children and Armed Conflict in the Democratic Republic of the Congo', S/2008/693 (10 November 2008) (2008 Secretary-General DRC Report), paras 77, 79 and 80.

[35] Colonel Engangela (aka Colonel 106) has been charged with insurrection, with further evidence being collected to sustain charges of forced recruitment of children under 15, abduction and illegal detention. Colonel Engangela was identified as Colonel Mabolongo (aka Colonel 106) in the 2007 Secretary-General DRC Report, n 29 above, para 30.

[36] Major Bwasolo Misaba was sentenced to five years' imprisonment for the recruitment of three children aged between 10 and 14.

recruitment of at least 300 children.[37] The Secretary-General has previously identified two of these individuals as violating parties.[38] The prosecution of Gedeon came in the wake of strong recommendations to that effect made by the Security Council Working Group on Children and Armed Conflict.

Unfortunately, it appears that, within the contexts of both international and municipal prosecutions, government authorities in the DRC are inclined to protect individuals from prosecution and punishment where it serves their own interests. This is indicative of a weak rule of law, which renders the utilisation of municipal machinery to prevent child soldiering less likely to succeed. It has previously been argued that the ICC operates on a basis of selective prosecution. As such, the necessary capacity to bring a majority of violating parties to justice should come from municipal courts and legal systems.[39] This approach, however, is unlikely to succeed where the rule of law in the relevant state is very weak. On a more positive note, on 17 February 2011, the Superior Council of Judiciary of the DRC announced the nomination of twelve judges, assigned to a new tribunal to address cases related to children.[40] However, it remains to be seen whether this tribunal will attain any success, notwithstanding the weak rule of law in the DRC and the numerous further systemic problems that render the protection that the law is supposed to offer children ineffective.

## IV. THE UNITED NATIONS AND THE PREVENTION OF CHILD SOLDIERING IN THE DRC

Virtually every relevant entity that forms part of the UN has engaged with the armed conflicts in the DRC. On the child soldier prevention front, the day-to-day activities of the UN peace mission in the DRC, the United Nations Organization Stabilization Mission in the Democratic Republic of the Congo (MONUSCO), relates to child soldier prevention on many levels. Additionally, the SRSG has consistently engaged with child soldiering in the DRC since the first SRSG was appointed in 1998. So, too, has the Security Council Monitoring and Reporting Mechanism, and as was noted in the previous section, the recommendations of this

---

[37] Kyungu Mutanga (aka Gedeon) is charged inter alia with the war crime of the military recruitment or use of children.

[38] Colonel Engangela (aka Colonel 106) was identified as Colonel Mabolongo (aka Colonel 106) in the 2007 Secretary-General DRC Report, n 29 above, para 38; Gedeon was identified as a child soldier recruitment violator in the 2007 Secretary-General DRC Report, n 29 above, paras 58 and 72.

[39] See generally Chapter 5.III.B.

[40] 'Report of the Secretary-General on the United Nations Organization Stabilization Mission in the Democratic Republic of the Congo', S/2011/298 (12 May 2011) (Second Secretary-General MONUSCO Report), para 49.

mechanism appear to have already shown a margin of success. Finally, in any country situation such as the DRC, where there are thousands of child soldiers and thousands more have recently been demobilised, a proper DDR programme is essential for various reasons. From a child soldier prevention point of view, proper DDR is one of the primary ways in which to prevent the re-enlistment of children. This problem is acute in a situation like the DRC, where the DDR process occurs during ongoing hostilities. Accordingly, DDR activities in the DRC are also specifically assessed in this section.

## A. Engagement by the United Nations Peace Mission in the DRC and UNICEF with Child Soldier Prevention

The UN peace mission in the DRC was formerly known as the United Nations Mission in the Democratic Republic of Congo (MONUC). However, on 1 July 2010, the mission was renamed the United Nations Organization Stabilization Mission in the Democratic Republic of the Congo (MONUSCO). This was done 'in view of the new phase that has been reached in the Democratic Republic of the Congo'.[41] The mandate of MONUSCO provides expressly that it must:

> Work closely with the Government to ensure the implementation of its commitments to address serious violations against children, in particular the finalization of the Action Plan to release children present in the FARDC and to prevent further recruitment, with the support of the Monitoring and Reporting Mechanism.[42]

The reason for discussing MONUSCO and UNICEF in the same section is that MONUSCO does not work with children directly, nor does it ever take charge of children. Instead, after relevant information has been gathered within MONUSCO, it is shared with implementing partners that are better able to work with children directly. Most notably, these partners include UNICEF, although various NGOs that operate autonomously from the UN system also partner with MONUSCO in this regard.

Insofar as child soldiers are concerned, the primary roles of the Child Protection Section are to gather and analyse data on instances of child soldiering, and to advocate for and educate people on the end of the military use and recruitment of children and the criminalisation of such use and recruitment. The Child Protection Section's function as the focal point for the sharing of information related to child soldier prevention in the DRC should not be underestimated. The lack of inter-agency and

---

[41] Security Council Resolution 1925 of 28 May 2010 para 1.
[42] Ibid, para 12(e).

inter-organisational coordination is one of the major challenges to the effectiveness of many humanitarian programmes. A number of NGO representatives have identified the lack of an inter-agency database on child soldiering within the DRC as a concern. This has two very negative effects. First, some work is duplicated in an environment where human resources are already overextended. Secondly, in some instances a specific entity might be able to act on a situation which they are not aware of. Estelle Nandy Ouattara, the child protection officer in the Bunia MONUC office, confirmed to me that no such inter-agency database existed at the time.[43]

MONUSCO boasts the largest child protection section in any peacekeeping mission. This includes specialised staff based in eastern DRC, Province Orientale and the mission's headquarters in Kinshasa. In addition, there are international and national staff members who are child protection officers based in eight field offices: Goma, Beni, Bukavu, Uvira, Dungu, Bunia, Kisangani and Kalemie.

It was reported that in 2010 MONUSCO/MONUC facilitated the release of 2006 children from armed groups.[44] This figure includes 393 children who were separated from FARDC units. Concern was raised, however, regarding the higher incidence of re-recruitment of former child soldiers, specifically by integrated former CNDP units and particularly in the Masisi territory.[45] Between January 2011 and the beginning of May 2011, the release of a further 376 children was documented by MONUSCO.[46]

UNICEF's approach in advocating for the protection of children's rights, which is their mandate, is not issue based, and aims not to categorise children.[47] Furthermore, UNICEF has an exceedingly strong emphasis on inspiring a collective response to issues on its agenda and therefore places heavy reliance on partners on the implementation level: 'UNICEF is expected to take a leadership role on child protection issues. This gives UNICEF a high degree of responsibility to act as an advocate, convener and partner, encouraging and not overshadowing the contributions of others.'[48] Advocacy and education accordingly play a central role in their initiatives.

---

[43] Interview conducted with Ms Ouattara on 13 November 2008, Bunia, DRC.

[44] 'Report of the Secretary-General on the United Nations Organization Stabilization Mission in the Democratic Republic of the Congo', S/2011/20 (17 January 2011) (First Secretary-General MONUSCO Report), para 53.

[45] Ibid.

[46] Second Secretary-General MONUSCO Report, n 40 above, para 49.

[47] 'UNICEF Child Protection Strategy', E/ICEF/2008/5/Rev.1 (3–5 June 2008), paras 37 and 55.

[48] Ibid, para 54; UNICEF, 'Core Commitments for Children in Emergencies', 3, available at www.unicef.org.

The five key 'focus areas' identified by UNICEF in order to meet its mandate are child survival and development; basic education and gender equality; HIV/AIDS and children; child protection; and policy advocacy and partnerships. The two focus areas most directly relevant to child soldiering are child protection and policy advocacy and partnerships, with basic education playing an indirect but significant role.

UNICEF's premise that 'successful child protection begins with prevention' signifies their philosophy that sustainable social change can only be achieved if a grassroots environment for the child can be established with sufficient community engagement and support and adequate social networks.[49] In this regard, the importance of education is specifically recognised.[50]

In the DRC, UNICEF is instrumental in the implementation of most of the significant initiatives related to children's protection from military use and recruitment, including the UN Monitoring and Reporting Mechanism, as well as the DDR programme in its relation to children. UNICEF approaches its mandate broadly and sees threats to child rights as all being interlinked. Correspondingly, they avoid categorising children by, for example, applying the label 'child soldier'.[51] With their resultant approach largely being focused on inspiring a collective response to issues on its agenda, it is impossible to quantify their actual successes on the ground. However, in the DRC, besides making huge headway in other sectors of child protection,[52] UNICEF, together with their partners, had begun the process of disarming and reintegrating 4,000 child soldiers in 2007.[53]

With an approved budget of more than US$1.4 billion for the period 1 July 2011 to 30 June 2012, MONUSCO can do more on the child protection front.[54] From a political and mandate point of view, it will be difficult for MONUSCO to directly enforce child soldier prohibitive norms. The same is true, to a lesser extent, of taking charge of children directly. However, MONUSCO can significantly increase training to the grass-roots NGOs on which they rely to take charge of children. This is specifically true regarding the reintegration phase of the DDR process regarding children. During my fieldwork I observed a clear lack of skills regarding the reintegration and social/psychological recovery of

[49] UNICEF Child Protection Strategy, n 47 above, 56.

[50] Ibid, paras 3 and 7.

[51] Interview conducted with Ms Ironside on 22 November 2008, Goma, DRC.

[52] For example, UNICEF and their partners have provided shelter to 180,000 families affected by armed conflict and/or natural disasters; the provision of safe water had been extended to 500,000 people by 2007; and 86 therapeutic feeding centres were servicing more than 45,000 children.

[53] NICEF West and Central Africa Office, DRC country profile, available at www.unicef.org/wcaro/Countries_1749.html.

[54] 'Approved Resources for Peacekeeping Operations for the Period from 1 July 2011 to 30 June 2012', A/C.5/65/19 (22 July 2011).

former child combatants in centres where children are housed. Indeed, in an interview I conducted with a senior representative from COOPI, in Bunia, I was told that, unless there was better communication between the civilian/humanitarian sector of MONUC (as it then was) and the military sector, only limited results would be achieved in preventing child soldiering.[55] As the civilian/humanitarian sector is responsible for transmitting the correct information to partners, however, it is the military sector that operates in the field, where they observe the presence of children with armed groups. Secondly, and more importantly, in delegating responsibility for matters such as taking charge of children, MONUC does not exercise proper control and safeguards to ensure that the organisation is capable of delivering what is required. Indeed, I was told that there were many instances in which MONUC had delegated such responsibility to organisations that exist on paper only.

NGOs such as the Don Bosco Ngangi centre for war orphans and at-risk children in Goma are doing remarkable work.[56] The centre currently houses 3,500 war orphans, and includes a programme for the reintegration of former child soldiers and a further 1,500 refugees. The centre also runs a medical centre, which cared for 19,000 patients in 2009 and has recently expanded its capabilities and is now able to do electrocardiograms and basic X-rays. However, the demand for such facilities far exceeds their availability. Also, the geographical location of such facilities determines whether they are available to specific children in need. The effect is that there are many grass-roots NGOs taking charge of children after their demobilisation that are in desperate need of further skills development regarding the reintegration and social/psychological recovery of such former child combatants. MONUSCO is well placed to provide such, together with other UN agencies, and it funds UNICEF, in particular, to contribute to this gap.

In an unprecedented move in 2013, the Security Council extended MONUSCO's mandate to include an offensive military component. The Security Council:

> Decides to extend the mandate of MONUSCO in the DRC until 31 March 2014, takes note of the recommendations of the Special Report of the Secretary-General on the DRC and in the Great Lakes Region regarding MONUSCO, and decides that MONUSCO shall, for an initial period of one year and within the authorized troop ceiling of 19,815, on an exceptional basis and without creating a precedent or any prejudice to the agreed principles of peacekeeping, include an 'Intervention Brigade' consisting inter alia of three infantry battalions, one artillery and one Special force and Reconnaissance company with headquarters in Goma, under direct command of the

[55] Interview conducted with Mr Andretti on 24 November 2008, Goma, DRC.
[56] See Project Congo, available at www.projectcongo.org/donboscongangi.html. I also visited the Don Bosco Ngangi centre numerous times during my stay in Goma.

MONUSCO Force Commander, with the responsibility of neutralizing armed groups as set out in paragraph 12(b) below and the objective of contributing to reducing the threat posed by armed groups to state authority and civilian security in eastern DRC and to make space for stabilization activities.[57]

The so-called Intervention Brigade was created after the initial rise of the M23 rebellion. M23 was responsible for the recruitment of child soldiers, and in the same resolution that created the Intervention Brigade, the Security Council strongly condemned such recruitment.[58] It is likely that members of the Intervention Brigade will engage in hostilities with forces that contain child soldiers. It should be clear that once a child engages in hostilities, he is targetable by opposition forces, as is the case with any other soldier or fighter. One hopes, however, that the Intervention Brigade will be able to conduct its operations in a manner that takes into account the presence of child soldiers in opposition forces.

## B. The Special Representative to the Secretary-General on Children and Armed Conflict

The SRSG's first field visit to the DRC took place during February 1999,[59] a mere sixteen months after the first SRSG was appointed. Most recently, the SRSG visited the DRC during April 2009.[60]

Most of the initial headway made by the SRSG came in the form of entering into dialogue with violating parties, and in so doing obtained concrete commitments to cease the use and recruitment of child soldiers. As early as 1999, the SRSG had obtained an undertaking from the Rassemblement Congolais pour la Démocratie (RCD) in the DRC to demobilise the child soldiers within its ranks. Of the thirty-six commitments obtained by the SRSG during his initial three year mandate, however, only nine were met. Neither the RCD nor any other group in the DRC was included in this group of nine.[61] A further tactic much utilised by the SRSG is naming and shaming violators. The merit of this tactic lies in negating the aspirations of armed groups to be seen as legitimate by exposing their unacceptable behaviour and methods. In her last annual report, the SRSG listed seven violating parties within the DRC.[62]

---

[57] Security Council Resolution 2098 of 28 March 2013, para 9.

[58] Ibid, paras 8, 15 and 22.

[59] 'Protection of Children Affected by Armed Conflict Note by the Secretary-General', A/54/430 (1 October 1999), para 93–94.

[60] 'Report of the Special Representative of the Secretary-General for Children and Armed Conflict', A/64/254 (6 August 2009), para 60.

[61] M Happold, *Child Soldiers in International Law* (Manchester, Manchester University Press, 2005) 40–41.

[62] 'Report of the Secretary-General, 'Children and Armed Conflict', A/65/820, S/2011/250 (23 April 2011) Annex 1. Forces armées de la République démocratique du Congo (FARDC);

Furthermore, the SRSG has placed a lot of emphasis on: global advocacy; supporting and facilitating dialogue between UN actors and parties to the relevant conflict; advocating for the implementation of concrete preventative measures; eliciting commitments to end violations by violating parties; facilitating the Monitoring and Reporting Mechanism; and advocating for the end of impunity in pursuit of fulfilling her mandate.

The DRC is one of only a few situations that have remained on the agenda of the SRSG since the creation of the office. In undertaking country visits, the role of the SRSG can best be described as inspiring. In facilitating and supporting measures aimed at the protection of children during armed conflict:

> It is important to stress that such visits are carried out to support the advocacy and programmatic work of operational partners on the ground, to raise the level of global awareness about their work, to help open further space for their protection dialogue and, where appropriate, to assist operational partners in unblocking political impasses to further advance protection agendas.[63]

During the country visit the SRSG undertook to the DRC in 2007, she managed to obtain the following commitments from the DRC authorities:

(a) To take measures, in consultation with the United Nations, to tackle the issues of child recruitment and sexual violence;
(b) To take all necessary measures to re-arrest commander Biyoyo;
(c) To take effective action to fight impunity of armed groups, such as those led by Laurent Nkunda and the *Forces démocratiques de libération du Rwanda*;
(d) To take steps, in consultation with the United Nations, to fight impunity.[64]

Yet, in 2011, the SRSG reported that the Government of the DRC:

> has not been forthcoming in engaging with the United Nations on an action plan to end the recruitment and use of children by the *Forces armées de la République démocratique du Congo* (FARDC), despite advocacy by child protection actors, including the country task force on monitoring and reporting, over the last several years. While efforts have been ongoing to professionalize FARDC, these efforts have not consistently involved a formal process to remove all children from FARDC units. Many children continue to be recruited and remain associated with FARDC units, particularly within former *Congrès national pour la défense du peuple* (CNDP) units. Many children

---

Forces démocratiques de libération du Rwanda (FDLR); Front des nationalistes et integra-tionalistes (FNI); Front de résistance patriotique en Ituri (FRPI); Mai-Mai groups in North and South Kivu, Maniema and Katanga who have not integrated into FARDC; Mouve-ment révolutionnaire congolais (MRC); and Non-integrated FARDC brigades loyal to rebel leader Laurent Nkunda. 'Annual Report of the Special Representative of the Secretary-General for Children and Armed Conflict, Radhika Coomaraswamy', A/HRC/9/3 (27 June 2008), Annex 1.

[63] 'Promotion and Protection of the Rights of Children: Report of the Special Representative of the Secretary-General for Children and Armed Conflict', A/62/228 (13 August 2007), para 26.

[64] Ibid, para 43.

released in 2010 reported that they had been recruited several times, even after family reunification. This reaffirms the urgent need for a political commitment at the highest levels of the Government in order to move forward on the action plan and ensure its coherence with ongoing security sector reform efforts. In a positive move, new military directives were issued by the '*Amani Leo*' chain of command ordering the release of all children remaining in FARDC units.

As stated previously, during my interview with former SRSG Coomaraswamy, she was resolute in her view that the proper approach to preventing child soldiering is the direct approach, as opposed to more broad-based approaches that rely on addressing deeper systemic problems such as extreme poverty and, indeed, the existence of armed conflict.[65] Direct engagement with violating parties in countries such as the DRC is the activity in which the SRSG engages most directly with child soldier prevention.

On the positive front, while the FARDC is not yet 'child free', and although there was a significant increase in child use and recruitment during late 2008, the mass and systematic recruitment of children by the government forces has ceased. Less success has been achieved in engaging with non-state entities. As Awich Pollar told me, such groups often profess not to use child soldiers whatsoever.[66] Where they acknowledge that there are children among their ranks, they are quick to give undertakings to demobilise these children and cease the use and recruitment of child soldiers, but slow to comply with their undertakings.

The SRSG has done a remarkable job in engaging with such groups and securing such commitments. However, where these groups persistently fail to comply with their obligations, showing a blatant disregard for international law, the SRSG can do little more than increase advocacy on the matter, and name and shame these parties in the Secretary-General's annual report on children in armed conflict to the Security Council, which is prepared by the SRSG. This in itself has proven to be not as effective as was initially hoped. For example, to date, the Secretary-General has appended lists of violating parties to seven of his annual reports to the Security Council. Of those parties included in the 2011 report, five were included consistently in the last four reports, spanning a five-year period.

A more forceful approach is required in order to induce compliance, not only with concrete commitments that have been made by these violating parties, but more importantly with international and municipal law. As was suggested in Chapter 6, the Security Council should take stronger action against such groups. Resolution 1332, adopted under

---

[65] See generally Chapter 6.II.D above.
[66] I Interviewed Mr Pollar on 1 February 2011 in Geneva, Switzerland.

the Chapter VII powers of the Security Council, was a welcome development.[67] This resolution called for 'an effective end to the recruitment,
training and use of children'.[68] However, it did not provide for any
form of sanction, or targeted action, against persistent violators. In my
view, this is a necessary component of a concerted effort to enter 'an
era of application'. Although the SRSG is the focal point within the UN
on children in armed conflict, her ability to force compliance is proportional to the strength of the mandate she has been afforded. Like any
other mechanism that contributes to the prevention of child soldiering,
her office is also dependent on other mechanisms, in order to create a
web of protection.

## C. The Security Council Monitoring and Reporting Mechanism

On 26 July 2005, the Security Council passed a Resolution calling for
the creation of a Monitoring and Reporting Mechanism on Children
and Armed Conflict (MRM).[69] The same Resolution also called for the
creation of a Security Council Working Group on Children and Armed
Conflict (Working Group).[70] The MRM focuses on six grave violations
of child rights, one of which is recruiting or using child soldiers.[71] No
new entities were established in the creation of the MRM; instead,
several key institutions were included, drawing from their respective
strengths and knowledge bases. Ultimately, the MRM functions on three
distinct levels: 'information-gathering, coordination and action at the
country level; coordination, scrutiny and integration of information and
preparation of reports at the Headquarters level; and concrete actions
to ensure compliance, to be taken particularly by bodies that constitute
"destinations for action"'.[72]

At the base of the activities of the MRM within any given country lies
the country task force. In 2005, seven countries were selected as pilot
countries in which to implement the MRM. There are groups which persistently violate international law by using or recruiting child soldiers in
each of these countries, and the DRC was included.[73] The DRC country

---

[67] Security Council Resolution 1332 of 14 December 2000.

[68] Ibid, Resolution 1332, para 10. V Popovski, 'Children in Armed Conflict: Law and
Practice of the United Nations' in K Arts and V Popovski (eds), *International Criminal
Accountability and the Rights of Children* (Cambridge, Cambridge University Press, 2006) 44,
states that 165 children were returned to UNICEF as a result of this resolution.

[69] Art 3 of UN Security Council Resolution 1612 of 26 July 2005.

[70] Ibid.

[71] 'Report of the Secretary-General on Children and Armed Conflict', A/59/695, S/2005/72
(9 February 2005) (2005 Security Council Report), para 68.

[72] Ibid, para 67.

[73] Ibid, Annexes 1 and 2. These countries included Burundi, Côte d'Ivoire, Democratic
Republic of Congo, Somalia and Sudan from Annex 1 and Nepal and Sri Lanka from

task force was set up the following year and the activities of the MRM began. The task force is jointly chaired by the country representative of UNICEF and the Deputy Special Representative to the Secretary-General for DRC,[74] and its membership consists of MONUSCO, UNICEF, UNHCR, ILO, Save the Children UK and CARE.[75] Assessing the role and success of the MRM in the DRC one needs to focus specifically on the three levels on which the MRM functions. The three levels of operation of the MRM are sequenced in such a way that each succeeding level is dependent on the preceding level. Accordingly, only after information has been gathered can the coordination of information and the preparation of reports occur, and only after this can concrete action be taken.

With regard to 'information-gathering, coordination and action at the country level', the more parties involved, the more information can be collected and the better the verification of such information. However, proper data management is imperative. UN entities operating in the DRC, in particular MONUSCO and UNICEF, have collaborated well in their efforts to contribute to the task force.[76] However, given the vastness of the DRC, it is not possible for the UN to act in isolation. The task force has had some difficulty in getting NGOs involved.[77]

The challenges facing this level do not end with collecting data. Data management and coordination between different agencies and organisations is a key concern. At the time that I conducted my fieldwork in the DRC, information sharing between different agencies and organisations, and even between different sections within MONUSCO, was handled on an ad hoc basis and dependent on informal agreements between staff members from the various organisation, agency or section. As stated above, NGOs in general and Estelle Nandy Ouattara, the child protection officer in the Bunia MONUC office,[78] confirmed to me that at that time there was no centralised database on the incidence of child recruitment in the DRC. It seems that the country task force has filled this gap to a significant extent. Other initiatives, such as the creation of Child Protection Working Groups in Goma, Bukavu and Bunia, have created a greater dimension of inter- and intra-agency information sharing, with members from any interested UN agencies and international or national

Annex 2. Furthermore, subsequently MRM task forces have also been set up in Chad, Myanmar, Philippines and Uganda.

[74] This is in conformity with 'Report of the Secretary-General on Children and Armed Conflict', A/59/695, S/2005/72 (9 February 2005), para 83.

[75] 'Getting It Done and Doing It Right: Implementing the Monitoring and Reporting Mechanism on Children and Armed Conflict in the DRC' (Watchlist on Children and Armed Conflict, January 2008) 3.

[76] The 1612 Reports Officer is a UNICEF staff member seconded to MONUC, thus facilitating better inter-agency coordination, ibid, 4.

[77] Ibid, 4–7.

[78] Interview conducted with Ms Ouattara on 13 November 2008, Bunia, DRC.

NGOs being permitted to join.[79] These working groups exist specifically to facilitate information exchange as envisaged by Security Council Resolution 1612. Such initiatives mitigate the challenges posed by the fact that there is a plethora of data collecting entities in the DRC operating within the same areas without knowing the operational details of each other. These include the Kinshasa level protection cluster; the provincial protection clusters; the protection monitoring project; the Humanitarian Advocacy Group; and the Joint-Initiative on Sexual Violence. The DRC task force's strength lies in these various entities' ability to collect, compile and report to the task force on the six grave violations.[80] However, to reap these benefits, the task force needs to better facilitate coordination between these data collection entities. When these entities act blind insofar as other agencies are concerned, duplication of data becomes a bigger issue, as does oversights. On the positive front, however, it appears that the DRC country task force has conducted itself well in this role.

The task force has relied heavily on MONUC/MONUSCO's child protection section to report instances of grave violations as an intermediary between the task force and the relevant party who reported on the violation to MONUC. This state of affairs is not ideal, specifically with regard to sustainability should MONUSCO's force be further reduced in line with the changing circumstances in the DRC.[81] Nevertheless, actionable information has been collected and handed up to the coordination level.

As stated, the second level, the 'coordination, scrutiny and integration of information and preparation of reports at the Headquarters level', is dependent on the success of country level information gathering. This level is the least problematic of the three and deserves little discussion in the context of the DRC case study, as the functions performed on this level are not severely affected by the specific country relevant to the task force handing up the information. The findings of the latest report compiled by the DRC country task force that was submitted by the Secretary-General to the Security Council in 2010 highlights that there has been a noticeable increase in the grave violations being committed against children in the context of armed conflict.[82] In total, the MRM documented 1,593 cases of child recruitment. Of this number, the FARDC was allegedly responsible for forty-two per cent of cases; the various Mai Mai groups accounted for twenty-six per cent; the PARECO for sixteen per cent; and lastly, the CNDP was responsible for ten per cent of cases.[83] Ninety-two per cent of these cases of recruitment took place in

---

[79] 2008 Secretary-General DRC Report, n 34 above, para 63.
[80] 2005 Security Council Report, n 71 above, para 79.
[81] Ibid, para 81.
[82] 'Report of the Secretary-General on Children and Armed Conflict in the Democratic Republic of the Congo', S/2010/369 (9 July 2010), para 15.
[83] Ibid, para 17.

the Kivu provinces.[84] Finally, a significant increase in the abduction of children for purposes of using them in armed conflict was emphasised. The LRA was identified as the primary culprit.[85]

The final level, 'concrete actions to ensure compliance, to be taken particularly by bodies that constitute "destinations for action"', falls within the ambit of the Security Council and its Working Group. The Working Group is tasked primarily with reviewing the reports of the MRM.[86] Reporting on these grave violations of child rights is the vehicle used by the MRM to bring such violations to the attention of 'destinations for action', thus the reports are the triggers for action. The main destinations for action are national governments, the Security Council, the General Assembly, the International Criminal Court, the Human Rights Commission, regional organisations, NGOs and civil society.[87] The measure for success of the MRM does not lie in the report but, rather, what comes of the report.

The Security Council has called upon its Working Group on Children and Armed Conflict to make recommendations to the Council on the promotion and protection of the rights of children affected by armed conflict.[88] The Working Group, as the primary conduit of information emanating from the Secretary-General's country reports, has performed efficiently in making recommendations on the basis of the country reports it reviews. As was stated earlier, the prosecution in a municipal DRC court of Mai Mai commander Gedeon for the use and recruitment of child soldiers came in the wake of strong recommendations to that effect made by the Working Group.

A lot of the MRM's potential is lost by not making concrete actionable and targeted suggestions in the Resolution 1612 Secretary-General's reports. The Working Group itself has also expressed this view.[89] For example, although various parties have failed for years to observe their obligations in international law to not use or recruit child soldiers, the recommendations made in the latest report on the DRC submitted by the Secretary-General are limited to calls on the parties to comply with their obligations themselves. Targeted action is required against such violating parties; the recommendations to the Security Council should express the need for such action.[90] Very significantly in this regard, in

---

[84] Ibid, para 22.

[85] Ibid, paras 39–41.

[86] Art 8 of the Security Council Resolution 1612.

[87] 2005 Security Council Report, n 71 above, para 107.

[88] Art 8(a) of the Security Council Resolution 1612.

[89] 'Letter Dated 8 September 2006 from the Permanent Representative of France to the United Nations Addressed to the President of the Security Council', S/2006/724 (11 September 2006).

[90] This is consistent with the argument I presented in relation to the Security Council in Chapter 6 above. See generally Chapter 6.II.C.

his latest report to the Security Council, dated 23 April 2011, the Secretary-General reported that:

> The Security Council Committee established . . . concerning the Democratic Republic of the Congo for the first time invited my Special Representative for Children and Armed Conflict to brief the Committee in May 2010. As a result, several individuals were included on the Committee's list of individuals and entities against whom targeted measures will be imposed on the basis of verified information regarding, inter alia, their recruitment and use of children. Further, on 2 December, the Security Council imposed sanctions on Forces armées de la République démocratique du Congo Colonel Innocent Zimurinda for grave violations against children, including the recruitment and use of child soldiers, the killing and maiming of children, sexual violations and denial of humanitarian access.[91]

This is a significant step, which is in accordance with the conclusions reached in Chapter 6. Furthermore, the development of the central monitoring and reporting database, as well as the country databases, significantly adds to the data required to address child soldiering effectively.

In 2013 it was reported that the MRMs figures indicate that 578 children were recruited into state and non-state forces during the preceding year.[92] This figure is incredibly low considering that past figures suggested that thousands of children were recruited annually, and it is important to note that the M23 movement commenced in 2012. As such, this low figure of recruitment occurred notwithstanding an escalation in armed activates.

## D. The Demobilisation, Disarmament and Reintegration of Child Soldiers in the DRC

The DDR programme has a dual role in child soldier prevention. First, it functions as a short-term preventative strategy in that children associated with fighting forces are removed from them. Secondly, it is a long-term preventative strategy in light of the role that DDR plays in conflict reduction and prevention. The National Program for Disarmament, Demobilization and Reintegration was preceded by the regional Ituri Disarmament and Community Reinsertion Program. Before the national programme was initiated, DDR activities, in relation to children, were carried out by UNICEF and NGOs with the assistance

---

[91] 'Report of the Secretary-General on Children and Armed Conflict', A/65/820, S/2011/250 (23 April 2011), para 205.
[92] The information below is based on the 'Report of the Secretary-General to the Security Council', A/67/845, S/2013/245 (15 May 2013).

of MONUSCO's Child Protection Section.[93] The national programme is not a UN initiative but, rather, was overseen by CONADER, a DRC state institution funded by the World Bank, with assistance from the UN and other organisations.[94] CONADER was dissolved by presidential decree on 14 July 2007 and replaced with UEPNDDR.[95] Because the peace process entails a reform of the national military, not all combatants from opposing armed groups are reintegrated into civilian life. Many are debriefed, retrained and integrated into mixed brigades of the reformed FARDC. This process is known as *bressage*. Thus there is a crucial point in the process where it is decided which route a specific candidate will follow. In the case of children, that route will always be DDR.[96] Child DDR ultimately entails that a given child be released from the fighting forces, reunited with her or his family, and ultimately reintegrated into her or his home community.[97] In the recent past, there have been many different DDR initiatives with regard to children, with involvement from grass-roots NGOs to UN agencies. UNICEF has played the most prominent role in this regard. However, a lack of inter-agency and inter-organisational coordination has resulted in little success being attained by these programmes.[98]

In the case of foreign nationals, both adults and children, they are repatriated to their home countries after demobilisation and disarmament. There is a significant number of foreign child combatants in the DRC, with the majority coming from Uganda, Sudan, Rwanda, Burundi and the Central African Republic. The DDR of foreign nationals falls outside of the scope of the national DDR programme. MONUSCO oversees the DDR of foreign nationals under its Disarmament, Demobilization, Repatriation, Reintegration and Resettlement programme.

Since its inception, the DDR process has been plagued by delays and inadequate service provision.[99] It was originally planned to be finalised by the time the national elections occurred on 30 July 2006.[100] Initially

---

[93] 'Global Report on Child Soldiers' *The Coalition to Stop the Use of Child Soldiers* (2008) 109.

[94] Commission nationale pour la démobilisation et la reinsertion.

[95] Unité d'exécution du programme national de désarmement, démobilisation et reinsertion.

[96] In terms of the joint operations plan, children below 18 are automatically vetted out of the armed forces and are thus demobilised.

[97] 'Children at War: Creating Hope for Their Future', AFR 62/017/2006 (Amnesty International, October 2006) 8.

[98] M Knight and A Özerdem, 'Guns, Camps and Cash: Disarmament, Demobilization and Reinsertion of Former Combatants in Transitions from War to Peace' (2004) 41(4) *Journal of Peace Research* 502.

[99] Multi-Country Demobilization and Reintegration Program, 'Quarterly Progress Report: DRC' (July–September 2005) 3 and 5.

[100] 'Children at War', n 97 above, 8.

the total number of soldiers were put at between 300,000 and 330,000,[101] with 150,000 soldiers in need of demobilisation. Of these 30,000 were children.[102] By the end of June 2006, CONADER's figures suggested that 72,737 adults and 19,054 children had been demobilised.[103] However, these figures do little to inform whether any real success had been attained. It is unclear whether the 150,000 figure was anywhere near accurate. In fact, most suggest it was inflated. There are also doubts about CONADER's accuracy in their figures regarding the numbers that have been taken into the DDR programme. Finally, of the people who passed through the DDR programme, it is unclear how many lied about being former combatants and also how many rejoined armed groups after having gone through DDR.

There is a real incentive for people to join the DDR programme who either have no real intention to demobilise or who lie about ever having been combatants to benefit from the programme. The DDR programme provides the participant with an initial US$110 payment, the *filet de sécurite* (security net); a further US$25 per month stipend for a one year period; and vocational training or other assistance in creating a livelihood for the person within civilian life.[104] However, after acting as an incentive to even those not in need of DDR, these payments have often not been made and further no vocational training has been provided to many people in the DDR programme,[105] adding to the disillusionment of former soldiers, many of whom were opposed to the government in their past military endeavours. On 7 July 2006, CONADER announced the cessation of the disarmament and demobilisation phases to the programme, due to lack of funds. The remaining funds were allocated to the reintegration phase, leaving thousands of children behind who are in need of demobilisation.

It goes without saying that the DDR of children necessarily implies unique approaches and more sensitive methods to ultimately attain the successful reintegration of a given child. To this end, the Cadre Opérationnel pour les Enfants Associés aux Forces et Groupes Armés (Operational Framework for the DDR of Children) was drafted by an inter-agency

---

[101] This was the figure put forward by the signatories to the 2002 peace process. It should be kept in mind that at that time parties to the process were still at war with each other. It is thus believed that these figures were inflated to create a stronger perception of the armed group's military strength.

[102] Multi-Country Demobilization and Reintegration Program, 'Quarterly Progress Report: DRC' (April–June 2006).

[103] Ibid.

[104] 'DRC: DDR and Reform of the Army', AFR 62/001/2007 (Amnesty International, January 2007) 18.

[105] Ibid.

group coordinated by UNICEF.[106] This operational framework provided CONADER with guidelines to the proper DDR of children.

In terms of the operational framework, the first phase of both DDR and army integration is for commanders to take their subordinates to military regroupment centres. This initial shared phase is known as *tronc commun*. However, because children are never offered direct cash payments, they frequently lie about their age and attempt to be absorbed into the adult DDR programme. At these regroupment centres the participants are disarmed, and those undergoing DDR are moved to CONADER/UEPNDDR orientation centres. Upon arrival, those under 18 are registered as children and are housed separately from adults. They are supposed to spend a maximum of only forty-eight hours at these centres.[107] Thereafter, they are entrusted to an accredited NGO, which is charged with their well-being. The children are then taken to transitional care structures run by the given NGO. Generally, children will spend three months at such structures, whereafter they are reunited with their families if possible. In terms of the operational framework, children below the age of fifteen are provided with basic education and those older than fifteen  with vocational training for one year.[108]

To a large extent, DDR programmes are outcome based, and CONADER's objectives in this regard are to

> remove all children from armed forces and groups; facilitate children's return to civilian life through reinsertion programmes; reinforce sustainable conditions for the protection of children through community ownership of protection mechanisms; develop specific strategies to reintegrate girls associated with armed forces and groups and prevent violations of children's rights.[109]

In order to succeed in these objectives, the operational framework requires CONADER to identify the children to be demobilised; verify their histories; document, research and ultimately reunite them with their families; reintegrate them with their families and communities; and finally monitor their situations.[110] Upon completion of the DDR process, children are issued with demobilisation certificates, proving their demobilisation and age. This practice has been noted as a success with regard to male children, though not with regard to females.[111]

During 2002, at the outset of the DDR programme, it was estimated that there were 30,000 children in need of DDR,[112] but as at September

---

[106] This group further consisted of representatives of MONUC, ministries of the transitional government and NGO experts.

[107] 'Children at War', n 97 above, 21.

[108] For a full assessment of the child DDR process in the DRC see ibid.

[109] 'Struggling to Survive: Children in Armed Conflict in the Democratic Republic of the Congo' (Watchlist on Children and Armed Conflict, April 2006) 46.

[110] Ibid.

[111] Ibid, 47.

[112] 'Children at War', n 97 above, 1.

2008 that estimated figure stood at 3,500.[113] CONADER's figures suggest that 30,000 children had been released by armed forces and groups by December 2006, and that 4,000 children were released between October 2006 and August 2007.[114] Thus, in terms of positive yield, the programme has attained some real success. However, the 'release' of children does not include their social reintegration into civilian life. By December 2006, CONADER figures showed that, of the 30,000 children released, 14,000 were still to receive any form of reintegration assistance. This often means that those children are worse off than they were while associated with fighting forces since, after demobilisation but before reintegration, many children had no form of income and nobody to look after them. This increased the number of homeless street children, and resulted in voluntary re-enlistment.

The main point of concern is the apparent inability of the DDR programme to demobilise female child soldiers. Of the 30,000 children estimated to need demobilisation, up to forty per cent (12,500) were thought to be girls.[115] Yet only an estimated twelve per cent of the children that went through the DDR process were female.[116] With regard to CONADER as an institution, there were great concerns. Amnesty International stated that they 'encountered pervasive pessimism among the child protection community about CONADER's limited capacity to effectively coordinate a comprehensive DDR process given its weak institutional foundations, shortage of technical experience, lack of decentralization and widespread reports of corruption inside CONADER'.[117]

The UEPNDDR succeeded CONADER immediately after the latte's dissolution on 14 July 2007. Ostensibly this substitution of organisations, at least in part, occurred as a result of the loss of faith in CONADER and the associated difficulties in securing further funding. This is evidenced by the fact that the UEPNDDR also functions on the operational framework established for CONADER during May 2004. Finally, regardless of the successes attained to date, child soldier recruitment bears a proportional relationship to the intensity of hostilities. As a result of the escalation in hostilities during August 2008, the number of children asso-

---

[113] 2008 Secretary-General DRC Report, n 34 above, paras 19–20; however, the Secretary-General warned that that figure may have increased due to the re-escalation of hostilities in North Kivu from 28 August 2008 onwards.

[114] 2006 Secretary-General DRC Report, n 33 above; 'Report of the Secretary-General on Children and Armed Conflict', A/62/609, S/2007/757 (21 December 2007).

[115] 'Forgotten Casualties of War: Girls in Armed Conflict' (Save the Children UK, 2005) 11.

[116] 2008 Global Report, n 93 above, 110.

[117] 'Struggling to Survive: Children in Armed Conflict in the Democratic Republic of the Congo' (Watchlist on Children and Armed Conflict, April 2006) 47.

ciated with fighting forces in the DRC re-escalated.[118] The figure stood at an estimated 3,500 before this escalation in hostilities.[119]

## V. SUMMARY

In the course of this chapter, I observed various positive developments in relation to the prevention of child soldiering in the DRC. Most significantly among these are the DDR of thousands of child soldiers on an annual basis, the ongoing prosecutions before the ICC and the better coordinated sharing of data that has been the result of the work of the country task force for the MRM. However, many of the results achieved to date are mixed. While the DRC was the first state to prosecute an individual for the use and recruitment of child soldiers, that individual has escaped justice and is serving in the national armed forces of the very state that convicted him. At the same time, the prosecution of Bosco Ntaganda before the ICC is a very welcome development. Nevertheless, many challenges remain. For the thousands of children who are absorbed into DDR programmes on an annual basis, thousands more slip through the cracks, and are not absorbed into these programmes. Moreover, not only are significant numbers of children still recruited on an annual basis, many of those children that have been absorbed into DDR programmes are re-recruited.

The practicalities in the DRC situation support my broad finding that, in order to be more effective, all mechanisms engaged with child soldier prevention must be continuously refined. Virtually every mechanism included in this chapter that is operational in addressing child soldiering in the DRC can be rendered more effective through such continuous reassessment and refinement. Worryingly, the mechanism that is currently underperforming most significantly—the most powerful mechanism engaged with child soldier prevention, which is underperforming in the majority of all mechanisms engaged with such prevention—is the Security Council itself. Consistent with the conclusions drawn in Chapter 6, the Security Council should take targeted action against those parties that persistently violate child soldier prohibitive norms. The sanctions imposed on Colonel Innocent Zimurinda of the Forces armées de la République démocratique du Congo is the most significant step in this regard to date. That notwithstanding, the effective prevention of child soldiering is dependent on contributions being made by every relevant mechanism, and not the refinement of one powerful mechanism.

---

[118] 2008 Secretary-General DRC Report, n 34 above, para 19–20.
[119] Ibid.

# 8

# *Conclusion*

T HE THESIS OF this book is that, in order for international law to be an agent through which 'an era of application' can be entered in the context of child soldier prevention, the focus must be shifted from norm creation to norm enforcement. This raises two questions. First, are the international law norms that prohibit the use and recruitment of child soldiers capable of enforcement in their current form? Secondly, what changes should be effected to the manner of enforcement of these norms in order to achieve a more significant degree of social change? In other words, what is needed for an era of application?

This chapter is divided into three parts. Parts I and II address the questions posed above. However, disjunctively, the conclusions reached regarding each of the research questions achieve little in plotting the central thesis of the study within the bigger scheme of eradicating the use and recruitment of child soldiers altogether. Therefore, part III not only serves to extrapolate the relevance of the conclusions reached regarding the two research questions, but does so analytically in relation to the nature of the child soldier problem, as detailed in the first two chapters of the study. Indeed, while Chapters 1 and 2 may feature less prominently in this chapter, they are still indispensable to the success of the study. 'An era of application', by definition, speaks to the reactive role of law, which is consistent with the instrumentalist approach I have adopted. For law to be used effectively as an instrument to achieve a desired outcome, and for it to react effectively to an undesired social reality, a thorough understanding of the nature and extent of that social reality or phenomenon is at the very least greatly beneficial and more likely imperative.

## I. THE ENFORCEABILITY OF INTERNATIONAL LAW NORMS PROHIBITING CHILD SOLDIERING

The various norms prohibiting the use and recruitment of child soldiers belonging to international humanitarian law (IHL), international human rights law (IHRL) and international criminal law (ICL) were individually assessed, in detail, in Chapters 3, 4 and 5. The reason for this assessment is that the nature and content of these norms impact heavily on the potential for their enforcement. The relationship between IHL and IHRL also impacts on the enforcement of these norms. In this context, war crimes in terms of ICL is seen as forming part of IHL, as norms belonging to both these regimes are subject to similar *chapeau* requirements, the existence of and nexus to armed conflict, and, unlike IHRL, both these regimes bind non-state actors in addition to state actors. Thus, for purposes of this section, reference to IHL includes ICL, unless stated otherwise.

## A. The Relationship between International Humanitarian Law and International Human Rights Law

In the context of child soldier prevention, I have emphasised the importance of the relationship between IHL and IHRL for a number of reasons, key among which are: first, that no other substantive norms that exist in both IHL and IHRL are defined substantively exactly the same. This is the case with Article 77(2) of Protocol I Additional to the Geneva Conventions and Article 38 of the Convention on the Rights of the Child (CRC), the two leading child soldier prohibitive norms from IHL and IHRL, respectively.[1] Yet, I argue that there is still potential for irreconcilable norm conflict between IHL and IHRL in relation to child soldier prevention. This serves well to indicate the complex nature of this relationship. Secondly, IHL applies during times of armed conflict, whereas IHRL applies during times of both peace and armed conflict. Thirdly, IHL binds state and non-state actors, whereas IHRL binds state actors only. Lastly, the regime to which the relevant norm belongs will largely dictate what avenues for enforcement are available.

The potential for norm conflict to which I refer relates to the different obligations the Optional Protocol to the Convention on the Rights of the Child on the Involvement of Children in Armed Conflict (CIAC Protocol) creates on parties depending on their status (state or non-state actors) on the one hand and the principle of equality of belligerents on the other.[2]

The likelihood of this potential norm conflict occurring is not remote, and the analysis thereof is not purely abstract or academic. Although the CIAC Protocol is a human rights law instrument, it expressly endeavours

[1] Convention on the Rights of the Child (entered into force 2 September 1990) 1577 UNTS 3; Protocol I Additional to the Geneva Conventions of 12 August 1949, and relating to the Protection of Victims of International Armed Conflicts, adopted 8 June 1977 (entered into force 7 December 1978) 1125 UNTS 17512.

[2] Optional Protocol to the Convention on the Rights of the Child on the Involvement of Children in Armed Conflict (CIAC Protocol) (entered into force 12 February 2002) 2173 UNTS 222. See generally Chapter 4.I above.

to regulate the conduct of parties during armed conflict as it prohibits the use of child soldiers in direct participation in hostilities. This instrument also prohibits the recruitment of child soldiers during peacetime. However, the importance of this instrument is perceived to be its focus on alleviating the suffering of children during armed conflict. Therefore, in any military engagement between a state armed force and a non-state actor, where the relevant state has ratified the CAIC Protocol, such a conflict of norms is inevitable. The Protocol will impose different obligations on state and non-state actors, and this will be irreconcilable with the equality of belligerents: 'the rules of international humanitarian law apply with equal force to both sides to the conflict, irrespective of who is the aggressor'.[3]

Further, status-dependent obligations add to the asymmetry that generally exists between state and non-state actors. This may prompt non-state actors to dissociate themselves from their IHL obligations, as they are not treated equally to state actors in terms of the law. It is important to keep in mind that one of the major challenges in preventing child soldiering is engagement with non-state actors. This norm conflict does not, however, render the norms contained in the Protocol unenforceable. If IHL is the *lex specialis* vis-à-vis IHRL in this context, then this norm conflict is to be resolved by applying the lowest common denominator to all parties to the conflict.

Unfortunately both the CRC and the CIAC Protocol failed to achieve their potential in preventing the exploitation of children by armed groups and forces. This, I conclude, is primarily due to a failure of the drafters of both instruments to appreciate the unique characteristics of IHRL as a legal regime, and specifically how these unique characteristics may contribute to the better protection of children from exploitation by military groups and forces. Much criticism was levelled against the CRC at the time of its adoption for directly adopting the IHL language contained in Additional Protocol I, and for failing to impose stricter obligations in relation to the prevention of the use and recruitment of child soldiers. However, it is not so much the failure of creating stricter standards that resulted in the CRC not achieving its potential as the failure of not creating norms better suited to the IHRL sphere of international law. In particular, unlike IHL, the CRC could have prohibited the use of children during situations falling short of armed conflict, such as internal disturbances and riots. Furthermore, although the CRC does prohibit the recruitment of children during times of peace, the language of the instrument should have reflected this expressly.

---

[3] C Greenwood, 'Historical Development and Legal Basis' in D Fleck (ed), *The Handbook of International Humanitarian Law* (Oxford, Oxford University Press, 2008) 11.

The prevailing consideration and motive in drafting the CIAC Protocol was lifting the standards of protection afforded to children, protecting them from military use and recruitment, while at the same time securing mass state subscription to the instrument. Unfortunately, to achieve this, the drafters of the instrument provided for less proscriptive regulation of child soldier use and recruitment by state actors than by non-state actors. In addition, neither of the problems I identified above in relation to the CRC, being the prohibition of the use of children in situations falling short of the IHL definition of armed conflict and the prohibition of child recruitment during times of peace, was rectified in the CIAC Protocol. Nevertheless, the shortcomings of the CRC and its Protocol do not result in a situation where the relevant norms are inherently incapable of being enforced. Instead, these shortcomings have resulted in the net of protection being cast more narrowly.

## B. Shortcomings of the Contemporary Prohibitions of Child Soldiering

There are shortcomings in the existing legal norms; some more worrying than others. In particular, the following elements appear in the most widely ratified instruments prohibiting child soldiering, including the CRC and Additional Protocol I: that 'all feasible measures' be taken that 'persons who have not attained the age of fifteen years' not be used to 'take a direct part in hostilities' and that states parties refrain from 'recruiting' such persons. As was the case in the previous section, these shortcomings generally result in protection being offered to fewer children, rather than inhibiting the enforceability of these norms. Moreover, often these shortcomings appear much more devastating than they are. This is certainly true of the 'all feasible measures' standard. Child soldier use is a continuous offence (continuous crime in criminal law terms), meaning the offence is committed for as long as a child participates directly in hostilities. The converse effect thereof is that a child's future status is not determined by whether all feasible measures were taken in the first instance where she/he was used for direct participation in hostilities. Instead, this assessment has to made *de novo* in each and every instance where the relevant child was used in direct participation in hostilities. It is highly unlikely that a child will be used for direct participation in hostilities on more than one occasion and that all feasible measures to ensure that the child does not so participate were taken in each instance. Moreover, it is highly exceptional that a child will be used in direct participation in hostilities only once. Thus, this standard has very little effect on the enforceability of these norms. The standard does, however, serve as a barometer for measuring the commitment of states to preventing child soldiering. Unfortunately, it was retained in relation to the regulation of child soldier use by state actors in the CIAC Protocol.[4]

The development of customary international law has already addressed some of these shortcomings, and will continue to do so in the future. The child soldier war crime is the only crime in the Rome Statute of the International Criminal Court (Rome Statute) that was not prohibited in terms of customary law, in the form it exists in the Rome Statute, at the time of the drafting and adoption of the Rome Statute.[5] Since then, in the *Child Recruitment* decision, the Special Court for Sierra Leone (SCSL) has held that this formulation of the crime is representative of customary international law.[6] Paradoxically, while the legal interpretation and analysis offered by the SCSL is often questionable, and never more so than in the *Child Recruitment* decision (this is an appropriate example of the adage 'hard cases make bad law'), the SCSL's work has had a tremendously positive effect on the development of child soldier prevention. Such positive developments include the recognition of the prohibition of the use and recruitment of child soldiers as a customary norm. The recognition of the Rome Statute formulation of the child soldier crime as forming part of customary international law extends the scope of protection previously offered to children from military recruitment, to include protection from military enlistment and conscription. This construct is broader than 'recruitment', and is broad enough to cover all instances of child soldier acquisition other than children taking up arms truly by their own initiative. Given the fact that there are only a very few states (as opposed to non-state actors) internationally that use children younger than eighteen (instead of fifteen) for direct participation in armed conflict, it is possible that there is an emerging rule of customary international law proscribing the use of children younger than eighteen in direct participation in armed conflict. Of course, this is subject to the *opinio juris* element of customary international law also being present.

Much headway has been made regarding impunity for the use and recruitment of child soldiers on the international sphere. The child soldier offence was one of the hallmarks of the SCSL, and the first case before the International Criminal Court (ICC) dealt exclusively with this crime.[7] Even though the success of the ICC is yet to be determined, and regardless of the many errors made during the *Lubanga* trial, it seems that there is no lack of commitment on the part of the Office of the Pros-

---

[4] Art 1 of the CIAC Protocol.

[5] Arts 8(2)(b)(xxvi) and 8(2)(e)(vii) of the Rome Statute of the International Criminal Court (entered into force 1 July 2002) 2187 UNTS 90.

[6] *Prosecutor v Sam Hinga Norman, Decision on Preliminary Motion Based on Lack of Jurisdiction*, SCSL-2004-14-AR72E (31 May 2004) (*Child Recruitment* decision).

[7] *Prosecutor v Thomas Lubanga Dyilo*, Trial Chamber I, judgment, ICC-01/04-01/06 (2012) (*Lubanga* judgment).

ecutor to pursue the prosecution of individuals for the use, enlistment or conscription of child soldiers.

Although there are shortcomings in the instruments that currently prohibit child soldiering, the elaboration of new such instruments is highly unlikely for many years to come. The tasks of drafting and adopting the CRC and the CIAC Protocol were monumental. Furthermore, there is less incentive for states to ratify any new such convention as, from a political perspective, they have already indicated their commitment to the protection of children and, in the context of the CIAC Protocol in particular, their non-recruitment and use during armed conflict. Therefore, hopes for the refinement of these norms rest on the development of customary international law. In this regard, mechanisms with the competence to interpret and apply customary child soldier prohibitions should periodically reassess the relevant state practice and associated *opinio juris* so as to ensure that proper account is taken of the potential development of the customary norm.

In summary, the norms proscribing the use and recruitment of child soldiers that are in existence at the moment are capable of enforcement. It is hoped that these norms will be refined over time, with a view to better protecting children. Nevertheless, a concerted effort is now required to address the application of these norms. The scope of application and the available enforcement mechanisms are determined by the legal regime to which the norms in question belong. The implications of the formal nature of the legal regime to which a particular norm prohibiting child soldiering belongs, be it IHL, IHRL or ICL, does not limit the enforceability of the specific norm. Rather, it dictates the scope of application and available enforcement mechanisms to which the legal regime is confined more broadly.

## II. THE REFINEMENT OF INTERNATIONAL LAW ENFORCEMENT MECHANISMS AIMED AT THE PREVENTION OF CHILD SOLDIERING

The likelihood that major changes to a small number of mechanisms will achieve significant results is minimal. Certainly, in this study I did not identify any mechanisms that hold the potential to prevent child soldiering on a broad-based scale by simply implementing extensive changes to the mechanism itself. Instead, all mechanisms that contribute to the prevention of child soldiering should be refined and reassessed on a continuous basis. Some mechanisms will, however, require more refinement than others. The mechanisms analysed in this study form part of the UN, the African Union and the ICC. The remainder of this section focuses on these entities and the various mechanisms that form part of them. Each mechanism analysed in this study is catalogued below, with specific emphasis being placed on the changes to the relevant mechanism that I argue will elevate its effectiveness in preventing child soldiering, should they be implemented.

## A. The Refinement of United Nations Mechanisms Aimed at Child Soldier Prevention

The UN is a massive organisation consisting of five principal organs and a host of agencies, funds and other entities. I refer to the entities that make up the UN system collectively as 'UN entities'. Many of these entities engage with child soldiering. However, the present analysis focuses on the Special Representative to the Secretary-General on Children and Armed Conflict (SRSG), the Committee on the Rights of the Child (CRC Committee) and the Security Council. The inclusion of these entities in this study was determined by two criteria: the relative strength of the entity and the entity's potential for direct engagement with child soldier prevention.

### i. The Special Representative to the Secretary-General on Children and Armed Conflict

The SRSG is the mechanism engaged with child soldier prevention that has arguably yielded the most tangible results to date. As was discussed in Chapter 7, for example, the phasing-out of the use and recruitment of child soldiers by the FARDC, the armed forces of the Democratic Republic of the Congo (DRC), was a direct result of negotiations with the DRC government initiated by former SRSG Otunnu. These negotiations culminated in a five-point action plan to cease the use and recruitment of child soldiers in the ranks of the FARDC, and this plan has seen extensive implementation. The SRSG is one of very few mechanisms engaged with child soldier prevention, the positive results of which can to some extent be measured on a quantitative basis. The deterrent effect of the ICC may be very real, yet it does not yield results that can be measured in a similar fashion. Caution should be heeded not to elevate the role of the SRSG in preventing child soldiering purely on the basis of measurable results; conversely, mechanisms the results of which are not similarly measurable should not be relegated by virtue of this alone.

The SRSG has invested more time and resources in direct engagement with child soldier prevention, ie engagement that may yield measurable results, than in indirect engagement. In the context of indirect engagement, the SRSG is mandated to act as a focal point within the UN system with responsibility for the coordination of initiatives and mechanisms aimed at child soldier prevention emanating from all entities making up the UN system. In this context, the SRSG should play a more meaningful role. Even though there is often considerable overlap in their efforts, there is little and often no cross-communication between the various UN entities engaged directly with child soldier prevention. There are various reasons why such communication should exist between these entities, including: they can benefit from each other's data and experience, and such interaction will better enable the different UN entities to make strategic decisions regarding which matters to take up and which not to. The Monitoring and Reporting Mechanism (MRM) cures this shortcoming to some extent, but only in countries where the MRM is active.

The SRSG engages with all of these entities; however, the entities may benefit greatly from engagement with each other. Given the level of effectiveness of the SRSG, criticism like this might seem trivial. However, this is wholly consistent with the broader conclusion reached in this section, that all mechanisms, regardless of their current level of effectiveness, should be reassessed and refined continuously.

## ii. The Committee on the Rights of the Child

The CRC Committee is a treaty body forming part of the UN human rights treaty system. For most of its history, the Committee's primary function was monitoring state compliance with the CRC. It was only very recently that the Protocol establishing an individual complaints mechanism for the Committee came into force. It is certainly hoped that such a complaints mechanism will elevate the effectiveness of the Committee.

## iii. The Security Council

The issue of children affected by armed conflict was formally placed on the agenda of the Security Council of the UN in 1998, since when the Security Council has continuously engaged with this issue. Most significantly, the Security Council has established a comprehensive Monitoring and Reporting Mechanism on Children and Armed Conflict (MRM) and Working Group on Children and Armed Conflict (Working Group). However, the MRM and Working Group have no power, in their own right, to enforce or apply international norms prohibiting child soldiering. Instead, they exist to inform the Security Council, which then has the power to take action by, for example, imposing targeted sanctions against violating parties. The Security Council has adopted one binding Resolution under its Chapter VII powers, which demanded the end of child soldier use and recruitment in the DRC.[8] This Resolution, however, did not go as far as creating targeted sanctions. There is clear evidence that a number of actors have persistently used and recruited child soldiers for a number of years. The potential of the Security Council to contribute to the prevention of the use and recruitment of child soldiers lies in its considerable power.

The Security Council threatened persistent violators with targeted sanctions for the first time in 2004.[9] This threat has been repeated on numerous occasions since then. By failing to act against such persistent violators, who have been identified by the Secretary-General in his annual report on children in armed conflict, the Security Council is likely reinforcing the view held by some that these are empty threats, and nothing more than political rhetoric. Regardless of debates around the different conceptions of childhood among different cultures, there are no violating parties today that justify their actions on the basis of any such arguments. Such violating parties use and recruit child soldiers as the benefits thereof outweigh the negative consequences—what Singer calls 'the decisional calculus behind the use of child soldiers'.[10] This will not be the case should the Security Council impose targeted sanctions, the review of which is conditional on the relevant violating party engaging with the SRSG to implement a plan phasing out the use and recruitment of child soldiers within a fixed time period. Indeed, of all the mechanisms engaged with child soldier prevention, I am of the view that the Security Council is best placed to affect this decisional calculus. This, however, is dependent on the Security Council taking the next step and following up its threats with action.

## B. The Refinement of African Union Mechanisms Aimed at Child Soldier Prevention

Within the African Union, both the African Court on Human and Peoples' Rights (African Court) and the African Committee of Experts on the Rights and Welfare of the Child (African Children's Committee) have subject-matter jurisdiction in relation to child soldier prohibitive norms. The African Court is the only regional human rights court that has such jurisdiction.

The African Children's Committee has been in existence for more than ten years, but has produced no real results to date. The relevance of this Committee for present purposes is its status as an African inter-governmental organisation, giving it the authority to transmit cases to the

---

[8] Security Council Resolution 1332 (14 December 2000).
[9] Security Council Resolution 1539 (22 April 2004), para 5(c).
[10] PW Singer, *Children at War* (Oakland, CA, University of California Press, 2006) 153.

African Court. The African Court has not yet developed jurisprudence on child rights. To enhance the future effectiveness of the Court in preventing child soldiering, more states should make declarations granting individuals and non-government organisations (NGOs) with observer status before the African Commission direct access to the Court. Of all the entities that have the authority to transmit cases to the Court, it is most likely that an individual or an NGO will transmit cases dealing with child soldier use and recruitment.

## C. The Refinement of the International Criminal Court in Relation to Child Soldier Prevention

In suggesting changes to enforcement structures, one of the considerations is the feasibility of changing the structure at all. In the context of the ICC, the process for amendment is such that small changes are not going to be made to the Rome Statute or the structure of the ICC. In any event, such changes are not required.

The potential of the Rome Statute to achieve far-reaching results rests on states parties incorporating the Rome Statute into their municipal law and prosecuting violators themselves. States should legislate for the use of universal jurisdiction in relation to the prosecution of war crimes, including the child soldier crime. This will increase the scope for the prosecution of the ICL child soldier crime exponentially. At the same time, the potential of the Rome Statute, in both the municipal and international spheres, is dependent on the extensive subscription to the Statute by states. Efforts to promote the ratification and municipal incorporation of the Rome Statute must be expanded.

An enforcement gap exists regarding the enforcement of child soldier prohibitive norms on non-state actors. This is so primarily because international law obligations are generally focused on state. IHL and ICL have a more significant role to play in this regard as, unlike IHRL, these regimes create obligations on non-state actors. Traditionally, however, there was no mechanism to enforce these obligations incumbent upon non-state actors. However, the ICC does have jurisdiction in relation to such actors, and will in all likelihood contribute to narrowing this gap. In terms of IHRL, the state in which such a non-state actor operates has a duty to prevent them from using or recruiting child soldiers. In practice, however, this is often impracticable as the state which is the duty-bearer is engaged in armed conflict with the relevant non-state actor and, moreover, there are numerous inherent difficulties in enforcing legal norms during ongoing armed conflict.

### III. CONCLUSION: SHIFTING FOCUS FROM NORM
### CREATION TO NORM ENFORCEMENT, THE
### REQUISITES FOR AN 'ERA OF APPLICATION'

The two questions posed at the outset of this chapter serve different purposes in that the first question relates to the viability of the thesis of the book whereas the second question analyses how the thesis is to be achieved. Should the conclusion of the first question have been negative, it would have been fatal to the thesis of the study—that international law can be an agent through which 'an era of application' can be entered in the context of child soldier prevention. The conclusion was, however, positive. The second question calls for further analysis, and a broader range of conclusions.

International law plays a dual role in addressing such matters as child soldiering. First, it plays a reactive role in the sense that violations of the relevant norms are redressed. Secondly, it plays a less tangible, anticipatory role in preventing violations from occurring altogether. This happens on both a micro- and a macroscale. On the microscale, the deterrent value of criminal prosecution plays a role in preventing the commission of at least some crimes in some circumstances. On the macroscale, the existence of specific rules of international law prevents the commission of some actions altogether. For example, in 1942 US President Roosevelt authorised the mass internment of people of Japanese ancestry, including a great number of US citizens.[11] In total, around 120,000 people were interned.[12] On the same authority, people of Japanese ancestry were excluded from designated areas, including the entire states of California and Oregon.[13] Since the commencement of the 'war on terror', there have been many calls from the far-right fringes of society for the internment of Muslim people in the US.[14] However, unlike the internment of people of Japanese ancestry during World War Two, these calls have been dismissed as emanating from fringe groups and not representing the views of the majority. Indeed, in a society based on fundamental human rights, such internment is unthinkable.[15]

---

[11] This was done on the authority of Executive Order 9066. See also *Korematsu v United States* 323 US 214 (1944). In this case the US Supreme Court, on a split verdict of six to three, upheld Executive Order 9066 as constitutional. Justice Roberts, Justice Murphy and Justice Jackson gave strong dissenting opinions. Justice Murphy stated in his dissent 'I dissent, therefore, from this legalization of racism'.

[12] WL Ng, *Japanese American Internment during World War II: A History and Reference Guide* (Westport, CT, Greenwood Press, 2002) xi.

[13] Ibid, 21.

[14] See, eg M Malkin, *In Defense of Internment: The Case for Racial Profiling in World War II and the War on Terror* (Washington, DC, Regenery Publishing, 2004).

[15] In view of the US detention facility at Guantanamo Bay, Cuba, it may be argued that internment is not as unrealistic as I suggest. Although detention at Guantanamo Bay is not based on legal process, it is nevertheless based upon intelligence implicating the specific detainees. The legality of such detention is undoubtedly questionable, but it is

As is clear from the analysis in Chapters 4–6, the era of application occurs very much in relation to the reactive role of law. This approach still fails to take account of deeper systemic problems that result in children joining armed groups, such as extreme poverty. Circumstances exist where it is sometimes the lesser of two evils for a child to be a child soldier as opposed to a child civilian.[16] Social change should not be limited to ending impunity and preventing the use and recruitment of child soldiers, but should also create an environment where choosing to be a child soldier is not more conducive to self-preservation than choosing to remain a civilian. To achieve this, the social milieu should be adjusted to the extent that not only are commanders discouraged from recruiting children, but the children themselves see no benefit in joining armed groups. To use the language of Andvig and Gates, social change should address not only the 'demand' of child soldiers, but also their 'supply'.[17] Such social change speaks to the anticipatory role of law.

As I stated earlier, social change is incremental. Achieving broad-based social change cannot be considered until extensive rights protection occurs. This implies that where the social phenomenon that is the subject of concern is a problem on a significant scale, international law's anticipatory role will only be effective once its reactive role has diminished the scope of the phenomenon. As is evidenced in Chapter 2, the use and recruitment of child soldiers is a problem of global proportions. The era of application is the next step in combating the child soldier phenomenon. Once this era of application is achieved, more work will still be required to prevent child soldiering. This work will need to focus more on the deeper systemic problems that cause children to join armed groups and forces, and, at the same time, will also need to focus more on the anticipatory role of international law. Norms forming part of international law are applied and enforced in both the municipal and international spheres. The municipal incorporation of international norms is one of the best avenues through which to secure application of these norms, and states should as a matter of course implement the international obligations to which they subscribe into their municipal law. However, the strength of the rule of law in the relevant state will largely determine whether the municipal law can be applied effectively. Children are generally used and recruited during armed conflict in states

---

not tantamount to the mass internment of people based on ethnicity alone, as was the case with Japanese internees during World War Two. See LM Olson, 'Guantanamo Habeas Review: are the D.C. District Court's Decisions consistent with IHL Internment Standards?' (2009–10) 42 *Case Western Reserve Journal of International Law* 197 for an analysis of detention at Guantanamo Bay in terms of IHL standards.

[16] See generally Chapter 2.III.A above.

[17] JC Andvig and S Gates, 'Recruiting Children for Armed Conflict' in S Gates and S Reich (eds), *Child Soldiers in the Age of Fractured States* (Pittsburgh, PA, Pittsburgh University Press, 2009) 77–78.

where the rule of law is very weak. Many of these challenges, as well as successes, are evident from the case study of the DRC presented in Chapter 7.

In the final analysis it is fitting to refer, as I did in Chapter 1, to former SRSG Otunnu's statement to the General Assembly some fifteen years ago:

> The Special Representative believes that the time has come for the international community to redirect its attention and energies from the juridical task of the development of norms to the political project of ensuring their application and respect on the ground. An 'era of application' must be launched. Words on paper cannot save children and women in peril. Such a project can be accomplished if the international community is prepared to employ its considerable collective influence to that end.[18]

The two aspects of this short quote with which I agree wholeheartedly are: (i) that the international community must redirect its focus from norm creation to norm enforcement; and (ii) that this goal is achievable if the international community employs its collective influence to that end. I disagree, however, that the task of developing norms is strictly 'juridical', and that the task of ensuring their application and respect is purely 'political'. The purpose of this study is not to restate Otunnu's views. Rather, the value this study adds to the knowledge on child soldier prevention is threefold. First, I conclude, after thorough analysis, that the positive law has developed to the extent that there is a body of international law that is capable of application. Secondly, I identify various entities, functionaries and mechanisms, the refinement of which will render international law more effective in preventing child soldiering. Concomitant to this, I draw specific conclusions in relation to how each of these entities, functionaries and mechanisms are to be refined. Finally, in analysing my findings in relation to each of these research questions, with the aim of addressing the central thesis, I conclude that the findings in this study are the next step in child soldier prevention, and a necessary component in eventually achieving broad-based social change. Nevertheless, such broad-based social change will not be truly achieved during 'an era of application' but, rather, during an era in which application is not necessary.

---

[18] 'Promotion and Protection of the Rights of Children: Protection of Children Affected by Armed Conflict Note by the Secretary-General' A/54/430 (1 October 1999), para 165.

# Bibliography

## BOOKS

Ang, F, *A Commentary on the United Nations Convention on the Rights of the Child: Article 38 Children in Armed Conflicts* (The Hague, Brill, 2005)

Arnold, R and Quenivet, N (eds), *International Humanitarian Law and Human Rights Law: Towards a New Merger in International Law* (The Hague, Brill, 2008)

Arts, K and Popovski V, *International Criminal Accountability and the Rights of Children* (Cambridge, Cambridge University Press, 2006)

Bernhardt, R, *Encyclopaedia of Public International Law Volume 2* (Amsterdam, Elsevier, 1992)

Bothe, M, Partch, K and Solf, W, *New Rules for Victims of Armed Conflicts* (The Hague, Martinus Nijohff Publishers, 1982)

Brett, R and McCallin, M, *Children: the Invisible Soldiers* (Stockholm, Rädda Barnen, 1998)

—— and Specht, I, *Young Soldiers: Why They Choose to Fight* (Boulder, CO, Lynne Rienner Publishers, 2004)

Byers, M, *Custom, Power and the Power of Rules* (Cambridge, Cambridge University Press, 1999)

Cassese, A, *International Criminal Law,* 2nd edn (Oxford, Oxford University Press, 2008)

Chesterman, S, *Law and Practice of the United Nations: Documents and Commentary* (Oxford, Oxford University Press, 2008)

Clark, JF (ed), *The African Stakes of the Congo War* (New York, Palgrave MacMillan, 2002)

Cohn, I and Goodwin-Gill, GS, *Child Soldiers: The Role of Children in Armed Conflict* (Oxford, Oxford University Press, 1994)

Cryer, R, *Prosecuting International Crimes: Selectivity and the International Criminal Law Regime* (Cambridge, Cambridge University Press, 2005)

—— et al, *An Introduction to International Criminal Law and Procedure* (Cambridge, Cambridge University Press, 2010)

Dallaire, R, *They Fight Like Soldiers, They Die Like Children* (London, Random House, 2010)

D'Amato, A, *The Concept of Custom* (Ithaca & London, Cornell University Press, 1971)

Detrick, S (ed), *The United Nations Convention on the Rights of the Child: A Guide to the 'Travaux Préparatoires'* (The Hague, Martinus Nijhoff Publishers, 1992)

——, *A Commentary on the United Nations Convention on the Rights of the Child* (The Hague, Martinus Nijhoff Publishers, 1999)

De Wet, E, *The Chapter VII Powers of the United Nations Security Council* (Oxford, Hart Publishing, 2004)

Doebbler, CFJ, *Introduction to International Human Rights Law* (CD Publishing, 2007)

Drumbl, MA, *Reimagining Child Soldiers in International Law and Policy* (Oxford, Oxford University Press, 2012)

Dugard, J, *International Law: A South African Perspective* (Cape Town, Juta & Co, 2005)

Ferdinandusse, WN, *Direct Application of International Criminal Law in National Courts* (Amsterdam, Asser Press, 2005)

Friedman, L (ed), *The Law of War* (New York, Random House, 1972)

Gates, S and Reich, S (eds), *Child Soldiers in the Age of Fractured States: Security Continuum: Global Politics in the Modern Age* (Pittsburgh, PA, University of Pittsburgh Press, 2009)

Goodwin-Gill, G and Cohn, I, *Child Soldiers: The Role of Children in Armed Conflicts* (Oxford, Oxford University Press, 1994)

Green, LC, *The Contemporary Law of Armed Conflict* (Manchester, Manchester University Press, 2000)

Happold, M, *Child Soldiers in International Law* (Manchester, Manchester University Press, 2005)

Heckman, JJ, Nelson, RL and Cabatingan, L (eds), *Global Perspectives on the Rule of Law* (London, Routledge, 2010)

Henckaerts, JM and Doswald-Beck, L, *Customary International Humanitarian Law Volume I: Rules* (Cambridge, Cambridge University Press, 2005)

—— and ——, *International Committee of the Red Cross: Customary International Humanitarian Law Volume II: Practice* (Cambridge, Cambridge University Press, 2005)

——, —— and Alvermann, C, *Customary International Humanitarian Law: Rules* (Cambridge, Cambridge University Press, 2007)

Henkin, L, *How Nations Behave* (New York, Columbia University Press, 1979)

Honwana, A, *Child Soldiers in Africa* (Philadelphia, PA University of Pennsylvania Press, 2007)

Kaldor, M, *New and Old Wars*, (Cambridge, Polity Press, 1999)

Kennedy, D, *The Dark Sides of Virtue: Reassessing International Humanitarianism* (Princeton, NJ, Princeton University Press, 2004)

Kittichaisaree, K, *International Criminal Law* (Oxford, Oxford University Press, 2001)

Klabbers, J, *An Introduction to International Institutional Law,* 2nd edn (Cambridge University Press, 2009)

Kuper, J, *International Law Concerning Child Civilians in Armed Conflict* (Oxford, Oxford University Press, 1997)

——, *Military Training and Children in Armed Conflict: Law, Policy and Practice* (The Hague, Martinus Nijhoff Publishers, 2004)

Lowe, AV, *International Law* (Oxford, Oxford University Press, 2007)

Lutz, EL and Reiger, C (eds), *Prosecuting Heads of State* (Cambridge, Cambridge University Press, 2008)

Makkonen, T (revised and updated by Kortteinen, J), *The Principle of Non-Discrimination in International Human Rights Law and EU Law* (Erik Castrén Institute, University of Helsinki, August 2005)

Malkin, M, *In Defense of Internment: The Case for Racial Profiling in World War II and the War on Terror* (Washington DC, Regenery Publishing, 2004)

Mendelson, MH, *The Formation of Customary International Law* (The Hague, Brill,1998)

Meron, T, *War Crimes Law Comes of Age* (Oxford, Oxford University Press, 1998)

Ng, WL, *Japanese American Internment during World War II: A History and Reference Guide* (Westport, CT, Greenwood Press, 2002)

Nikken, P, *La Proteccion Internacional de los Derechos Humanos: Su Desarrollo Progresivo* (Madrid, Institudo Interamericano de derechos humanos, 1987)

Piaget, J, *The Child's Conception of the World* (London, Routledge & Kegan Paul, 1928)

——, *The Moral Judgment of the Child* (London, Kegan Paul, Trench, Trubner & Co. 1932)

—— *The Child's Construction of Reality* (London, Routledge and Kegan Paul, 1955)

—— and ——, *The Growth of Logical Thinking from Childhood to Adolescence* (New York, Basic Books, 1958)

—— and ——, *The Early Growth of Logic in the Child: Classification and Seriation* (London, Routledge & Kegan Paul, 1964)

Pinker, S, *The Better Angels of Our Nature: Why Violence has Declined* (New York, Penguin, 2011)

Rosen, DM, *Armies of the Young: Child Soldiers in War and Terrorism* (Brunswick, Rutgers University Press, 2005)

Sadat-Akhavi, SA, *Methods of Resolving Conflicts between Treaties* (The Hague, Martinus Nijhoff Publishers, 2003)

Schabas, W, *An Introduction to the International Criminal Court* (Cambridge, Cambridge University Press, 2001)

——, *The International Criminal Court: A Commentary on the Rome Statute* (Oxford, Oxford University Press, 2010)

Schwarzenberger, G, *The Frontiers of International Law* (London, Stevens & Sons, 1962)

Singer, PW, *Children at War* (Oakland, University of California, 2006)

Soanes, C and Stevenson, A (eds), *Concise Oxford English Dictionary* (2006)

Van Bueren, G, *The International Law on the Rights of the Child* (The Hague, Martinus Nijhoff Publishers, 1995)

Van Bueren, G, *The International Law on the Rights of the Child* (The Hague, Martinus Nijhoff Publishers, 1998)

Verheyde, M, *A Commentary on the United Nations Convention on the Rights of the Child: Articles 43–45: the UN Committee on the Rights of the Child* (The Hague, Martinus Nijhoff Publishers, 2006)

Viljoen, F, *International Human Rights Law in Africa* (Oxford, Oxford University Press, 2007)

Villiger, ME, *Customary International Law and Treaties* (Amsterdam, Kluwer Law International, 1997)

Wessells, M, *Child Soldiers: From Violence to Protection* (Boston, Harvard University Press, 2006)

## CHAPTERS IN BOOKS

Alston, P, 'Critical Appraisal of the UN Human Rights Regime' in P Alston (ed), *The United Nations and Human Rights: A Critical Appraisal* (Oxford, Oxford University Press, 1992)

Ames, B, 'Methodological Problems in the Study of Child Soldiers' in S Gates and S Reich (eds), *Child Soldiers in the Age of Fractured States: Security Continuum: Global Politics in the Modern Age* (Pittsburgh, PA, University of Pittsburgh Press, 2009)

Andvig, JC and Gates, S, 'Recruiting Children for Armed Conflict' in S Gates and S Reich (eds), *Child Soldiers in the Age of Fractured States: Security Continuum: Global Politics in the Modern Age* (Pittsburgh, PA, University of Pittsburgh Press, 2009)

Becker, J, 'Child Recruitment in Burma, Sri Lanka and Nepal' in S Gates and S Reich (eds), *Child Soldiers in the Age of Fractured States: Security Continuum: Global Politics in the Modern Age* (Pittsburgh, PA, University of Pittsburgh Press, 2009)

Bothe, M, 'War Crimes' in A Cassese, P Gaeta and JRWD Jones (eds), *The Rome Statute of the International Criminal Court: A Commentary Volume I* (Oxford, Oxford University Press, 2002)

Boyden, J, 'Anthropology Under Fire: Ethics, Researchers and Children in War' in J Boyden and J De Berry (eds), *Children and Youth on the Front Line: Ethnography, Armed Conflict and Displacement* (Oxford, Berghahn Books, 2004)

Cottier, M, 'Article 8(2)(b)(xxvi)' in O Triffterer (ed), *Commentary on the Rome Statute of the International Criminal Court* (Oxford, Hart Publishing, 2008)

Danilenko, M, 'ICC Jurisdiction and Third States' in A Cassese (ed),
    *International Criminal Law* (Oxford, Oxford University Press, 2003)

Dunn, KC, 'A Survival Guide to Kinshasa: Lessons of the Father, Passed
    Down to the Son' in JF Clark (ed), *The African Stakes of the Congo
    War* (New York, Palgrave MacMillan, 2002)

Gamba, V and Cornwell, R, 'Arms, Elites, and Resources in the Angolan
    Civil War' in M Berdal M and DM Malone (eds), *Greed and
    Grievance—Economic Agendas in Civil Wars* (Boulder, CO, Lynne
    Rienner Publishers, 2000)

Greenwood, C, 'Historical Development and Legal Basis' in D Fleck (ed),
    *The Handbook of International Humanitarian Law* (Oxford, Oxford
    University Press, 2008)

Grunfeld, F, 'Child Soldiers' in J Willems (ed), *Developmental and
    Autonomy Rights of Children. Empowering children, caregivers and
    communities* (New York, Intersentia, 2002)

Harhoff, F, 'Sense and Sensibility in Sentencing—Taking Stock of
    International Criminal Punishment' in O Engdahl, P Wrange and O
    Bring (eds), *Law at War: The Law As It Was and the Law As It
    Should Be* (The Hague, Martinus Nijhoff Publishers, 2008)

Harrington, J, 'The African Court on Human and Peoples' Rights' in MD
    Evans and R Murray (eds), *The African Charter on Human and
    Peoples' Rights: the System in Practice, 1986–2006* (Cambridge,
    Cambridge University Press, 2008)

Jonah, JOC, 'The United Nations' in A Adebajo and I RashidI (eds), *West
    Africa's Security Challenges: Building Peace in a Troubled Region*
    (Boulder, CO, Lynne Rienner Publishers, 2004)

Kane, I and Motala, AC, 'The Creation of a New African Court of Justice
    and Human Rights' in MD Evans and R Murray (eds), *The African
    Charter on Human and Peoples' Rights: the System in Practice,
    1986–2006* (Cambridge, Cambridge University Press, 2008)

Karp, J, 'Reporting and the Committee on the Rights of the Child' in AF
    Bayefsky (ed), *The Human Rights Treaty System in the 21st Century*
    (Amsterdam, Kluwer Academic Publishers, 2000)

Kuper, J, 'Children and Armed Conflict—Some Problems in Law and Policy'
    in D Fottrell (ed), *Revisiting Children's Rights: 10 Years of the UN
    Convention on the Rights of the Child* (Amsterdam, Kluwer Law
    International, 2000)

Kuper, J, 'Military Training and International Criminal Accountability' in K
    Arts and V Popovski (eds), *International Criminal Accountability and
    the Rights of Children* (Cambridge, Cambridge University Press, 2006)

Mundis, D, 'Blockburger Test' in A Cassese (ed), *The Oxford Companion to
    International Criminal Justice* (Oxford, Oxford University Press, 2009)

Ober, J, 'Classical Greek Times' in M Howard, GJ Andreopoulos and MR
    Shulman (eds), *The Laws of War: Constraints on Warfare in the
    Western World* (New Haven, CT, Yale University Press, 1994)
Piragoff, DK, 'Mental Element' in A Cassese et al (eds), *Commentary on the
    Rome Statute of the International Criminal Court* (Oxford, Oxford
    University Press, 1999)
Popovski, V, 'Children in Armed Conflict: Law and Practice of the United
    Nations' in K Arts and V Popovski (eds), *International Criminal
    Accountability and the Rights of Children* (Cambridge, Cambridge
    University Press, 2006)
Prout, A and James, A, 'A New Paradigm for the Sociology of Childhood'
    in A Prout and A James (eds), *Constructing and Reconstructing
    Childhood: Contemporary Issues in the Sociological Study of
    Childhood* (New York, Routledge, 1990)
Schmitt, MN, 'Direct Participation in Hostilities and 21st Century Armed
    Conflict' in H Fischer (ed), *Crisis Management and Humanitarian
    Protection: Festschrift für Dieter Fleck* (Berlin, Berliner Wiss.-Verl,
    2004)
Schwebel, SM, 'Commentary' in MK Bulterman and M Kuijer (eds),
    *Compliance with Judgements of International Courts* (Amsterdam,
    Kluwer Law International, 1996)
Sen, A, 'Global Justice' in JJ Heckman, RL Nelson and L Cabatingan (eds),
    *Global Perspectives on the Rule of Law* (New York, Routledge, 2010)
Singer, PW, 'The Enablers of War: Causal Factors behind the Child Soldier
    Phenomenon' in S Gates and S Reich (eds), *Child Soldiers in the
    Age of Fractured States: Security Continuum: Global Politics in the
    Modern Age* (Pittsburgh, PA, University of Pittsburgh Press, 2009)
Stone, L, 'Implementation of the Rome Statute in South Africa' in C Bhoke
    and J Biegon (eds), *Prosecuting International Crimes in Africa*
    (Pretoria, Pretoria University Law Press, 2011)
Von Hebel, H and Robinson, D, 'Crimes within the Jurisdiction of the Court'
    in RS Lee (ed), *The International Criminal Court: The Making of
    the Rome Statute — Issues, Negotiations, Results* (Amsterdam, Kluwer
    Law International, 1999)
Viljoen, F, 'Communications under the African Charter: Procedure and
    Admissibility' in MD Evans and R Murray (eds), *The African Charter
    on Human and Peoples' Rights: the System in Practice, 1986–2006*
    (Cambridge, Cambridge University Press, 2008)

JOURNAL ARTICLES

Akehurst, M, 'The Hierarchy of the Sources of International Law' (1974–75)
    XLVII *British Yearbook of International Law* 273

Ames, B, 'Methodological Problems in the Study of Child Soldiers' (2009)
    *Child Soldiers in the Age of Fractured States* 16
Ancker III, CJ and Burke, MD, 'Doctrine for Asymmetric Warfare' [July–
    August 2003] *Military Review* 18
Bassiouni, MC, 'Repression of Breaches of the Geneva Conventions under
    the Draft Additional Protocol to the Geneva Conventions of August
    12, 1949' (1977) 8 *Rutgers-Cam Law Journal* 185
——, 'The Normative Framework of International Humanitarian Law:
    Overlaps, Gaps and Ambiguities' (2000) 75 *International Law Studies
    Series* 3
Benvenisti, E, 'The Legal Battle to Define the Law on Transnational
    Asymmetric Warfare' (2009–10) 20 *Duke Journal of Comparative &
    International Law* 339
Bethlehem, D, 'The Relationship between International Humanitarian Law
    and International Human Rights Law in Situations of Armed Conflict'
    (2013) (2)2 *Cambridge Journal of International and Comparative Law*
    180
Boothby, B, 'And for Such Time as: The Time Dimension to Direct
    Participation in Hostilities' (2009–10) 42 *New York University Journal
    of International Law & Policy* 741
Boudreault, LS, 'Les reserves apportees au Protocole additionnel 1 aux
    Conventions de Geneve sur le droit humanitaire' (1989–90) 6 *Revue
    quebecoise de droit international* 105
Bowring, B, 'Fragmentation, Lex Specialis and the Tensions in the
    Jurisprudence of the European Court of Human Rights' (2009) 14
    *Journal Conflict & Security Law* 485
Breen, C, 'When Is a Child Not a Child? Child Soldiers in International
    Law' (2007) 8(2) *Human Rights Review* 83
Brett, R, 'Girl Soldiers Denial of Rights and Responsibilities' (2004) 23(2)
    *Refugee Survey Quarterly* 30
Brooks, RE, 'The New Imperialism: Violence, Norms, and the 'Rule of Law''
    (2002–03) 101 *Michigan Law Review* 2275
Buergenthal, T, 'International and Regional Human Rights Law and
    Institutions: Some Examples of Their Interaction' (1977) 12 *Texas
    International Law Journal* 321
——, 'The Normative and Institutional Evolution of International Human
    Rights' (1997) 19 *Human Rights Quarterly* 703
Cassel, D, 'Does International Human Rights Law Make a Difference?'
    (2001) 2 *Chicago Journal of International Law* 121
Cassese, A, 'The Statute of the International Criminal Court: Preliminary
    Reflections' (1999) 10 *European Journal of International Law* 144
Chirwa, DM, 'The Merits and Demerits of the African Charter on the
    Rights and Welfare of the Child' (2002) 10 *International Journal of
    Children's Rights* 157

Daskal, JC, 'The Geography of the Battlefield: A Framework for Detention and Targeting Outside the "Hot" Conflict Zone' (2013) 161 *University of Pennsylvania Law Review* 1165

De Beco, G, 'The Optional Protocol to the Convention on the Rights of the Child on a Communications Procedure: Good News' (2013) 13 *Human Rights Law Review* 367

Dennis, MJ, 'Application of Human Rights Treaties Extraterritorially to Detention of Combatants and Security Internees: Fuzzy Thinking All Around?' (2005–06) 12 *ILSA Journal of International & Comparative Law* 472

De Wet, E, 'The Prohibition of Torture as an International Norm of *Jus Cogens* and Its Implications for National and Customary Law' (2004) 15 *European Journal of International Law* 97

Dhanapala, J, 'Multilateral Cooperation on Small Arms and Light Weapons: From Crisis to Collective Response' (2002–03) 9 *Brown Journal World Affairs* 163

Doebbler, CFJ & Scharf, MP, 'Will Saddam Hussein Get a Fair Trial' (2005–06) 37 *Case Western Reserve Journal of International Law* 21

Draper, GIAD, 'Human Rights and the Law of War' (1971–72) 12 *Virginia Journal of International Law* 326

——, 'Humanitarian Law and Human Rights' (1979) *Acta Juridica* 193

Dror, Y, 'Law and Social Change' (1958–59) 33 *Tulsa Law Review* 787

Drumbl, M, 'Collective Violence and Individual Punishment: The Criminality of Mass Atrocity' (2004–05) 99 *North-Western Law Review* 539

Duy Phan, H, 'A Blueprint for a Southeast Asian Court of Human Rights' (2008–09) 10 *Asian–Pacific Law & Policy Journal* 384

Eno, RW, 'The Jurisdiction of the African Court on Human and Peoples' Rights' (2002) 2 *African Human Rights Law Journal* 223

Fombad, CM, 'The Separation of Powers and Constitutionalism In Africa: The Case of Botswana' (2005) 25 *British Columbia Third World Law Journal* 301

Fitzmaurice, G, 'The Law and Procedure of the International Court of Justice 1951–4: Treaty Interpretation and other Treaty Points' (1957) *British Yearbook of International Law* 33 237

Garraway, C, '"To Kill or Not to Kill?" Dilemmas on the Use of Force' (2009) 14 *Journal of Conflict & Security Law* 500

Geiß, R, 'Asymmetric Conflict Structures' (2006) 88(864) *International Review of the Red Cross* 757

Gormley, WP, 'The Codification of *Pacta Sunt Servanda* by the International Law Commission: The Preservation of Classical Norms of Moral Force and Good Faith' (1969–70) 14 *St Louis University Law Journal* 370

Green, LC, '"Grave Breaches" or Crimes against Humanity' (1997–98) 8 *USAFA Journal of Legal Studies* 19

Greenwood, C, 'International Humanitarian Law and the *Tadić* Case' (1996)
  7 *European Journal of International Law* 265

Gutteridge, JAC, 'The Geneva Conventions of 1949' (1949) 26 *British
  Yearbook of International Law* 298

Happold, M, 'The Optional Protocol to the Convention on the Rights of
  the Child on the involvement of children in armed conflict' (2000) 3
  *Yearbook of International Humanitarian Law* 226

——, 'Excluding Children from Refugee Status: Child Soldiers and Article
  1F of the Refugee Convention' (2001–02) 17 *American University
  International Law Review* 1131

——, 'Child Soldiers: Victims or Perpetrators?' (2008) 29 *University La
  Verne Law Review* 56

Hart, J, 'The Politics of Child Soldiers' (2006–07) 13 *Brown Journal World
  Affairs* 217

Hathaway, OA, 'Do Human Rights Treaties Make a Difference?' (2001–02)
  111 *Yale Law Journal* 1935

Helle, D, 'Optional Protocol on the involvement of children in armed conflict
  to the Convention on the Rights of the Child' (2000) *International
  Review of the Red Cross* 839

Henkin, L, 'Columbia Human Rights Law Review Twenty-Fifth Anniversary
  Issue Human Rights: The Next Twenty-Five Years' (1993–94) 25
  *Columbia Human Rights Law Review.* 259

——, 'Human Rights and State Sovereignty'' (1995–96) 25 *Georgia Journal
  of International & Comparative Law* 31

Kennedy, D, 'The International Human Rights Movement: Part of the
  Problem?' (2002) 15 *Harvard Human Rights Journal* 101

Killander, M, 'Interpreting Regional Human Rights Treaties' (2010) 13 *Sur—
  International Journal on Hum Rights* 145

Kingsbury, B, 'The Concept of Compliance as a Function of Competing
  Conceptions of International Law' (1998) 19 *Michigan Journal of
  International Law* 345

Knight, M and Özerdem, A, 'Guns, Camps and Cash: Disarmament,
  Demobilization and Reinsertion of Former Combatants in Transitions
  from War to Peace' (2004) 41(4) *Journal of Peace Research* 502

Koh, HH, 'Why Do Nations Obey International Law?' (1997) 106 *Yale Law
  Journal* 2599

Konge, P, 'International Crimes & Child Soldiers' (2010) 16 *Southwestern
  Journal of International Law* 41

Krieger, H, 'A Conflict of Norms: The Relationship between Humanitarian
  Law and Human Rights Law in the ICRC Customary Law Study'
  (2006) 11 *Journal Conflict & Security Law* 265

Kuntz, JL, 'The Laws of War' (1956) 50 *American Journal of International
  Law* 313

Kuper, J, 'Children in Armed Conflict: The Law and Its Uses' (2000) 43(1) *Development* 32

Kurth, ME, 'The *Lubanga* Case of the International Criminal Court: A Critical Analysis of the Trial Chamber's Findings on Issues of Active Use, Age, and Gravity' (2013) (5)2 *Göttingen Journal of International Law* 431

Lindroos, A, 'Addressing Norm Conflicts in a Fragmented Legal System: The Doctrine of *Lex Specialis*' (2005) 74 *Nordic Journal of International Law* 27

Lloyd, A, 'Evolution of the African Charter on the Rights and Welfare of the Child and the African Committee of Experts: Raising the Gauntlet' (2002) 10 *International Journal of Children's Rights* 179

Mann, H, 'International Law and the Child Soldier' (1987) 36 *International & Comparative Law Quarterly* 32

Matheson, MJ, 'The Sixth Annual American Red Cross–Washington College of Law Conference on International Humanitarian law: A Workshop on Customary International Law and the 1977 Protocols Additional to the 1949 Geneva Conventions' (1987) 2 *American University Journal of International Law & Policy* 415

McCormack, TLH, 'Selective Reaction to Atrocity' (1996–97) 60 *Albany Law Review* 681

Melzer, N, 'Keeping the Balance between Military Necessity and Humanity: A Response to Four Critiques of the ICRC's Interpretive Guidance on the Notion of Direct Participation in Hostilities' (2009–10) 42 *New York University Journal of International Law & Policy* 831

Meron, T, 'A Report on the NYU Conference on Teaching International Protection of Human Rights' (1980–81) 13 *New York University Journal of International Law & Policy* 881

——, 'Norm Making and Supervision in International Human Rights: Reflections on Institutional Order' (1982) 76 *American Journal of International Law* 754

——, 'The Humanization of Humanitarian Law' (2000) 94 *American Journal of International Law* 239

Musah, AF, 'Small Arms: A Time Bomb Under West Africa's Democratization Process' (2002–03) 9 *Brown Journal World Affairs* 239

Neumayer, E, 'Do International Human Rights Treaties Improve Respect for Human Rights?' (2005) 49(6) *The Journal of Conflict Resolution* 925

Olowu, D,'Protecting Children's Rights in Africa: A Critique of the African Charter on the Rights and Welfare of the Child' (2002) 10 *International Journal of Children's Rights* 127

Olson, LM, 'Practical Challenges of Implementing the Complementarity between International Humanitarian and Human Rights Law— Demonstrated by the Procedural Regulation of Internment in Non-

International Armed Conflict' (2007–09) 40 *Case Western Reserve Journal of International Law* 437

——, 'Guantanamo Habeas Review: Are the D.C. District Court's Decisions Consistent with IHL Internment Standards?' (2009–10) 42 *Case Western Reserve Journal of International Law* 197

Orakhelashvili, A, 'The Interaction between Human Rights and Humanitarian Law: Fragmentation, Conflict, Parallelism, or Convergence?' (2008) 19 *European Journal of International Law* 161

Parks, WH, 'Part IX of the ICRC Direct Participation in Hostilities Study: No Mandate, No Expertise, and Legally Incorrect' (2009–10) 42 *New York University Journal of International Law & Policy* 769

Peters, K and Richards, P, 'Why we Fight: The Voices of Youth Combatants in Sierra Leone' (1998) 68 *Africa* 2

Prud'homme, N, 'Lex Specialis: Oversimplifying a More Complex and Multifaceted Relationship?' (2007) 40 *Israel Law Review* 356

Punyasena, W, 'Conflict Prevention and the International Criminal Court: Deterrence in a Changing World' (2006) 14 *Michigan State Journal of International Law* 39

Quénivet, N, 'The Liberal Discourse and the "New Wars" of/on Children' (2012–13) 38 *Brook. Journal of International Law* 1053

Rosen, DM, 'Who is a Child? The Legal Conundrum of Child Soldiers' (2009–10) 25 *Connecticutt Journal of International Law* 81

Ross, ML, 'How Do Natural Resources Influence Civil War? Evidence from Thirteen Cases' (2004) 58(1) *International Organization* 35

Samb, M, 'Fundamental Issues and Practical Challenges of Human Rights in the Context of the African Union' (2009) 15 *Annual Survey of International & Comparative Law* 61

Sassòli, M and Olson, LM, 'The Relationship between International Humanitarian and Human Rights Law Where it Matters: Admissible Killing and Internment of Fighters in Non-international Armed Conflicts' (2008) 90(871) *ICRC Review* 605

Schabas, WA, '*Lex Specialis*? Belt and Suspenders? The Parallel Operation of Human Rights Law and the Law of Armed Conflict, and the Conundrum of Jus ad Bellum' (2007) 40 *Israel Law Review* 592

Schmitt, MN, 'Deconstructing Direct Participation in Hostilities: The Constitutive Elements' (2009–10) 42 *New York University Journal of International Law & Policy* 697

Scobbie, I, 'Principle or Pragmatics? The Relationship between Human Rights Law and the Law of Armed Conflict' (2009) 14 *Journal Conflict & Security Law* 449

Seneviratne, L, 'Accountability of Child Soldiers: Blame Misplaced' (2008) 20 *Sri Lanka Journal of International Law* 29

Seneviratne, W, 'International Legal Standards Applicable to Child Soldiers' (2003) 15 *Sri Lanka Journal of International Law* 39

Simon, WH, 'Solving Problems vs. Claiming Rights: The Pragmatist Challenge to Legal Liberalism' (2004–05) 46 *William & Mary Law Review* 127

Singer, PW, 'Talk is Cheap: Getting Serious about Preventing Child Soldiers' (2004) 37 *Cornell International Law Journal* 561

Sloth-Nielsen, J and Mezmur, BD, 'Out of the Starting Blocks: The 12th and 13th Sessions of the African Committee of Experts on the Rights and Welfare of the Child' (2009) 9 *African Human Rights Law Journal* 336

Smidt, M, 'The International Criminal Court: An Effective Means of Deterrence?' (2001) 167 *Military Law Review* 156

Smith, A, 'Child Recruitment and the Special Court for Sierra Leone' (2004) 2 *Journal of International Criminal Justice* 1141

Somer, J, 'Jungle Justice: Passing Sentence on the Equality of Belligerents in Non-international Armed Conflict' (2007) 89(867) *ICRC Review* 655

Stohl, R, 'Targeting Children: Small Arms and Children in Conflict' (2002–03) 9(1) *The Brown Journal of World Affairs* 281

Stohl, R, 'Reality Check—The Danger of Small Arms Proliferation' (2005) 6 *Geo Journal of International Affairs* 71

Tacsan, J, 'The Effectiveness of International Law: An Alternative Approach' (1996) 11(1) *International Legal Theory* 3

Tamanaha, BZ, 'The Tension between Legal Instrumentalism and the Rule of Law' (2005–06) 33 *Syracuse Journal of International Law & Commerce* 131

Ubombana, NJ, 'Towards the African Court on Human and Peoples' Rights: Better Late than Never' (2000) 3 *Yale Human Rights and Development Law Journal* 45

Van der Vyver, JD, 'The International Criminal Court and the Concept of Mens Rea in International Criminal Law' (2004) 12 *University Miami International & Comparative Law Review* 57

Van Schaack, B, 'The Principle of Legality in International Criminal Law: Legality & International Criminal Law' (2009) 103 *American Society for International Law Proceedings* 101

Verri, P, 'Combattants armés ne pouvant se distinguer de la population civile' (1982) 21(1–4) *RDPMDG* 345

Viljoen, F, 'Supra-national Human Rights Instruments for the Protection of Children in Africa: The Convention on the Rights of the Child and the African Charter on the Rights and Welfare of the Child' (1998) 31 *Comparative and International Law Journal of Southern Africa* 199

Vlassenroot, K, 'Citizenship, Identity Formation & Conflict in South Kivu: The Case of the Banyamulenge' (2002) 29(93/94) *Review of African Political Economy* 499

Waschefort, G, 'Drawing the Boundaries between Terrorism and Crimes against Humanity' (2007) 22(2) *South African Public Law* 457

——, 'Justice for Child Soldiers? The RUF Trial of the Special Court for Sierra Leone' (2010) 1 *International Humanitarian Legal Studies* 189

——, 'The Pseudo Legal Personality of Non-state Armed Groups in International Law' (2011) 36 *South African Yearbook of International Law* 226

——, 'Beyond Fragmentation: An Issues-Based Approach to "Human Rights"' (2012) 37 *South African Yearbook of International Law* 61

Watkin, K, 'Opportunity Lost: Organized Armed Groups and the ICRC Direct Participation in Hostilities Interpretive Guidance' (2009–10) 42 *New York University Journal of International Law & Policy* 641

Weisburd, AM, 'Customary International Law: The Problem of Treaties' (1988) 21 *Vanderbilt Journal of Transnational Law* 1

West, H, 'Girls with Guns: Narrating the Experience of War of FRELIMO's "Female Detachment"' (2000) 73 *Anthropological Quarterly* 4

Wouters, J and Verhoeven, S, 'The Prohibition of Genocide as a Norm of Ius Cogens and its Implications for the Enforcement of the Law of Genocide' (2005) 5 *International Criminal Law Review* 401

## COMMENTARIES

Pictet, J, *Commentary on the Geneva Conventions of 12 August 1949* Vol IV (International Committee of the Red Cross, 1955)

——, *Commentary, IV Geneva Conventions Relative to the Protection of Civilian Persons in Time of War* (International Committee of the Red Cross, 1958)

Sandoz, Y, Swinarski, C and Zimmermann, B (eds), *Commentary on the Additional Protocols of 8 June 1977 to the Geneva Conventions of 12 August 1949* (International Committee of the Red Cross, 1987)

Sassòli, M and Bouvier AA et al, *How Does Law Protect in War: Cases, Documents and Teaching Materials on Contemporary Practice in International Humanitarian Law* (International Committee of the Red Cross, 1999)

## NON-GOVERNMENTAL ORGANISATION PUBLICATIONS

'Children at War: Creating Hope for their Future', AFR 62/017/2006 (Amnesty International, October 2006)

Des Forges, A, 'Leave None to Tell the Story: Genocide in Rwanda' (Human Rights Watch, 1999)

'DRC: DDR and Reform of the Army', AFR 62/001/2007 (Amnesty International, January 2007)

Florquin, N and Berman, EG (eds), 'Armed and Aimless: Armed Groups, Guns and Human Security in the ECOWAS Region' (Small Arms Survey, May 2005)

'Forgotten Casualties of War: Girls in Armed Conflict' (Save the Children UK, 2005)

'Getting it Done and Doing it Right: Implementing the Monitoring and Reporting Mechanism on Children and Armed Conflict in the DRC' (Watch List on Children and Armed Conflict, January 2008)

Melzer, N, Interpretive Guidance on the Notion of Direct Participation in Hostilities under International Humanitarian Law (International Committee of the Red Cross, 2009)

Mukundi Wachira, G, 'African Court on Human and Peoples' Rights: Ten Years on and Still no Justice' (Report of the Minority Rights Group International, 2008)

Reich, SF and Achvarina, A 'Why Do Children Fight? Explaining Child Soldier Ratios in African Intra-State Conflicts' (Ford Institute, 2005)

'Struggling to Survive: Children in Armed Conflict in the Democratic Republic of the Congo' (Watch List on Children and Armed Conflict, April 2006)

Veale, A 'From Child Soldier to Ex-Fighter: A Political Journey. Demobilisation and Reintegration of Female Ex-Combatants, Ethiopia' (Institute for Security Studies, 2003)

Viljoen, F (ed), 'Judiciary Watch Report: The African Human Rights System: Towards the Coexistence of the African Commission on Human and Peoples' Rights and African Court on Human and Peoples' Rights' (Nairobi, Kenyan Section of the International Commission of Jurists, 2006)

'Quarterly Progress Report: DRC' (Multi-Country Demobilization and Reintegration Program, July–September 2005)

'Quarterly Progress Report: DRC' (Multi-Country Demobilization and Reintegration Program, April–June 2006)

INTERNATIONAL INSTRUMENTS

ILO Forced Labour Convention No 29 (entered into force 1 May 1932) 39 UNTS 55

Convention for the Amelioration of the Condition of the Wounded in Armies in the Field, Geneva (22 August 1864)

Universal Declaration of Human Rights, GA res 217A (III), UN Doc A/810, 71 (1948)

Charter of the United Nations (entered into force 24 October 1945) 1 UNTS XVI

European Convention on Human Rights and Fundamental Freedoms (entered
into force 4 November 1950) 213 UNTS 221

Convention for the Protection of Human Rights and Fundamental Freedoms
(entered into force of 3 September 1953) ETS 5, 213 UNTS 222

Declaration of the Rights of the Child, General Assembly Resolution 1386
(XIV), 14 UN GAOR Supp. (No 16) at 19, UN Doc A/4354 (1959)

Declaration on the Protection of Women and Children in Emergency
and Armed Conflict, General Assembly Resolution 29/3318 of 14
December 1974

International Covenant on Civil and Political Rights (entered into force 23
March 1976) 999 UNTS 171

ILO Minimum Age Convention No 138 (entered into force 19 June 1976)
1015 UNTS 297

Protocol I Additional to the Geneva Conventions of 12 August 1949, and
relating to the Protection of Victims of International Armed Conflicts,
adopted 8 June 1977 (entered into force 7 December 1978) 1125
UNTS 17512

Protocol II Additional to the Geneva Conventions of 12 August 1949, and
relating to the Protection of Victims of Non-International Armed
Conflicts, adopted 8 June 1977 (entered into force 7 December 1978)
1125 UNTS 609

African Charter on Human and Peoples' Rights (entered into force on 21
October 1986) 1520 UNTS 217

Convention against Torture and Other Cruel, Inhuman or Degrading
Treatment or Punishment (entered into force on 26 June 1987) 1465
UNTS 85

Convention on the Rights of the Child, General Assembly Resolution 44/25
(12 December 1989) (entered into force 2 September 1990) 1577
UNTS 3

Vienna Declaration and Programme of Action' A/CONF.157/23 (12 July
1993)

Convention on the Prohibition of the Use, Stockpiling, Production and
Transfer of Anti-Personnel Mines and on their Destruction (entered
into force on 18 September 1997) 2056 UNTS 211

Nouakchott Draft of the Protocol to the African Charter on Human and
Peoples' Rights on the Establishment of an African Court on Human
and Peoples' Rights (1997) OAU Doc OAU/LEGAL/EXP/AFCHPR/
PRO (2)

Convention on the Prohibition of the Use, Stockpiling, Production and
Transfer of Anti-Personnel Mines and on their Destruction (entered
into force 1 March 1999) 36 ILM 1507

The African Charter on the Rights and Welfare of the Child (1990), OAU
Doc CAB/LEG/24.9/49 (entered into force 29 November 1999)

ILO Worst Forms of Child Labour Convention No 182 (entered into force 19 November 2000) 2133 UNTS161

Optional Protocol to the Convention on the Rights of the Child on the Sale of Children, Child Prostitution and Child Pornography (entered into force 18 January 2002) 1577 UNTS 3

Optional Protocol to the Convention on the Rights of the Child on the Involvement of Children in Armed Conflict (entered into force 12 February 2002) 2173 UNTS 222

Rome Statute of the International Criminal Court (Rome Statute) (entered into force 1 July 2002) 2187 UNTS 90

Elements of Crimes of the Rome Statute of the International Criminal Court (2002) ICC-ASP/1/3

Protocol to the African Charter on Human and Peoples' Rights on the Establishment of an African Court on Human and People's Rights (entered into force 25 January 2004) OAU Doc OAU/LEG/EXP/ AFCHPR/PROT (III)

## UNITED NATIONS RESOLUTIONS

### General Assembly

General Assembly Resolution 57 (I), 11 December 1946
General Assembly Resolution 31/169, 1 January 1979
General Assembly Resolution 48/157, 20 December 1993
General Assembly Resolution 49/75K, 15 December 1994
General Assembly Resolution 57/77, 12 December 1996
General Assembly Resolution A/RES/63/117, 10 December 2008

### Security Council

Security Council Resolution 1071, 30 August 1996
Security Council Resolution 1314, 11 August 2000
Security Council Resolution 1332, 14 December 2000
Security Council Resolution 1379, 20 November 2001
Security Council Resolution 1460, 30 January 2003
Security Council Resolution 1539, 22 April 2004
Security Council Resolution 1612, 26 July 2005
Security Council Resolution 1882, 4 August 2009
Security Council Resolution 1998, 12 July 2011
Security Council Resolution 2002, 29 July 2011
Security Council Resolution 2068, 19 September 2012
Security Council Resolution 2098, 28 March 2013
Security Council Resolution 2143, 7 March 2014

## Human Rights Council Resolutions

Human Rights Council Resolution A/HRC/RES/11/1, 17 June 2009

## Commission on Human Rights Resolution

Commission on Human Rights Resolution 1994/91, 9 March 1994

## Other Resolutions

'Human Rights in Armed Conflicts' Resolution XXIII adopted by the
    International Conference on Human Rights, Teheran, 12 May 1968

### INTERNATIONAL AND REGIONAL REPORTS

'21st Session of the African Committee of Experts on the Rights & Welfare
    of the Child' (15–19 April 2013), ACERWC//RPT (XXI)
'Children of War: Report from the Conference on Children in War', Raoul
    Wallenberg Institute Report No 10 (1991)
'Coalition to Stop the Use of Child Soldiers', Child Soldiers Global Report
    2001
'Draft Statute for the International Criminal Court and Draft Final Act',
    United Nations Diplomatic Conference of Plenipotentiaries on the
    Establishment of an International Criminal Court, A/CONF.183/2/
    Add.1, 21 (1998)
'Guide to the Optional Protocol on the Involvement of Children in Armed
    Conflict' (UNICEF and Coalition to Stop the Use of Child Soldiers,
    2003)
'Human Security Report 2005: War and Peace in the 21st Century' (Liu
    Institute for Global Issues, University of British Columbia, 2005)
'Louder Than Words: An Agenda to End State Use of Child Soldiers' (Child
    Soldiers International, 2012)
'Promotion and Protection of the Rights of Children', Report of the Special
    Representative of the Secretary-General for Children and Armed
    Conflict, A/62/228, 13 August 2007
'Report of the Mapping Exercise Documenting the Most Serious Violations
    of Human Rights and International Humanitarian Law Committed
    within the Territory of the Democratic Republic of the Congo between
    March 1993 and June 2003' (Office of the High Commissioner for
    Human Rights, 2010)

'Report of the Secretary-General on Children and Armed Conflict to the
    Security Council' (26 April 2012), A/66/782, S/2012/261
'Report of the Secretary-General on Children and Armed Conflict to the
    Security Council' (15 May 2013) A/67/845, S/2013/245
'The State of the World's Children' (UNICEF, 2005)
16th Session of the African Committee of Experts on the Rights and Welfare
    of the Child (ACERWC), ACERWC/Rpt (XVI), 9–12 November 2010
Annual Report of the Secretary-General on Children in Armed Conflict,
    Security Council, A/59/695 S/2005/72, 9 February 2005
Annual Report of the Special Representative of the Secretary-General for
    Children and Armed Conflict, Radhika Coomaraswamy, A/HRC/9/3, 27
    June 2008
Approved resources for peacekeeping operations for the period from 1 July
    2011 to 30 June 2012, A/C.5/65/19, 22 July 2011
Coalition to Stop the Use of Child Soldiers, 'Child Soldiers Global Report
    2008'
Coalition to Stop the Use of Child Soldiers, Child Soldiers Global Report
    2004, 2004
Committee on the Rights of the Child, 'Report on the Forty-Eighth Session',
    CRC/C/48/3, 16 November 2009
Committee on the Rights of the Child, 'Report on the Second Session',
    CRC/C/10 (19 October 1992)
Committee on the Rights of the Child, 'Report on the Third Session',
    CRC/C/16, 5 March 1993
Concluding Observations of the Committee on the Rights of the Child:
    Democratic Republic of the Congo, CRC/C/COD/CO/2, January 2009
Coomaraswamy, R, 'Report of the Special Representative of the Secretary-
    General for Children and Armed Conflict', A/64/254, 6 August 2009
Drahoslav Štefánek, D (Chairperson-Rapporteur), 'Report of the Open-Ended
    Working Group to Explore the Possibility of Elaborating an Optional
    Protocol to the Convention on the Rights of the Child to Provide a
    Communications Procedure', A/HRC/13/43, 21 January 2010
Koskenniemi, M, 'Fragmentation of International Law: Difficulties Arising
    from the Diversification and Expansion of International law', Report
    of the Study Group of the International Law Commission, A/CN.4/
    Law682, 13 April 2006
Letter dated 8 September 2006 from the Permanent Representative of France
    to the United Nations addressed to the President of the Security
    Council, S/2006/724, 11 September 2006
Machel, G, 'Promotion and Protection of the Rights of Children: Impact of
    Armed Conflict on Children', UN Doc A/51/306, 26 August 1996
Mission Report: Visit of the Special Representative for Children and Armed
    Conflict to The Democratic Republic of the Congo, 14–21 April 2009

Nowak, M, 'Study on the Phenomena of Torture, Cruel, Inhuman or Degrading Treatment or Punishment in the World, Including an Assessment of Conditions of Detention', A/HRC/13/39/Add.5, 5 February 2010

Otunnu, O, 'Promotion and Protection of the Rights of Children: Protection of Children Affected by Armed Conflict', A/53/482, 12 October 1998

Otunnu, O, 'Protection of Children Affected by Armed Conflict Report of the Special Representative of the Secretary-General for Children and Armed Conflict', A/54/430, 1 October 1999

Otunnu, O, 'Protection of Children Affected by Armed Conflict, Report of the Special Representative of the Secretary-General for Children and Armed Conflict', A/58/328, 29 August 2003

Report by Ndiaye, BW, Special Rapporteur, on his mission to Rwanda from 8 to 17 April 1993, E/CN.4/1994/7/Add.1, 11 August 1993

Report of the International Law Commission (ILC), Fifty-Sixth Session, UN Doc A/59/10, 2004

Report of the Preparatory Committee on the Establishment of an International Criminal Court, A/CONF.183/2/Add.1, 14 April 1998

Report of the Secretary General on Children and Armed Conflict in the Democratic Republic of the Congo, S/2008/693,10 November 2008

Report of the Secretary-General on Children and Armed Conflict in the DRC, S/2006/389, 13 June 2006

Report of the Secretary-General on Children and Armed Conflict in the Democratic Republic of the Congo, S/2007/391, 28 June 2007

Report of the Secretary-General on Children and Armed Conflict in the Democratic Republic of the Congo, S/2010/369, 9 July 2010

Report of the Secretary-General on Children and Armed Conflict, A/61/529–S/2006/826, October 2006

Report of the Secretary-General on Children and Armed Conflict, A/63/785, S/2009/158, 26 March 2009

Report of the Secretary-General on Children and Armed Conflict, A/64/742, S/2010/181, 13 April 2010

Report of the Secretary-General on Children and Armed Conflict, A/65/820, S/2011/250, 23 April 2011

Report of the Secretary-General on Children and Armed Conflict, S/2002/1299, 26 November 2002

Report of the Secretary-General on Children and Armed Conflict, Security Council, A/58/546–S/2003/1053, 10 November 2003

Report of the Secretary-General on Children and Armed Conflict, Security Council, A/62/609–S/2007/757, 21 December 2007

Report of the Secretary-General on the Establishment of a Special Court for Sierra Leone, S/2000/915, 4 October 2000

Report of the Secretary-General on the United Nations Organization Stabilization Mission in the Democratic Republic of the Congo, S/2011/20, 17 January 2011

Report of the Secretary-General on the United Nations Organization Stabilization Mission in the Democratic Republic of the Congo, S/2011/298, 12 May 2011

Report of the Secretary-General's Panel of Experts on Accountability in Sri Lanka, 31 March 2011

Report of the Special Representative of the Secretary-General for Children and Armed Conflict, A/66/256 93, August 2011

Report of the United Nations Fact Finding Mission on the Gaza Conflict, A/HRC/12/48, 25 September 2009

Revised proposal for a draft optional protocol prepared by the Chairperson-Rapporteur of the Open-ended Working Group on an Optional Protocol to the Convention on the Rights of the Child to provide a communications procedure, A/HRC/WG.7/2/4, 13 January 2011

UNICEF Child Protection Strategy, E/ICEF/2008/5/Review1, 3-5 June 2008

United Nations Diplomatic Conference of Plenipotentiaries on the Establishment of an International Criminal Court, Committee of the Whole, 'Summary Record of the 4th Meeting', A/CONF.183/C.1/SR.4, 20 November 1998

## OFFICIAL STATEMENTS

Otunnu, OA, '"Era of Application": Instituting a Compliance and Enforcement Regime for CAAC', statement before the Security Council, 23 February 2005

Redmond, R (UNHCR spokesperson), comments made at press briefing at the Palais des Nations in Geneva, 24 March 2009

## INTERNATIONAL AND REGIONAL PRINCIPLES

Cape Town Principles on Best Practices on the Prevention of Recruitment of Children into the Armed Forces and on Demobilisation and Social Reintegration of Child Soldiers in Africa, 1997

Brussels Principles against Immunity and for International Justice, Principle 13, Combating Impunity: Proceedings of the Symposium held in Brussels from 11 to 13 March 2002

Paris Commitments and the Principles and Guidelines on Children Associated with Armed Forces or Armed Groups, 2007

CASES

## Nuremberg Tribunal

*Trial of Wilhelm List and Others* Case No 47 United Nations War Crimes
 Commission, Law Reports of Trials of War Criminals, Volume VIII
 (1949)

## Permanent Court of International Justice

*Lotus* case (*France v Turkey*) PCIJ (1927) Series A No 10

## International Court of Justice

*Asylum (Colombia v Peru)*, ICJ Reports, 1950
*Anglo-Norwegian Fisheries (United Kingdom v Norway)*, ICJ Reports 1951
*North Sea Continental Shelf (Federal Republic of Germany v Denmark;*
 *Federal Republic of Germany v Netherlands)*, ICJ Reports, 1969
*Continental Shelf (Libyan Arab Jamahiriya v Malta)*, ICJ Reports, 1985
*Military and Paramilitary Activities in and against Nicaragua (The Republic*
 *of Nicaragua v The United States of America)*, ICJ Reports, 1986
*South-West Africa (Ethiopia v South Africa; Liberia v South Africa) Second*
 *Phase*, ICJ Reports, 1966
*Legality of the Threat or Use of Nuclear Weapons*, Advisory Opinion, ICJ
 Reports, 1996
*Case Concerning the Arrest Warrant of 11 April 2000 (Democratic Republic*
 *of the Congo v Belgium)*, ICJ Reports, 2002
*Legal Consequences of the Construction of a Wall in the Occupied*
 *Palestinian Territory*, ICJ Reports, 2004
*Armed Activities on the Territories of the Congo (DRC v Uganda)*, ICJ
 Reports, 2005

## International Criminal Tribunal for Rwanda

*Prosecutor v Akayesu* ICTR-96-4-T (1998)
*Prosecutor v Kayhishema and Ruzindana* ICTR-95-1-T (1999)
*Prosecutor v Rutaganda* ICTR-96-3-T (1999)
*Prosecutor v Musema* ICTR-96-13-T (2000)
*Prosecutor v Semanza* ICTR-97-20-T (2003)

## International Criminal Tribunal for the former Yugoslavia

*Prosecutor v Duško Tadić*, Decision on the Defence Motion for Interlocutory Appeal on Jurisdiction IT-94-1-AR-72 (2 October 1995)
*Prosecutor v Tihomir Blaškić* IT-95-14-T (5 November 1996)
*Prosecutor v Anto Furundžija*, Trial Chamber II, ICTY-IT-95-17/1-T10 (10 December 1998)
*Prosecutor v Blaškić* IT-95-14-A (29 July 2004)
*Prosecutor v Stakić* IT-97-24-T (2003)

## International Criminal Court

*Prosecutor v Bosco Ntaganda*, Warrant of Arrest, ICC-01/04-02/06 (2006)
*Prosecutor v Thomas Lubanga Dyilo*, Warrant of Arrest, ICC-01/04-01/06 (2006)
*Prosecutor v Lubanga Confirmation of Charges* ICC-01/04-01/06 (2007)
*Prosecutor v Germain Katanga and Mathieu Ngudjolo Chui*, Arrest Warrant, ICC-01/04-01/07 (2007)
*Prosecutor v Katanga and Ngudjolo Confirmation of Charges* ICC-01/04-01/07 (2008)
*Prosecutor v Lubanga*, Warrant of Arrest, ICC-01/04-01/06 (2006)
*Prosecutor v Lubanga*, Trial Chamber Judgment, ICC-01/04-01/06 (2012)

## Special Court for Sierra Leone

*Prosecutor v Norman, Fofana and Kondewa*, Indictment, SCSL-2004-14-PT (11-21) (5 February 2004)
*Prosecutor v Sam Hinga Norman*, Decision on Preliminary Motion Based on Lack of Jurisdiction, SCSL-2004-14-AR72E (31 May 2004)
*Prosecutor v Charles Taylor*, Prosecutor's Second Amended Indictment, SCSL-03-01-PT (2007)
*Prosecutor v Brima, Kamara and Kanu*, Trial Chamber II, SCSL-04-16-T (20 June 2007)
*Prosecutor v Fofana and Kondewa*, Trial Chamber I, SCSL-04-14-T (2 August 2007)
*Prosecutor v Brima, Kamara and Kanu*, Appeals Chamber, SCSL-04-16-A (22 February 2008)
*Prosecutor v Fofana and Kondewa*, Appeals Chamber, SCSL-04-14-A (28 May 2008)
*Prosecutor v Sesay, Kallon and Gbao*, Trial Chamber I, SCSL-04-15-T (2 March 2009)

*Prosecutor v Sesay, Kallon and Gbao*, Appeals Chamber, SCSL-04-15-A (26 October 2009)


**African Commission on Human and Peoples' Rights**

*Frederick Korvah v Liberia* Communication 1/88, *Frederick Korvah v Liberia*, Seventh Activity Report 1993-1994, Annex IX


**Inter-American Commission on Human Rights**

Inter-American Commission on Human Rights communication, *Juan Carlos Abella v Argentina*, Case No 11, 137, Annual Report 1997, OAS Doc OAE/Ser.L/V/II.98. Doc 7 rev (13 April 1998)


**Inter-American Court on Human Rights**

*'Mapiripán Massacre' v Colombia* Inter-American Court of Human Rights (15 September 2005)


**Municipal Cases**

*Blockburger*, US Supreme Court, 1932, 284 US, 299 US SCt 180
*Korematsu v United States* 323 US 214 (1944)
*Regina v R* (1992) 1 AC 599 (House of Lords)
*S v Makwanyane and Others* 1995 (3) SA 391 (CC)
*R v Bow Street Metropolitan Stipendiary Magistrate and others, Ex Parte Pinochet Ugarte (Amnesty International and Others Intervening) (No 3)*, [1999] 2 All ER 97, 177 (HL)
*The Public Committee against Torture in Israel v Government of Israel et al* HCJ 769/02 (11 December 2005)


**Press Releases**

Special Court for Sierra Leone Public Affairs Office, 'Special Court Prosecutor Says He Will Not Prosecute Children' (2 November 2002)
ICC press release, 'Prosecutor Receives Referral of the Situation in the Democratic Republic of Congo', ICC-OTP-20040419-50 (2004)

Coomaraswamy, R, 'Press Conference by Special Representative for Children and Armed Conflict' (UN Department of Public Information, News and Media Division, New York, 16 March 2007)

ICC press release, 'Warrant of Arrest against Bosco Ntaganda Unsealed', ICC-CPI-20080429-PR310 (2008)

Human Rights Watch press release, 'DR Congo: ICC-Indicted War Criminal Implicated in Assassinations of Opponents' (13 October 2010)

'Special Representative of the Secretary-General for Children and Armed Conflict—Chad Signs an Action Plan to End Recruitment and Use of Children in its National Army and Security Forces', OSRSG/061611-12 (16 June 2011)

## United Nations Comments

Comments by the Committee on the Rights of the Child on the proposal for a draft optional protocol prepared by the Chairperson-Rapporteur of the Open-ended Working Group on an optional protocol to the Convention on the Rights of the Child to provide a communications procedure, A/HRC/WG.7/2/3 (13 October 2010)

## Internet Sources

African Committee of Experts on the Rights and Welfare of the Child, www.acerwc.org

Committee on the Rights of the Child—Working Methods, individual Communications, www2.ohchr.org

Echevarria II, AJ, *Fourth Generation War and Other Myths* (US Government, 2005), www.StrategicStudiesInstitute.army.mil

Lasker, J, 'Inside Africa's PlayStation War', http://towardfreedom.com

UNICEF news note, 'UNICEF Welcomes Decision by the Somali Transitional Federal Government to Ratify the Convention on the Rights of the Child' (20 November 2009), http://www.unicef.org

Talmadge, R, 'John Lincoln Clem', *The Handbook of Texas Online* (2001)

The United Nations Children's Fund (UNICEF) Report on Children in Conflict, www.unicef.org/protection/files/Armed_Groups.pdf

Parliamentarians for Global Action, 'A Deterrent International Criminal Court—The Ultimate Objective', www.pgaction.org/uploadedfiles/deterrent%20paper%20rev%20Tokyo.pdf

Project Congo, www.projectcongo.org/donboscongangi.html

UNICEF, Core Commitments for Children in Emergencies, www.unicef.org

UNICEF, West and Central Africa Office: DRC country profile, www.unicef.org/wcaro/Countries_1749.html

## News Sources

Fawke, M, 'UNHCR visits Congolese Towns Attacked by Lord's Resistance Army' (UNHCR, 2008)
'Rwanda: How the Genocide Happened' (BBC, 1 April 2004)


## Newsletters

Banks, MD, 'Avery Brown (1852–1904), Musician: America's Youngest Civil War Soldier', *America's Shrine to Music Newsletter*, February 2001
'Children and Armed Conflict', *Watchlist on Children and Armed Conflict Newsletter*, November 2001


## Newspaper/Magazine Sources

Dao, J, 'The War on Terrorism Takes an Aim at Crime', *New York Times*, 7 April 2002
Ganguly, D, 'Female Assassins Seen in Sri Lanka', *Associated Press*, 5 January 2000
——, 'Female Fighters Used in Sri Lanka', *Associated Press*, 10 January 2000
Grillo, I, 'In Teenage Killers, Mexico Confronts a Bloody Future', *Time*, 8 December 2010
Lind, WS et al, 'The Changing Face of War: Into the Fourth Generation', *Marine Corps Gazette*, October 1989
Mamou, J, 'Soldier Boys and Girls', *Le Monde diplomatique*, November 2001
Parker, DB and Freeman, A, 'David Bailey Freeman', *Cartersville Magazine*, 2001
Sanger, DE, 'Bush, On Offense, Says He Will Fight to Keep Tax Cuts', *New York Times*, 6 January 2002
Thompson, R, 'Village Honours It's Boy Soldier', *Cincinnati Enquirer*, 6 November 1999
Waschefort, G, 'Child Soldiers: The Legacy of East African Conflict', *De Kat*, July/August 2009
Wilson, S, 'Columbian Fighters Drug Trade is Detailed', *Washington Post*, 25 June 2003

## Workshop Presentations/Forum Proceedings

Becker, J, 'Small Arms and Child Soldiers', presentation at Workshop for 'Putting Children First: Building a Framework for International Action to Address the Impact of Small Arms', New York, 20 March 2001

Hogg, CL, 'The Liberation Tigers of Tamil Eelam (LTTE) and Child Recruitment', Coalition to Stop the Use of Child Soldiers forum on armed groups and the involvement of children in armed conflict, Chateau de Bossey, Switzerland, 4–7 July 2006

Restoy, E, 'The Revolutionary United Front (RUF): Trying to Influence an Army of Children', Coalition to Stop the Use of Child Soldiers forum on armed groups and the involvement of children in armed conflict, Chateau de Bossey, Switzerland, 4–7 July 2006

## Speeches/Addresses

Kennedy, JF, 'Civil Rights Address', 11 June 1963

Grant, JP, 'Child Health and Human Rights', address to the Committee on Health and Human Rights Lecture Programme, Institute of Medicine, 1994

## Miscellaneous

Declaration of the United Kingdom of Great Britain and Northern Ireland, upon ratification of the CIAC Protocol (24 June 2003), http://treaties.un.org

Declaration of the United States of America, upon ratification of the CIAC Protocol (23 December 2002), http://treaties.un.org

Declaration of Vietnam, upon ratification of the CIAC Protocol (20 December 2001), http://treaties.un.org

Kuper, J, 'Implementing the Rights of Children in Armed Conflict: Progress and Dilemmas', Public Lecture, School of Oriental and African Studies, 5 March 2010

Kuper, J, 'International Law Concerning Child Civilians in Armed Conflict', PhD Thesis, 1996

Lieber Code: Instructions for the Government of Armies of the United States in the Field, General Order No 100 (1863)

Report of Rapporteur to Committee Three of the Drafting of Additional Protocol I to the Geneva Conventions, OR XV 465. CDDH/407/Rev 1

The Hague Regulations Concerning the Laws and Customs of War on Land (18 October 1907)

US Code—10 USC § 505: Regular components: qualifications, term, grade

# *Index*

www.ingramcontent.com/pod-product-compliance
Lightning Source LLC
Chambersburg PA
CBHW050415280326
41932CB00013BA/1866